D1601607

Hanging by a Thread

Social Change in Southern Textiles

JEFFREY LEITER, MICHAEL D. SCHULMAN,
AND RHONDA ZINGRAFF, EDITORS

ILR Press
Ithaca, New York

Cover design by Kat Dalton
Cover photo, King mills and worker housing, Augusta, Georgia, ca. 1912–1915, courtesy of Georgia Department of Archives and History

Library of Congress Cataloging-in-Publication data

Hanging by a thread : social change in southern textiles / Jeffrey
   Leiter, Michael D. Schulman, and Rhonda Zingraff, editors.
      p. cm.
   Includes bibliographical references and index.
   ISBN 0–87546–173–5 (case : alk. paper).
   ISBN 0–87546–174–3 (pb. : alk. paper).
   1. Cotton textile industry—Southern States—Employees—History.
2. Cotton textile industry—Southern States—History. 3. Southern
States—Social conditions—1865–1945. I. Leiter, Jeffrey, 1948–
II. Schulman, Michael D. III. Zingraff, Rhonda, 1950–
HD8039.T42U6476   1991
331.7′67721′0975—dc20   90–27040

Copies may be ordered through bookstores or from
ILR Press
School of Industrial and Labor Relations
Cornell University
Ithaca, NY 14851–0952

Printed on acid-free paper in the United States of America
5 4 3 2 1

Contents

Tables and Figures

Preface

In October 1990, as this book was being prepared for publication, President George Bush issued the fourteenth veto of his administration. The target was legislation passed by Congress which would have limited textile, apparel, and shoe imports. Insisting that the domestic textile industry was performing well, President Bush argued that import restrictions would jeopardize global economic progress. Advocates for the bill, whether elected officials or industry representatives, decried the veto with predictions of continued job losses. As editors, this news symbolized to a great extent our rationale for producing this volume. The clashing perspectives and conflicting interests that underlay this bill and its veto were familiar to those who have studied the historical and contemporary struggles of textile firms, their workers, and the communities that have been their homes. The news read like another chapter in a continuing saga of conflict and change. Some expect we are nearing the end of the story, while others believe the end is nowhere in sight. Most will agree, however, that these have been critical times for textiles.

We envisioned this book as a way to illuminate the historical roots and current dynamics of the southern textile industry. By the mid-1980s it was apparent that the industry had undergone a vast restructuring and that the human consequences were immense. The domestic economy of the United States had grown vulnerable to deindustrialization. The Midwest was termed the rustbelt, and the southern sunbelt was experiencing capital flight to more profitable locations across the border or overseas. Both our scholarly and civic interests led us to decide that the transformation of southern textiles was a story that needed to be told.

Our collaboration in the study of southern textiles began in 1980, when we surveyed employees of the J. P. Stevens plants in Roanoke Rapids, North Carolina. This was an especially provocative research site because of a lengthy battle between the company and the Amal-

gamated Clothing and Textile Workers Union (ACTWU), which had
been certified to represent the workers in an election seven years
before but still had no contract settlement with Stevens. As we began
to share the results of that research, we met other colleagues with
similar interests in textile communities across the South. Some were
sociologists; some were historians or political scientists. We valued
these cross-disciplinary associations and concluded that a book designed to explain the circumstances in southern textiles ought to
contain cross-disciplinary insights.

We sought contributions for *Hanging by a Thread* from those sociologists, historians, and political scientists whose expertise could inform readers of the crises faced by the industry at various times, by
the communities where mills were located, and by the people whose
lives were embedded in both. We sought historical and comparative
analyses so that the picture of the textile experience in the South
could be framed by a broad recognition of social, cultural, economic,
and political forces. As editors, we have been fortunate to assemble
these chapters from contributors who have our admiration and ap-
preciation. We want to acknowledge their cooperation in all respects
but also to applaud the energy and commitment they display in
their studies of this topic. Their work has enlivened our own and, in
some cases, has for many years enriched our own.

Our assessments of the developments in and the forecasts for the
industry and communities have been vastly improved by our conver-
sations with Clyde Bush of the ACTWU. We met him while planning our initial forays into Roanoke Rapids years ago and found a
combination facilitator and interpreter in whom we have had confidence ever since. We are grateful also for our associations with Keir
Jorgensen of the ACTWU in New York, who has always responded
to our requests for information.

Our publication agreement with ILR Press has been a model experience. Fran Benson, Andrea Fleck Clardy, Trudie Calvert, and
Erica Fox provided constructive advice and encouragement and
splendid support services. We hope they recognize how much we
value their contributions. The way they do their jobs has truly enhanced the way we did ours.

Our gratitude to Judy Teander is of giant proportion. She has
distinguished herself as a manuscript manager extraordinaire. She
knows how much we appreciate her labors, for which WordPerfect is
both a process and a description, but we want everyone to know that
her intelligent attention to detail is in evidence throughout this
book.

PART I

Introduction

1

Southern Textiles: Contested Puzzles and Continuing Paradoxes

Michael D. Schulman and Jeffrey Leiter

This book brings together the research of sociologists and historians on textiles and textile workers in the southern United States. "Hanging by a thread" is a metaphor that describes the past and the uncertain future of the southern textile industry, its workers, families, and communities. Both the industry and the lives of its workers are fragile: job security and profits have followed volatile production cycles, and pressures to cut costs have intensified demands on workers. Changes in the world economy, in corporate organization, and in the labor process are causing a restructuring of the industry. Even if a transformed industry enters a new period of prosperity, the process may leave many firms, people, and communities dangling from tenuous socioeconomic threads.

We believe the southern textile industry provides a case study of the forces that cause change in social and industrial organization. The issues and questions that appear repeatedly in both sociological and historical analyses of this industry can be viewed in light of different sociological concepts. Yet the application of theoretical concepts to historically specific situations or cases reveals contradictions and new complexities.

One may ask, Why study the textile industry? It is not a high-tech industry at the forefront of industrial restructuring; technological change and modernization have come relatively recently to the numerous mills scattered throughout the southeastern United States. It is not a growth industry in which the United States has a comparative advantage but a sick industry with shrinking employment.

People who study the textile industry—and the contributors to this book are only a few of the many who do—believe that it is the prototype for the analysis of industrialization, modernization, and the development of capitalism. It is also an exemplar for studies of the socioeconomic consequences of these transformations at the level of the individual worker, family, community, and society. Textiles are central to an understanding of Western development and to the analysis of many contemporary developing societies in which the textile industry serves as the base for a transition from agrarian to industrial economies.

In many countries, industrialization began in the textile industry. Expanding markets offered opportunities for entrepreneurs, and the mechanization of spinning and weaving and their relocation from the home to the factory made possible great increases in cloth production. Early industrial cities, such as the Manchesters on both sides of the Atlantic, frequently were centers of textile manufacturing.

The textile industry was often central to classic analyses of industrialization. Adam Smith (1976) compared spinning and weaving to illustrate the impact of capital investment on the relative returns to labor and capital. David S. Landes (1969) demonstrated the technological, organizational, and market forces behind industrialization in explaining the centralization of British textiles in Lancashire mills. Neil J. Smelser (1959) analyzed structural differentiation in textile production and textile families to illustrate the fundamental social changes wrought by the Industrial Revolution, and Tamara K. Hareven (1982) amplified Smelser's analysis by providing insights into the shifting balance of family and managerial forces on the textile workplace. Alfred D. Chandler (1977) pointed to the integrated production of textiles as the earliest use of large factories in the United States and the harbinger of a widespread managerial revolution. Robert Blauner (1964) used textiles as the paradigmatic example of machine-tending technology, which, along with assembly lines, was the source of greatest alienation for industrial workers.

Just as these analyses of industrialization used the textile industry to illustrate their arguments, so have interpretations of social transformation. The problems of precapitalist production that led to the reorganization of work around the wage-labor exchange, the dilemmas factory owners faced in the resistance of their workers, and the managerial and technological innovations owners undertook to extract greater profits were all widely and clearly experienced in textiles. Friedrich Engels (1962) stressed the poverty of the textile proletariat in mid-nineteenth-century Manchester. E. P. Thompson (1967) used early mill management practices and workers' responses to establish how the factory discipline of industrial capitalism fundamentally altered producers' lives. Stephen A. Marglin (1974) and Richard C. Edwards (1979) argued that the earliest factories were not created to harness machinery to water power but rather to increase control over spinners and initially involved no technological change from cottage yarn production. Dan Clawson (1980) used the example of textiles to show that technological changes are chosen and forgone in the process of class struggle. Liston Pope (1942) and Dale Newman (1980) investigated how paternalistic authority is used to control labor by considering textile communities.

One aspect of capitalist transformation has been the incorporation of peripheral areas and markets into the capitalist world economy. Textiles, as a consumer and producer of important trade commodities, has been central to this process. Textile production, because it required relatively little start-up capital and supplied necessities for proletarianized producers, served to facilitate accumulation in core areas of the capitalist world economy (Wallerstein 1980). Subsequently, the low value added in textile production with the resultant low profits, low wages, and low modernization rates has led to its transfer from the core into more peripheral areas, be they in the Third World (Chirot 1977) or in regions of the United States (Bluestone and Harrison 1982). U.S. textiles are now produced largely in the South, where the industry relocated starting after Reconstruction and accelerating after World War I.

Concentration of the industry in the South raises compelling questions and issues that may be labeled contested puzzles and continuing paradoxes. Contested puzzles are ongoing scholarly debates among researchers from different theoretical paradigms and intellectual traditions. Continuing paradoxes refer to the social reality behind the scholarly debates: phenomena whose complexity and historical specificity defy easy categorization and explanation. Sociological theory provides a fundamental set of concepts for isolating the essence or common factor that defines the poles of each contested puzzle. Theoretical concepts isolate certain aspects of social phenomena for intensive scrutiny, and their explanatory power is tested by applying them to the analysis of continuing paradoxes. This dialectical tension between puzzles and paradoxes is one reason sociologists and historians find the study of southern textiles central for investigation. Although the six contested puzzles and continuing paradoxes identified here do not constitute the universe of southern textile scholarship, they do represent a core set of concerns that are addressed in this volume.

Social Class versus New Men of Power in the New South

The textile industry in the U.S. South is a product of post–Civil War industrialization. Textile plants and mill villages sprang up during the 1880s following the destruction of the agricultural-slave basis of the southern economy. A major problem facing mill owners was the composition of the labor force for the new mills. Blacks were considered unfit for industrial labor in the mills and were needed as agricultural workers in the cotton sharecropping/debt peonage system. Blacks worked the land to produce cotton, and whites worked in the mills to produce cloth (Williamson 1984). In addition, since oppression of blacks was legitimated by the concept of the natural superiority of whites, employment of blacks even in unskilled positions on an equal basis with whites risked questioning the ideological underpinnings of white dominance (Boyte 1972). Concurrent with textile industrialization, southern agriculture was experiencing a depression. A steady increase in sharecropping and tenancy and reliance on one-crop (cotton) agriculture combined to proletarianize white yeomen and tenants as the price of cotton fell (Mitchell 1921). Landless and impoverished white farmers and their families left agriculture to become textile workers in the newly created mill villages.

Traditional interpretations suggest that the textile boom was the work of a new group of industrialists who drew capital and support from community mill-building efforts (Woodward 1971). Other scholars argue that mill owners were members of the pre–Civil War dominant class: former owners of slaves and plantations, professionals, and merchants who either had retained land and capital or had accumulated capital through the sharecropping and tenancy systems of post–Civil War agriculture (Billings 1979; Wiener 1978). The heart of this puzzle involves the stratification system that developed in the post–Civil War South. Did the textile boom represent a clean break with plantation-based class and social structures, or did pre–Civil War systems of power and privilege reappear during southern industrialization?

If planters played a minor part in the textile boom, one might argue that the traditional agrarian plantation-based social structure had been destroyed and replaced with capitalist industrial systems, resulting in both social mobility and new class positions for owners of capital, former slaves, and white farmers and workers (Wood 1986). Alternatively, if planters became merchants and textile mill owners, one might argue that plantation-based systems were recreated in the post–Civil War textile boom (Mandle 1978) and that relative positions in the stratification system remained the same though the roles of specific groups changed.

Although the contested puzzle over the structural inequalities of the New South involves historically specific phenomena, it is also a continuing paradox because of its importance for understanding the complexity of stratification in southern textiles. On one hand, textile industrialization fundamentally changed the pre–Civil War economic, social, and political structures. On the other hand, the post–Civil War replacements for these structures seem to have had much in common with their predecessors. Questions involving the interrelationship between agriculture and industry (e.g., was sharecropping a form of wage labor or a noncapitalist form of production?), stratification by race and gender (e.g., how did race and gender stratify workers?), dominant class control (e.g., were planters a ruling class or an elite?), and paternalism (e.g., does it persist?) need to be analyzed within the context of the social origins of the New South. This combination of continuity and discontinuity forms the heart of the paradox. Change obviously occurred, but was it a change in the form or the substance of social relations?

Paternalism versus Bureaucratic Authority over Labor

The interpenetration of workplace and community social structures to create unique systems of control over labor is a major theme that characterizes both sociological and historical analyses of southern textiles. Given the hierarchical, inegalitarian, and conflict-generating aspects of social relations between mill owners and workers, how was and is class conflict experienced? What systems of control over labor involving the mill and the community were specific to southern textiles? Are these systems still evident today, or have they been replaced by other control structures?

Dominant classes in all systems of stratification attempt to obtain stability by getting members of subordinate classes to accept and identify with the system. One of the most stable bases for the legitimation of systems of stratification is tradition. Traditional authority applies both to the sanctity of old rules and to those holding positions of power who embody the rules (Newby 1977). Paternalism was the form of traditional authority in southern textile mill villages.

Paternalism involves both hierarchical differentiation between classes and the identification of the subordinate class with members of the dominant class (Newby 1975). It occurs when the dominant class has extended its control beyond the workplace into the community through a complex web of interrelationships. Paternalistic relations are most likely to emerge in isolated, one-industry, rural communities in which powerful members of the dominant class are personally identifiable and are involved in the everyday activities of workers' lives and there is an ideology that stresses the organic bonds between workers and employers (Norris 1978).

Early mills in the U.S. South were situated in geographically isolated towns, where the labor force was white, unskilled, and recruited from the farm population. Workers, many of them women and children, were often members of the same family or kin (Newman 1978). The mill was central to village life, providing housing and welfare activities and sponsoring community organizations. The dominant ideology within the mill village portrayed workers and owners as organically bound together in a "white family."

One aspect of the contested puzzle about paternalism involves the extent of control. Some argue that the extension of mill owners' control beyond the factory served to destroy any autonomous social space or institutions that workers might have developed on their own. The total determination of this social experience prevented workers from developing any autonomous culture or consciousness of themselves as a class (Cash 1941). While acknowledging the structural reality of paternalism, others argue that the paternalistic textile mill village was also subject to the informal expectations stemming from the workers' rural farm origins. Subsistence strategies common to rural farm life continued in the mill villages. Textile workers may not have been class conscious, but they did establish community- and occupation-based cultural forms, which at times appeared reconciled to paternalism but could serve as a basis for resistance when owners attempted to change the work process (Hall et al. 1986).

Another aspect of this contested puzzle involves the legacy of paternalistic structures. During the 1940s, local ownership of southern textile mills declined as a wave of consolidation hit the industry and most mill housing was sold (Herring 1949). Though the traditional mill village no longer exists, some argue that the ideology of paternalism persists through mechanisms of cultural transmission, socialization, and the continuing employment of older workers and their kin (Roy 1965). The heavy hand of the paternalistic past prevents workers from mobilizing and protesting. Others argue that the paternalistic legitimation of authority based on tradition has been supplanted by bureaucratic systems of control. Bureaucratic systems of authority are legitimated according to codified sets of rules and procedures institutionalized in rational-legal organizations. The penetration of market relations produces rational-legal norms and values in both the workplace and the community. Owners become anonymous managers, and workers become organizational role-players. Mill towns fade and are replaced by industrial communities in which work and family are separate. A relative degree of affluence compensates for alienation in the labor process (Leiter 1982).

The continuing paradox of systems of control over labor involves the alternation between paternalistic and bureaucratic systems of control. Despite mergers, consolidations, and plant closings, most southern textile mills remain relatively small and the industry competitive. Workers may personalize authority relations even in mills owned by nonlocal corporations. Outside owners may appeal to traditional paternalistic symbols in attempts to retain authority and defeat unions. Alternatively, the emergence of new industries has drawn white workers out of textiles. New workers, especially blacks, may come from communities that have not been under the paternalistic control of mill owners. New machines and technology have revamped the production process and changed production relations. Foreign competition and industry consolidation have reduced the number of positions and heightened employment insecurities. These changes are indicative of changes in the systems of control over labor. Yet, paradoxically, many of the vestiges of the past paternalistic system seem to persist.

Quiescence versus Militancy in Labor Struggles

Labor relations in the southern textile industry can be characterized as long waves of quiescence broken by relatively short but bitter outbursts of conflict, followed by a reformation of previous owner-worker relationships. Despite repeated attempts, starting with the Knights of Labor in the 1880s and currently involving the Amalgamated Clothing and Textile Workers Union, successful unionization efforts have been rare in southern textiles (Mitchell 1931; Raynor 1977; Johnson and Scurlock 1986a; Hodges 1986). The low levels of unionization among southern textile workers and the historical record of strikes and unionization attempts form the core of the next contested puzzle and continuing paradox.

Explanations of the lack of union support among southern textile workers highlight the interpenetration of community and workplace social structures. The "labor force integration" perspective argues that southern textile workers were tied to the mill through employment of family members and through the mill's extraeconomic control over community institutions (Simpson 1981). Worker-controlled social structures capable of generating an autonomous working-class consciousness and culture simply did not exist in the mill village.

This bleak picture of labor docility has been challenged by both historians and sociologists. Historical studies of strikes contradict the picture of southern workers as deferential individualists. Workers organized and went out on strikes when wages, working conditions, or the labor process were changed by mill owners (Pope 1942; McLaurin 1971). Instead of preventing organization, the preindustrial cultural traditions of mutual aid and support common to the mill village provided a basis for worker mobilization. Though not necessarily a class-conscious proletariat, southern workers resisted the capitalist rationalization of workplace and community life (Beatty 1984). Lack of resources, repression by both owners and the state, and poverty undermined the ability of workers to mount continuous struggles. Contemporary repression by sophisticated antiunion management consulting firms and a declining labor market for textile workers also serve to depress workers' mobilization.

Sociological studies attempt to identify the social bases for class consciousness, militancy, and union support among southern textile workers. Workers' social location outside the workplace, according to their age, education, race, and gender, and within the mill, according to their skill, length of employment, and job dissatisfaction, affect union support and militancy (Reif et al. 1988). Further, even workers who do not manifest strong levels of union support may simply be acknowledging the structure of power that confronts them rather than consensually adopting the ideologies of owners and managers (Leiter 1986). Many of the characteristics that led to militancy and union support among other workers can be shown to have been present among southern textile workers.

Although the characteristics that can produce labor militancy and quiescence have been identified and historical case studies have demonstrated the potential for militancy, the lack of widespread unionization creates a continuing paradox. In certain historical conjunctures, characteristics of the workers, the community, and the workplace have all come together to produce militancy among southern textile workers. Yet such mobilizations have been at best sporadic and fragile.

Segmentation versus Homogenization among Textile Workers

Until the 1960s, southern textile workers were overwhelmingly racially homogeneous. Some blacks did work in segregated workplaces in certain mills during the nineteenth century, but by the beginning of the twentieth century, the textile work force was exclusively white except for a scattering of blacks in menial positions (Williamson 1984). In the 1960s large numbers of blacks, both men and women, began to enter the mill work force (Rowan 1970; Hughes 1976). Industrialization in the South created other opportunities for white workers, and the breakdown of legal segregation allowed blacks to enter the mills in significant numbers. Another contested puzzle centers around the internal stratification of the southern textile work force, particularly around the issue of race and gender divisions.

Growth in the number of black textile workers has segmented the work force and provided a social base for worker mobilization. The traditional web of cross-class ties in the paternalistic community did not envelop blacks because they were excluded from mill employment. Therefore, black workers who entered the mills in the 1960s came from rural farm backgrounds. Racially cohesive institutions such as churches and the accomplishments of the civil rights movement gave them experience with collective action (Frederickson 1982). Black support has been fundamental to recent union successes, yet race has been used by management as an issue to balkanize workers by charging that unions are agents for a "black takeover." This strategy has dissuaded some whites from supporting unions (Cramer 1978).

Gender is another division in the internal stratification of the southern textile work force. As a competitive, low-paying industry, southern textiles has historically employed many women; close to half of all recent operative positions have been filled by females. Families with large numbers of females or widows with families moved from farm to factory because textile work was one of the few avenues of employment open to women (Newman 1978). Mills employed women and children as part of a family wage system that bound the labor of entire families to a mill. Family labor also provided household survival strategies such as gardening that further served to lower the reproduction costs of labor power (Wood 1986).

Traditional analyses argue that because of their family and household responsibilities women view work as a secondary concern; they
are housewives, housekeepers, and mothers as well as workers and
therefore harder to organize than men (Blauner 1964; Fiorito and
Greer 1982; Kornhauser 1961). This viewpoint has been challenged
by both sociological and historical studies. Historical research has
shown that women have been actively involved in major unionization campaigns and strikes from the 1880s to the present (Foner
1979; Kenneally 1981). Sociological studies find that gender differences in union support, militancy, and other work-based attitudes
diminish or disappear when other variables such as pay and job status are held constant (Crosby 1982; Schulman et al. 1985).

Although race and gender divide the southern textile work force,
countervailing economic forces may be decreasing the importance
of this polarization. With industrial restructuring and the decline in
the number of jobs, differences in job characteristics and employment between blacks and whites and between males and females
may diminish. Thus the continuing paradox of worker segmentation
concerns the increasing or decreasing significance of economic class
relative to race and gender.

Uneven Development versus Regional Specialization

The migration of the New England textile industry to the South
started at the turn of the century and intensified during the 1940s.
The majority of American textile mills are now located in the South
in small to medium-sized communities, where the mills dominate
the local economy (Avery and Sullivan 1985). The textile industry
moved to the South to take advantage of a large pool of inexpensive,
unorganized labor (Stelzer 1961). The relocation of the industry and
the current pattern of geographical dispersion across rural areas
form the core of the next contested puzzle: how do social location
and the social organization of production interact to produce an uneven distribution of industrial forms?

Some argue that industrial relocation to rural areas is part of the
process of uneven development inherent in capitalist development.
The textile industry relocated to the South to obtain higher rates of
surplus value than were possible in New England. Wages were lower
in the South because of surplus labor, the employment of multiple
family members, and lower costs for the reproduction of labor
power as a result of household subsistence activities (Wood 1986).

Alternatively, the question of southern industrialization can be
analyzed as a process of regional specialization. Labor costs were

lower in the South because the standard of living was lower. Labor-intensive industries like textiles need cheap labor, especially when there is a high degree of competition. Low-cost transportation and fuel and location near sources of raw materials were additional advantages that served to lower production costs in the South. The textile industry, facing a variety of competitive pressures, moved south in response to market forces so as to become more efficient (Williamson 1974).

The contested puzzle of spatial organization has assumed new significance as a consequence of deindustrialization and industrial restructuring. Fewer workers are needed in southern textiles as the mills have begun to automate and change product lines in response to foreign competition. The puzzle of uneven development or regional specialization now involves a world economy and thus remains a continuing paradox.

Deskilling versus Technological Modernization

The basic elements of production—raw materials, labor power, and technology—are transformed into useful products through the labor process. The organization of the labor process involves both coordination (by directing each person's labor so that it integrates with the labor of others) and control (by converting the labor power purchased in the market into useful labor). Both coordination and control are accomplished within the workplace itself and involve workers and owners/managers in continuing conflict regarding the timing of work tasks, control over the quality of products, and the manner in which workers are rewarded or punished (Edwards 1979).

The majority of jobs in southern textiles have been unskilled or semiskilled machine tending, employing large numbers of workers in repetitive tasks using obsolete technology. Low wages (or high rates of surplus value) allowed mill owners to ignore technological change for many years, but increased foreign competition has forced them to adopt new technology and reorganize the labor process (Rowan and Barr 1987). The contested puzzle over technological change revolves around the issue of deskilling versus automated efficiency.

Technological change can result in shifting skill and control over the labor process from the work force to the machines. The adoption of electric motors and the reorganization of the labor process along the principles of scientific management fundamentally changed the textile industry during the early part of the twentieth century (Hall et al. 1987). Skilled jobs such as weaving were turned into semiskilled machine-tending jobs, and workers could no longer control the pace of work. This process, called deskilling, fundamentally changes the work process and degrades the worker by diminishing skill requirements. It also gives owners more opportunities for exploitation by giving them greater control over workers, whose skills are becoming increasingly easy to reproduce (Braverman 1974).

Alternatively, technological change has been interpreted as part of the modernization process inherent in a market economy. Manufacturers under competitive pressures attempt to reduce costs by adopting new technologies that make them more efficient. Shifts in market forces change the relative costs of raw materials, labor, and capital. Manufacturers respond to these shifts by substituting abundant resources for scarce ones. Technological change allows for maximal use of the existing productive resources (Kuznets 1973). In some industries, automation has increased the number of skilled positions, resulting in higher wages and greater bureaucratic control over the labor process (Burawoy 1979).

The contested puzzle of deskilling versus modernization is also a continuing paradox because a new wave of automation began in the mills in the late 1970s. New machines have revamped the textile production process by combining several operations, increasing machine speed, and decreasing the number of workers (Office of Technology Assessment 1987). Automated technology has changed the labor process, leading to the possible erosion of existing systems of control over labor and to a change in the isolated, rural nature of the industry by consolidating workers into fewer plants (Schulman 1983). Proponents of technological change argue that it will save southern textiles by making the industry more competitive and by creating better-quality jobs. Critics charge that the technological changes being promulgated will further deskill jobs and thereby increase the competition in the labor market for an already shrinking number of jobs.

History and Sociology in the Study of Southern Textiles

The contested puzzles and continuing paradoxes of southern textiles are not just academic exercises. Rather, their resolution is central for understanding why the southern textile industry is "hanging by a thread." Both history and sociology are necessary to explain the current process of industrial restructuring in southern textiles. Historians and sociologists sometimes have different theoretical and methodological perspectives, which would imply that the two disciplines take contending approaches to the study of social phenomena. Leading members of both disciplines, however (e.g., Giddens 1979; Braudel 1980), emphasize the need for a unified approach.

The unifying approach, called "structuration" by Anthony Giddens (1979), is "built around the idea of the 'fundamentally recursive character of social life' and [is] designed precisely to express 'the mutual dependence of structure and agency' in terms of process in time" (Abrams 1982, p. xvii). This approach tries to escape or at least inform the paradox of human agency by which we actively create structures which then constrain our action but in turn are reproduced across time by human action. History and sociology can be united by conceiving of this dilemma historically as a process of structuring in time and in space (Abrams 1982). This balancing of structural and conjunctural explanations attempts "to make sense of the unfolding of unintended as well as intended outcomes in individual lives and social transformations" (Skocpol 1984, p. 1).

"The integration of time and place into the very argument marks off historical analysis" (Tilly 1981, p. 7). Minimally, historical analysis corrects misconceived sociological analyses that generalize while ignoring specific contexts. In addition, historical analysis provides the basis for theorizing. Arthur Stinchcombe (1978) argues that the construction of theory should be an inductive process rooted deeply in historical specifics by which a causal sequence is discovered in the historical facts, an analogy made to other causal sequences about facts of other times or places, and the analogy systematized as a concept, which in combination with other concepts yields theory.

But "historical materials are not raw evidence awaiting sociological analysis" (Tilly 1981, p. 6), a stance that would subsume history as elaborate data collection within sociology. Rather, historical considerations delimit, focus, and explain the interplay of action and structure. Thus, in Tilly's research program, the repertoire of collective action available in response to the pressures of state-making and proletarianization is specified by time and place.

The integration of history and sociology involves blending the narrative, which historians stress, with the sociologist's emphasis on causal theory. This is harder than it sounds. All too often, the appearance of analysis is obtained by the literary sleight of hand of simply assigning names or categories to facts. This verges on imposing theory on specifics, rather than drawing theory out of specifics. When causal theory is drawn out of the facts, however, the causal links must be very carefully demonstrated (Stinchcombe 1978).

Putting together a causal account from the facts requires combining a historian's insight with a sociologist's care about measurement and causal inference, which form the links between data and theory. Measurement and causal inference are, therefore, central aspects of the sociological side of social science history or of historical sociology, whichever we choose to call the enterprise in question. The essays in this book elaborate the issues and questions identified in this opening chapter. These themes are not divided between the historians and the sociologists or between those who report on the past and those who report on the present. Rather, both the historians and the sociologists treat these themes throughout the volume.

Overview of the Volume

We have divided the contributions to this volume into five parts, with this chapter constituting part I. Part II deals with the development of the textile industry in the South and the specific problems of labor force recruitment. Gary Freeze details the recruitment of the early textile labor force from the ranks of disadvantaged women. The changing importance of women, as workers, as strikers, and as community members, is a frequent theme throughout the volume. Gay Gullickson contrasts French and U.S. southern patterns of labor recruitment and organization, again with special attention to gender. Hers is the first of three comparative chapters that throw southern textiles into sharp relief. Phillip Wood asks why textile industrialization was so much more successful in the U.S. South than in the Canadian Maritimes. His answer points to differences in landownership that explain the greater exploitation of powerless wage workers and hence higher profits in the U.S. South.

The essays in part III deal with labor force integration and labor-capital struggles. Bryant Simon's study of unionization in Greensboro, North Carolina, focuses on the stretch-out introduced by management at the end of the 1920s, when paternalism began to erode and workers had to choose between loyalty and change. Linda Frankel analyzes the interplay of gender, religion, and unionization in Henderson, North Carolina, in the late 1950s. The ultimate defeat of the protracted 1958–61 strike is still remembered in the region with great disappointment. Bennett Judkins and Bart Dredge contrast the work of the Brown Lung Association in the 1970s with its situation in the early 1980s to help us understand the difficulties union organizers have faced. They base their analysis on resource mobilization theory, which currently dominates sociological studies of social movements.

The next three chapters, constituting part IV, focus on current trends and contemporary problems. Roger Penn and Jeffrey Leiter contrast the declining proportion of females in the British textile labor force with the increasing proportions of both females and blacks in southern U.S. textile factories. These trends are explained by differences in emerging occupational structures in and out of textiles. Julia Bonham assesses the prospects and problems of injecting productive flexibility into textiles via robotics and computerization. Her research makes use of trade publications to analyze management's response to import competition. Finally, John Gaventa and Barbara Smith frame a case study of deindustrialization in southern textiles in the larger problem of capital flight. The Tennessee community they studied is just one stop on the path of a particular firm from Michigan to Mexico.

In part V, Rhonda Zingraff picks up these tensions to trace the roots of the current crisis in southern textiles. She gives us both the texture and the context for the precarious fix facing textile workers, communities, and firms.

The essays in this volume do not present a single theoretical or empirical approach to southern textiles. Differences of style, method, and theoretical explicitness persist. Nevertheless, the questions raised and the answers suggested by the historians and sociologists included here are questions and answers of common interest. Our aim is to present a broad and coherent study of the structuring of human action in southern textiles.

PART II

Industrialization and Labor Recruitment

2

Poor Girls Who Might Otherwise Be Wretched: The Origins of Paternalism in North Carolina's Mills, 1836–1880

Gary R. Freeze

Women have always worked in southern cotton mills, and men have always run them. Gender relations have been part of labor relations in southern textiles since the first stages of industrial development before the Civil War. This essay argues that gender relations significantly influenced the evolution of a management ethic among pioneer North Carolina textile proprietors and helped shape the paternalism they practiced. This original paternalism then served as a rationale for managerial policies in the later corporate phases of cotton mill growth.

The first North Carolina manufacturers, like their successors, sought low-wage labor. In the antebellum phase of industrialization, mill owners employed, as one proprietor advised another, "all the widow women that has got a family of girls or other families that are mostly girls" as they could (Webb 1851). Because both proprietors and workers came mainly from the agrarian society of the surrounding countryside, both brought with them traditional attitudes about how "girls" and their widowed mothers should be treated inside and outside the factory. Evidence suggests that this dynamic led to the paternalism that long governed labor relations in the state.

In paternalistic social relations, the mill owners or operators took a personal, interventionist stance toward their workers. Paternalism often has been equated with company welfare policies because in many early mills the company provided housing, stores, and community facilities such as churches, schools, and playgrounds. These policies not only served the manufacturer's interests as a mechanism of social control but often fostered a sense of community among workers and ameliorated some of the traumas of adaptation to industrial discipline. On a deeper level, however, paternalism was a form of traditional authority legitimated by social perceptions. Manufacturers acted paternalistically, they claimed, because it was in the best interests of "our people." Their benevolent acts implied an underlying presumption that the workers would have been in a worse condition had the owner not intervened. At the same time, the coercive side of paternalistic behavior was justified by the assumption that inequality was natural (Gert and Culver 1976, 1979; Fotian 1979; Kleinig 1983). Assessing the particular way gender helped establish this underlying presumption is the central inquiry of this essay.

Historians of the southern textile industry have yet to examine all the social forces that shaped labor relations in the region's factories. Early historians of the cotton mills argued that paternalistic benevolence was a principal motivation behind the fabled "community crusades" that brought factories to so many southern piedmont towns after the Civil War (Mitchell 1921; Herring 1929; Rhyne 1930; Lemert 1933). Cotton mills, the proponents of a New South proclaimed, would regenerate local economies and uplift the prospects of "poor whites" as well as enrich the manufacturers. The idea that the paternalism of the postbellum South was led by men of titanic social qualities remained the dominant view among scholars well into the twentieth century. This interpretation has drawn constructive and corrective criticism from more recent investigators (McLaurin 1971; Billings 1979; Carlton 1982; Escott 1985; Hall et al. 1987), who have found that the benevolent pattern of labor relations in the New South was often slow to flower. Not until the twentieth century were progressive welfare policies adopted to ameliorate the conditions of workers. Thus the revisionists have questioned the traditional interpretation that the founders of the southern textile industry held genuinely paternalistic attitudes toward the first generations of workers.

The revisionists have been correct to emphasize the pecuniary motivations of the early industrialists, but they have often overlooked evidence which suggests that the general social atmosphere of the early cotton mills was conducive to a paternalism that served the interests of both workers and owners. The self-image of the first mill owners as benevolent benefactors, though clearly self-serving, was nevertheless logically grounded in the still-dominant agrarian values of the traditional South. "Ideologies of management," one student of the Industrial Revolution has suggested, "can be explained only in part as rationalizations of self-interest; they also result from the legacy of institutions and ideas" (Bendix 1974, p. 444). Often, the revisionists have not gone far enough back in time to examine the rationales that shaped social relations among the owners and operatives of the first factories. In the case of North Carolina, which was the leading southern textile state by the early 1900s, the roots of paternalism were deeply embedded in the peculiar social structure of the largely female mill villages dating to the 1830s, as an examination of the early industry will show.

Beginnings of the North Carolina Textile Industry

North Carolinians first began to talk about the prospects for cotton manufacturing in the 1790s, during the earliest days of America's Industrial Revolution, but not until the War of 1812 led to an expanded demand for domestic cloth was a spinning factory built in the state. Because the wealthy kept their investments in agriculture, only three more factories were erected before 1830. A decline in the price of most farm commodities in the late 1830s, combined with the political successes of the Whig party (which advocated internal improvements, including railroads, banks, public schools, and factories), led to the real beginning of the textile industry. More than a dozen factories were planned and built from 1836 to 1840, and more followed as agricultural prices remained depressed. In 1850, the state boasted twenty-eight cotton factories worth together just over $1 million. The return of higher cotton prices during the 1850s led to the closing or reorganization of quite a number of the factories, but new mills were also built. In 1860, there were thirty-nine cotton factories scattered across the piedmont, from Rocky Mount on the fall line to Patterson at the Blue Ridge. The greatest concentration of factories was at Fayetteville, where seven were in operation (Griffin 1954).

The great majority of North Carolina's early cotton mills were small. Some, like the spinning factory at Swift Island on the Pee Dee River, had fewer than twenty hands at work. Only Cedar Falls on the Deep River and Rockfish on the creek of that name near Fayetteville employed more than one hundred people at any one time. The factories themselves seldom rose more than two or three stories and ran on water power, which forced them to close temporarily when summers were dry. Only the factories in Salem (now Winston-Salem) and Concord had steam boilers, which allowed them to run in all seasons and were novelties that drew amazed farmers from as far away as one hundred miles (Griffin 1954; Freeze 1988).

The size and number of cotton mills remained stable from the 1830s to the 1870s. Until the railroads opened up the piedmont in the 1850s, marketing the yarn and cloth the factories made was often difficult and haphazard. The treacherous roads of the piedmont interior hindered distribution over long distances. In 1856, for example, a mountain merchant announced the "unfortunate termination to our trade" with Cedar Falls proprietors because cloth had arrived mildewed on a rain-delayed delivery wagon (Cowles 1856). As a consequence, most of the factory trade was conducted locally. Often, the store, run in conjunction with the factory, bartered bundled yarn and coarse cloth for the commodities produced by nearby farmers. Only around Fayetteville, a river town with access to the seaport of Wilmington, were the early manufacturers able to capitalize on outside markets. Although the advent of the railroad promised the "spirit of improvement" for many factories, the rise in cotton prices in the 1850s, followed by the economic upheavals of the Civil War and Reconstruction, retarded the marketing potential of the piedmont industry until the late 1870s (Griffin 1954).

Because of the stagnant nature of the early industry, the labor force changed little in size, identity, or structure from the 1830s to the 1870s (see table 2.1). Virtually all the workers were white; only in Rocky Mount and Salem were slaves used temporarily as operatives. Most factories had two or three female workers for every male hand. The vast majority of these workers were young; seldom were any hands other than the male bosses over the age of thirty. In Cedar Falls, where employment records have survived, almost three-fourths of the 104 workers in September 1850 were female. Two-thirds of the workers were teenagers, and six were girls aged eleven and twelve. Two thirty-year-old women were the oldest hands in the factory. Superintendent James F. Marsh, an in-law of the factory's principal owner, was the oldest male at age twenty-nine (Briggs 1975, pp. 35–65). The social structure at Cedar Falls mirrored the organization of labor elsewhere. Although a disabled older male might be given a sinecure such as "fire watchman" if his children were also mill hands, the vast majority of workers in any antebellum factory were typically young, female, and unmarried.

The relative youth of so many mill hands meant that, aside from the male bosses, few were heads of families or households. Rather,

TABLE 2.1. Gender Composition of the Work Force during the First
Phase of Textile Industrialization in North Carolina, 1840–1880

Census year	Number of factories	Number of operatives	Males[a]	Females[a]	Children[b]
1840	24	1,219	n/a	n/a	n/a
1850	28	1,619	442	1,117	n/a
1860	39	1,755	440	1,315	n/a
1870	33	1,459	258	916	279
1880	49	2,602	875	1,727	741

Source: Compendium of the Tenth Census (Washington, D.C.: U.S. Government Printing Office, 1882), 5:188–89.
[a]The census defined male operatives as those age fifteen and up, female hands as
those age sixteen and up.
[b]Although children were not counted until 1870, the population schedules of the
antebellum period confirm their significant presence in the factory work forces, an
indication that the totals are approximations of an ever-shifting population.

the typical operative in the early factories was a dependent of adults
who came to the mill village because they needed to put members of
the family to work to make ends meet. From the beginning, wages
in North Carolina cotton mills were low, and during the antebellum
period able-bodied men could find farm work that paid as well and
gave them more control of their time and labor than did the long
hours of "wage slavery" in the factories (Earle and Hoffman 1980).
Yeoman farmers in the piedmont generally preferred that members
of their families not take factory employment. Although only a mi-
nority of the farmers could be considered truly prosperous, almost
all tenaciously valued their autonomy and took pride in the agrarian
traditions of their culture (Cecil-Fronsman 1983, pp. 182–90). Thus
the first mill villages were populated only by those families who for
some reason had lost their traditional livelihood and therefore
needed the economic security of the factory wage.

A precise definition of the social status of the families in North
Carolina's first mill villages is difficult because most factory records
have been lost. The federal population census of 1860, which for the
first time identified the occupations of female industrial workers,
provides the clearest perspective on the identities of early mill village residents. Although only twenty-one of the thirty-nine mill villages in the state could be isolated in the enumeration, enough
factory households were counted to indicate certain patterns of social structure. In all, 765 workers were enumerated in 333 households, representing about 43 percent of the total work force
reported that year. A variety of household structures characterized
mill hand families, but three types predominated: those headed by

TABLE 2.2. Social Structure of Households in the Mill Villages of Randolph County, 1860, by Occupation of the Head of Household

Occupation of household head	Number of households[a]	Workers in residence[b]	Percentage of offspring in work force[c]
Widowed housekeeper	30	56	46
Artisan/tradesman	17	42	31
Farmer/farmhand	8	14	8
Factory boss	7	2	0
Male factory hand	3	4	1
Day laborer	2	2	2
Totals	67	120	

Sources: Census of the United States, 1860: Population Schedule Manuscripts, Randolph County; Time book, Elliott & Marsh Co., Cedar Falls, N.C., both in North Carolina State Archives, Raleigh.

[a] Includes all households enumerated in which at least one member listed his or her occupation as factory hand. The total does not include households headed by a manufacturer if no other person in residence worked in the factory.

[b] Includes all workers in the household: adult factory hands, employed offspring, and boarders. Of the 120 workers found, only 13 were boarders. I did not trace the social origins of the boarders.

[c] Includes only the children of the household head.

artisans, by laborers, and by widows. The most striking characteristic of the society of most mill villages was the widespread predominance of widows and their children. Women headed 40 percent of mill village households, and their offspring made up the same proportion of all workers enumerated. These figures are out of proportion to the frequency of families headed by females in the greater piedmont society (Census of the United States 1860).

The proportion of widows in the mill villages varied, of course, from place to place. In Concord widows headed half the households clustered around the home of the factory owner, whereas at Long Island on the Catawba River only one widow and her family were found in the twelve factory houses. Generally, the proportion of families headed by widows within a mill village community ranged from one-third to one-half. Widows were most likely to predominate in the smaller rural villages located on piedmont streams. The disproportion of widowed families in the early mill villages was particularly great in Randolph County (see table 2.2). Four industrial communities were established around the Deep River factories, all of which held enclaves of widows. Five widows lived in a row along the river bottom at Cedar Falls in 1860. In nearby Franklinsville, ten of the twenty-three mill hand households were kept by a widow who sent her children off to the factories each morning. Living around them were cobblers, coopers, wagon makers, carpenters, day laborers, and blacksmiths, who also sent their children to the mills. In addition, a small number of farm children walked into the towns each day to work.

The Factory as a Refuge

The demographics of the early mill villages in North Carolina helped engender a perception that those who went to work in the factory did so because their lives in agrarian society had become unstable and untenable. The Reverend J. A. Baldwin, who at the end of the nineteenth century became one of the state's first agitators for child labor restrictions, recalled that North Carolinians generally regarded a cotton mill as a place for the "afflicted," where families like those left fatherless took refuge when material circumstances had reduced them to poverty (Baldwin 1899). Many regarded the factory as something akin to an asylum for the impoverished and dependent within a culture that, in the words of one of its historians, still had "the tang of the soil" in its mind (Thompson 1900).

The notion of the factory as a refuge from want was articulated throughout the nineteenth century. As early as 1828 a North Carolina correspondent to *DeBow's Review* argued that the development of manufacturing jobs would provide "an honorable alternative" for impoverished whites otherwise reduced to "mere machines" as were Negro slaves. A legislative committee in 1828 recommended state aid for manufacturing because, it claimed, factories would "build up flourishing villages in the interior of our state and improve not only the physical, but the moral and intellectual conditions of our citizens." Underlying the assumption that factories could fulfill a redemptive purpose was the perception that those who entered the factories needed to do so because they were, as a Fayetteville resident observed in 1837, "generally of a class who formerly suffered for want of even the common necessities of life." Benson J. Lossing, a northerner touring the state in the late 1840s, noted after visiting the Alamance Factory that "this cotton mill . . . is a real blessing, present and prospective, for it gives employment and comfort to many poor girls who might otherwise be wretched." The sense of the factory as asylum was confirmed by the experiences of the Civil War home front, when many North Carolinians suffered. "It is a feature of this institution," a journalist noted of the Rocky Mount factory in 1863, that those "who have been reduced by the calamities of war" found "light and honorable employment for their children" (Griffin 1960, pp. 35–38).

The predominance of widows and their daughters in the emerging factory communities, it seems, was a major reason these observers saw the factories as socially redemptive. Gender as much as class provided a logical basis for such attitudes. Most of the owners and the observers were literate, affluent men who were products of an agrarian, patriarchal culture deeply imbued with principles of evangelical benevolence (Calhoon 1979). Their patriarchal assumptions about social order produced, at the least, a benignly paternalistic regard toward widows.

Women in antebellum North Carolina, it must be remembered, lived in a patriarchal world. Common law, as inherited from English precedent and applied in the antebellum courts, regarded women as barely more than an extension of their husbands' or fathers' property (Johnson 1937; DeHart-Mathews 1984). The death of a husband or father mitigated the bonds of dependence only if the survivors were securely and amply provided for. Lack of a will, for example, relegated the widow and orphans (as the fatherless were legally regarded) to the control of the county courts. Life could go on as before if the committee of men charged with overseeing the widow's dower behaved in a competent manner. But lingering debts, the lack of new income, or other vicissitudes of life could, and often did, impoverish the widow and her family. When the traditional forms of agrarian social benevolence failed, one of the few alternatives for the widow was to repair to a cotton factory where her children could collectively obtain a living. Hence it was logical for the surrounding agrarian society to view her decision in the context of patriarchal benevolence because the men who owned the factory were offering an honorable alternative to the social disgrace of dependent poverty.

The experience of one North Carolina widow exemplified the asylum theme. James Carrigan was a modestly prosperous farmer in northwestern Cabarrus County when he died in 1843 without a will, some debts still unpaid, and, as his executors were to learn, without clear title to his family's land. In addition, he left a family divided within itself. The set of children from Carrigan's first marriage had little regard for his second wife, Elizabeth Killbrough Carrigan, although the surviving family letters never explain why. Upon Carrigan's death, his widow and her four children were made wards of the local county court. The widow received "thirds in the lands of her deceased husband," which amounted to 112 acres, and "the year's allowance" of $119 in cash, a bed, a pair of cotton cards, and a spinning wheel "as her absolute property" to allow her to make a living (Cabarrus County 1843).

Despite the efforts of the dower committee, matters did not go well for the Carrigans. A brother of her deceased husband sued Elizabeth Carrigan for possession of the family farm, and eventually the widow and her children were forced to rent a nearby house. In 1852, Samuel Carrigan, Elizabeth's son, told a stepbrother, "Mother is old now and is not able to make her living so Wee have to worke veary hard in deed to get our living." For awhile, Elizabeth Carrigan boarded out her children and moved to the nearby town of Concord, probably to take in sewing. By 1855, to keep her family intact, she moved to "the factory in Gaston County twelve miles from Charlotte," she told a stepson, "as I thought Mary and Cornelia [two daughters] cood make more to work in the factory." She asked for money to help pay for the moving expenses but asserted, "I think after a while Mary and Cornelia can make a nough to doo us." In 1860, the federal census taker found Elizabeth Carrigan, age sixty-two, still living with her two daughters, now in their late twenties, in the Mountain Island factory village. Mrs. Carrigan died during the Civil War, and both daughters eventually married nearby farmers, thus completing the cycle of refuge and redemption which the mill experience supposedly provided (see the years 1852–59 in Carrigan 1843–62).

Far too little is known about most widows who came to North Carolina's first cotton mill villages to assert whether their experience was similar to that of Elizabeth Carrigan. Many, like her, did seem to have been uprooted and dislocated from their families. In 1850, for example, the census takers in North Carolina often gave the county of birth for residents. As many as half the widows in the mill villages had been born elsewhere. Most of them were reduced by economic want. Of all the widows found in the mill villages of 1860, only two—Bethany York in Franklinsville and Charity Kizziah in Concord—owned the homes they occupied. None of the widows enumerated in 1860 owned more than $100 in personal property, an indication of their relative poverty in a society in which most farm families were considered comfortable if they owned personal possessions worth $500. "Times is veary hard here now," Elizabeth Carrigan wrote a stepson in 1857 during a slump in the textile market. "Provisions is that deare thatt it takes all they [i.e., the Mountain Island factory families] can make to get something to eat" (see the year 1857 in Carrigan 1843–62).

Relations between Workers and Mill Owners

Since the first operatives left a meager literary record of their lives, it is difficult to gauge the general attitude of laborers toward the mill owners or to measure the extent to which owner and operative interacted on a personal basis. Ambiguities clearly characterized all social interaction within the factory environment. For example, mill owners in Gaston County passed down the oral tradition that Jaspar Stowe, son of the founder of the Stowe Factory, often took the female hands of the nearby Woodlawn Factory fishing in the mill pond (Ragan 1969). Stowe doubtless enjoyed the company, but he also put his social graces to work to induce "the factory gals" to switch to his mill. His fishing partners likely knew what he was about. After so much trial in her life, Elizabeth Carrigan clearly regarded Thomas Tate, owner of the Mountain Island factory, as a patron. "Mr. Tate has been veary kind to me and his family to," she told a stepson in 1862 shortly before her death. In contrast, Jane Phifer, who worked alongside the Carrigan sisters in the factory, recalled that the only time anyone saw the owner was on the first of the month, when the head of each operative household was called into the office to be told how much in arrears the family was at the company store (Goodloe 1881).

Whether all the early manufacturers were self-consciously paternalistic in their approach to factory management is difficult to discern. Thomas Tate of Mountain Island, for example, left no record of what he thought about his supposed kindness to the widow Carrigan. Edwin M. Holt, whose family started many of the factories in Alamance County, was one of the very few industrialists to leave a diary, but he seldom mentioned his hands in it, and there is other evidence to suggest that Holt factory operatives were let go once their exploitable usefulness was lost (Beatty 1986). The most recent search of the records left by the early manufacturers indicates that few pioneer industrialists regarded themselves as the benevolent benefactors the public perceived them to be (Escott 1985). In this area of analysis the revisionists have come full circle back to the findings of the first historian of the industry, who learned from oral traditions passed down by the early manufacturers that "the attitude of the mill owners . . . toward the social welfare of the operatives" was "by no means uniform" and depended on "the personal expression of the man in charge" (Thompson 1906, pp. 60–62).

The few extant company records provide some evidence of paternalistic policies. In establishing labor regulations, some proprietors took pains to conduct factory affairs to suit the social norms common for the time. The most paternal of the rules acknowledged the special problems of imposing discipline on young and female workers. In 1842, the owners of the Concord factory, in passing policies for the governance of the hands, required not only punctuality and attention to duty but good behavior as well. "No hand will be allowed to quarrel or fight in the factory," the proprietors ordered, and "no running about, playing, throwing bobbins, or leaving the work to talk will be allowed." The need for further order in the Concord factory was demonstrated in 1850, when it was resolved that any male hand "who shall utter any slanderous word reflecting upon the good name of any female engaged in the establishment . . . shall forthwith be discharged" (Concord Manufacturing Company 1839–60).

Some factory proprietors not only assumed a parental position inside the factory but extended their intervention into the private lives of their young operatives as well. As early as the 1840s, when public education was introduced to North Carolina, mill owner Henry B. Elliott of Cedar Falls in Randolph County encouraged the younger children of mill hand families to attend. The proprietors of the two factories in nearby Franklinsville proselytized their Methodism in a "flourishing Sunday and Bible school" aimed at the operatives. George Makepeace, the industrial pioneer who was factory superintendent at Franklinsville in 1849, proudly boasted that "like the girls of Lowell," his female operatives were encouraged to save their money. Makepeace provided an incentive for thrift by borrowing workers' savings, at interest, for use by the factory. Some of the hands held notes on the company in excess of $100 ("The Deep River Factories" 1848).

One of the more dramatic instances of cotton mill owners asserting social control occurred in Franklinsville, where local manufacturers did not hesitate to assume that they knew what was best for their operatives' religious interests. In 1850, the factory owners forbade their operatives to attend church services "under the guise of True Wesleyanism" because they were afraid that the antislavery rhetoric of the egalitarian Wesleyan missionaries would affect deferential behavior in the factories. The policy backfired, leading to a breakdown in the "morale of organization" and eventually to an arsonist burning down one of the factories. Several of the dismissed hands, who had been examined in a manner similar to a church disciplinary trial, were reinstated (Nicholson 1952, pp. 51–52).

Clearly, the predominantly female work force of the early mills was amenable to patriarchal social relations. Paternalism was not an invention of mill owners but rather a transferral of the traditional relations of patriarchy to a new setting. Although paternalism was not ubiquitous in the early North Carolina textile industry, the evidence does suggest that the social environment in the first factory communities contained the elements that often led to paternalism. The residents of antebellum North Carolina regarded the factories as asylums from economic want for "afflicted" families of widows and orphans. The presence of so many young factory hands from the households of widows helped the novice manufacturers justify their measures of social control. Men bred in an agrarian society could easily argue that the factory girls "might otherwise be wretched" without the "honorable alternative" of spinning and weaving.

Further, the attitudes of the owners of the early factories significantly affected later labor relations. After 1880, when the scope and structure of markets in the industry began to change, growth necessitated the introduction of new labor sources. Widows and their families continued to come to the factories as before, but those who had previously forsworn such work came in far greater numbers. Agriculture in the North Carolina piedmont underwent severe trials during the 1880s and 1890s, when commodity prices fell steadily and credit tightened. Many farm families lost their land. Rather then sink into long-term tenancy, they migrated to the factories to relieve their poverty. There, these new workers, generally young men bred on farms, encountered not only the unfamiliar rigors of industrial discipline but the stigma of paternalistic assumptions as well. The young men, like the widows' daughters who preceded them, became objects of condescension. The proponents of a New South who organized cotton mills in most piedmont cities built on the framework of social relations developed in the antebellum industry. The best known of the post–Civil War paternalists in North Carolina, John Milton Odell, was a conscious disciple of the policies and attitudes adopted by the early manufacturers in his native Deep River valley. The mills the Odell family helped build in such industrial centers as Durham, Greensboro, Salisbury, Concord, and Gastonia became seedbeds for many of the company welfare policies of the early twentieth century (Freeze 1988).

Thus the imprint of the notion of the factory as asylum persisted to shape modern textile workers. Scholars have only begun to unravel the ways in which the experiences of southern mill hands in the twentieth century stem from patterns set in the earliest factories of the 1830s and 1840s, when getting "all the widow women" and their daughters made both social and business sense.

3

Technology, Gender, and Rural Culture: Normandy and the Piedmont

Gay L. Gullickson

The cotton textile industries in Normandy and the U.S. piedmont developed along different paths. The manufacture of cotton cloth was introduced into Normandy at the turn of the eighteenth century and progressed gradually from a rural to an urban and from a cottage to a factory industry. By midcentury, the cotton industry rivaled farming as a source of income in much of Normandy, and peasants and rural villagers divided their work time between the putting-out merchants, the large farmers who employed them as day laborers and harvesters, and their own small plots of land. This period of large-scale rural manufacturing, now known as proto-industrialization, died out in two phases, as first spinning (beginning in the 1790s) and then weaving (beginning in the 1830s) was mechanized and moved into more urban factories. By the 1840s, families that had combined cottage manufacturing with farming for generations began to find themselves forced to choose between full-time farming and migration to the mills of Rouen.

In the American South, there was no proto-industrial period when people combined cottage manufacturing with farming, and only a handful of spinning mills provided yarn for rural weavers in the early nineteenth century. By 1850 a few mills combining yarn and cloth production under one roof had appeared in the piedmont, but their production had little impact on the regional economy and was overshadowed by the textile mills of New England. Then, in the 1880s, a new group of merchants began to build textile mills, and poor white farm families were drawn off the land and into the factories. A new phenomenon—the mill town—appeared, and men and women who heretofore had relied entirely on farming for their subsistence moved to towns, operated machinery, and depended on factory work and wages for survival.

Despite the different developmental patterns of the Normand and piedmont cotton industries, shared assumptions about gender, childhood and work, and technological stagnation between the 1840s and 1920s produced remarkably similar work experiences for women and men and girls and boys on both sides of the Atlantic. To be sure, important variations did exist. Most notably, perhaps, Normand mill owners never exercised as much control over their workers as piedmont mill owners could and did in their isolated company towns. But despite the longer history of cotton spinning and weaving in Normandy and the cultural and agricultural differences between these two regions (Protestant versus Catholic, slave versus nonslave, tobacco and cotton versus wheat, rye, and cows), the similarities in the workers' experiences raise interesting questions about the roles of technology and culture in determining the organization of work and the division of labor (see Hartmann 1976; Phillips and Taylor 1980). The purpose of this chapter is to examine these questions.

The conclusions reached here are tentative. I have greater knowledge of the French textile industry in both its proto-industrial and industrial phases than of the piedmont industry, and I have used both archival and secondary sources for France but only secondary sources for the piedmont. I realize such a procedure is fraught with danger, but the monographic literature on the piedmont is so well grounded in archival and oral sources that I have felt confident in relying on it.

In addition, the sources available to French and American historians for the textile industry vary considerably. The registers of births, deaths, and marriages that were meticulously kept in France by priests and local officials make it possible for historians to reconstruct the families of textile workers. Supplemented with the few local memoirs that were written, government and private reports, and tax and notarial records, the parish and civil registers reveal a great deal about the economic, social, and demographic experiences of cottage workers during the proto-industrial period. What we do not have for France are letters or diaries or interviews that would give us a sense of what people thought and how they felt about their

work and their lives. Nor do we have reliable accounts of living conditions and family life. We can make only tentative, and one hopes
logical, guesses at the impact of economic changes on families and
individuals.

For the piedmont, the situation is different. American historians
have interviewed mill workers and their children, and many of their
experiences have been preserved in their own words. There is no
comparable oral history source for France. Yet, though American
historians have done some quantitative studies of the labor force in
the piedmont, there have been no detailed family reconstitution
studies such as exist for France. Despite these differences in source
material, comparisons seem possible and enlightening.

The Proto-industrial Village and the Mill Town

NORMANDY

The Seine River, winding slowly toward the English Channel from
Paris, passes through the old province of Normandy, dividing it into
two distinct sections. Rouen, the capital of the province, lies midway
to the Channel, on the northern bank of a large loop in the river.
Connected to both the domestic markets of Paris and the export
markets of England, Spain, and Portugal by short water routes,
Rouen was an important commercial center in eighteenth- and
nineteenth-century France (Levainville 1913, pp. 188–93).

North of the city lies the *pays de Caux*, a large triangular-shaped
plateau covered with grain fields and woods and traversed by a major road leading from Rouen to Dieppe on the Channel. From at
least the beginning of the seventeenth century, the peasants of the
Caux provided labor for the Rouen textile merchants, who hired
traveling porters to transport raw materials to the countryside and
completed goods back to the city for finishing and sale.

In the late seventeenth century, the number of *cauchois* peasants
who alternated between work in agriculture and cottage industry increased substantially as the Rouen merchants entered the expanding
world cotton trade (Archives Nationales [hereafter abbreviated AN]
F12 560; Dardel 1939, pp. 77–80). Spinners who had previously
spun locally produced wool and linen readily switched to the
cleaner, better-smelling, and more easily worked cotton, and weavers
began to ply their linen warps with cotton wefts. By the 1760s, the
cotton industry was expanding rapidly and the wool industry was in
full-scale decline (AN F12 560; Archives Departementales de la

Seine Maritime [hereafter abbreviated ADSM] 6MP5110; Sion 1909, pp. 12, 168–86; Dardel 1939, pp. 52, 77–80). The half-cotton, half-linen fabric produced in the Caux (called *siamoise* because it reminded people of Oriental fabric) was not of high quality, and its major purchasers were peasants, urban workers, and colonial planters who bought it to clothe their slaves. *Siamoises* came in red, white, and blue solids and red and white and blue and white stripes and checks[1] (AN F12 650: Reybaud 1862, pp. 268–69; Sion 1909, pp. 174–75; Fohlen 1956, p. 193).

By 1782, there were more than 188,000 spinners and weavers working within a fifteen-league radius of Rouen, and the *pays de Caux* was one of France's largest cotton cloth–producing regions[2] (Mollat 1979, pp. 218–23; AN F12 560). The scale on which *siamoises* were produced, their sale in national and international rather than local markets, and the use of a rural labor force that worked at home with traditional tools—spinning wheels and hand looms—makes the textile industry of the Caux a classic proto-industry.[3]

From its beginning, the cotton industry divided work on the basis of sex, as had the wool and linen industries before it. Spinning was designated women's work and weaving, men's work. The origins of this division of labor in the Caux and elsewhere in Europe are unclear, but it meshed nicely with the common assignment of nonharvest field work to men. Since at least eight spinners were necessary for every weaver, the textile industry provided more work for women and farming provided more work for men[4] (AN F12 560). Less skilled weavers spent as much as half the year working in the fields, which helped them subsist during periods when warps and shuttle yarn were difficult to obtain. Spinners and the most skilled weavers left their looms only during the harvest season, when virtually everyone in rural villages poured into the fields to cut and

---

1. Some pure cotton cloth was produced in the Caux in this period, but the cotton fibers produced by hand spinning were generally too weak to withstand the pressure applied to warp threads in the weaving process.

2. Rouen's midcentury population was only fifty to sixty thousand.

3. Franklin Mendels defined the concept of proto-industrialization in 1972. Proto-industries were generally much larger than the cottage industries that preceded them and that produced goods for local markets. Proto-industries were organized by urban merchants who put raw materials out into the countryside to be transformed into finished goods by peasants and villagers working in their own homes. These industries dominated local labor markets, employed large numbers of rural residents, and produced goods for sale in national and international (not local) markets (1972, p. 241).

4. Goy estimated nine and a half workers per loom or roughly eight spinners and carders to every weaver.

gather the grain crops. In addition to spinning and working on the harvest, the sexual division of labor within the family assigned a variety of tasks to rural women, including gardening, raising barnyard animals, gathering firewood, cooking, and child care[5] (Gullickson 1986, pp. 72, 75).

The significance of spinning as an employer of female labor, and hence as a source of income for the families of the Caux, can be seen in a cluster of villages known administratively in the eighteenth century as the canton of Auffay. Located along the eastern edge of the region, about halfway between Rouen and Dieppe (a total distance of sixty-two kilometers), the twenty-one villages ranged in size from tiny Bazomesnil with an adult population of only 96 to the village of Auffay with an adult population of 668 in 1796. This part of the Caux lay well within the range of the Rouen putting-out merchants, and three-quarters of the women in the villages worked as spinners. In the small village of Sevis, an astounding 98 percent of the women (120 out of 123) were spinners, and in no village were fewer than 60 percent of the women engaged in spinning. In comparison, only 15 percent of the male residents of the canton were weavers, and in only one village did weavers constitute as much as 40 percent of the male population[6] (ADSM L367).

In general, men earned more than women in Normandy in the eighteenth century, and textile workers were no exception. Spinners and weavers were paid by the piece, and their earnings varied according to the quality and quantity of their work (ADSM 6MP5122). Although estimates vary, even the highest earnings of female spinners were lower than the earnings of the most unskilled male weavers, and weavers were among the poorest of male villagers.[7] Nevertheless, women's earnings were crucial to their families' economic survival because most men's earnings were too low for them to support two adults, much less a family. Women's earnings from spinning helped their families survive the seasonal fluctuations in the demand for farm labor; paid the rent on small parcels of land, cottages, and

---

5. One of the attractions of the proto-industrial system for merchants was that they could pay rural workers less than their urban counterparts, partially because there were no guild restrictions outside of the cities and partially because cottage manufacturing was not the rural workers' only source of income.

6. Children under the age of twelve were not listed in the census.

7. Daily estimates (in sous) are as follows: Goy: spinners, 10–15, weavers, 20; Sion: spinners, 8–12, weavers, 20; Evrard: spinners, 12–14, weavers, 15–18; Bouloiseau: spinners, 8–15, weavers, 30–40 (AN F12 560; ADSM 6MP5154; Sion 1909, pp. 184–85, 310; Evrard 1947, pp. 349–50; Bouloiseau 1956, pp. 405–6).

workshops; and made it unnecessary for men to look for work as urban laborers during the winter months. Without women's earnings, many families would have been forced to choose between sending sons and daughters away from home to work, making the husband/ father a seasonal migrant, and moving out of the region. Women's earnings thus helped keep the family together and, in some cases, enabled widows to maintain their own households, although survival for these women could not have been easy[8] (ADSM L367, 6M23, 6M64, 6M83).

The procedure in the Caux was for women to sell their completed yarn in the local textile markets or back to the merchant from whom they had received the raw cotton on credit. Yarn merchants then sold the completed yarn to cloth merchants who had the thread washed and dyed and put it back out into the countryside to be woven. In the Auffay region, spinners rose in the middle of the night to carry their skeins of yarn several miles in leather backpacks to the textile market in Bacqueville, where trading began at dawn. Fabric was too heavy to be carried to markets and was retrieved by the same traveling porters who distributed spun yarn and prepared warps to the weavers (Mars 1876, pp. 38–39; Dardel 1939, p. 96; Fohlen 1956, pp. 148–53).

Income from the textile industry made life better than it would have been otherwise, but it did not make it easy. For most spinners, life was a matter of incessant work; small, damp, crowded houses; worry about the harvest and the availability of cotton; and fears about childbirth, illness, and death. Ironically, if the accounts of nineteenth-century reformers are at all accurate, even this fairly grim life would have looked good to later generations of textile workers who lived in Rouen and its industrial suburbs.

At the end of the eighteenth century, the textile industry underwent a series of dramatic changes. Competition from English textile merchants, whose fabric was now being produced with machine-spun yarn and was consequently lower in price and higher in quality than French fabric, forced the Rouen merchants to introduce machines or face bankruptcy. Although the early spinning jennies were small enough to be placed in cottages, the era of cottage machine spinning was short-lived. Larger machines soon replaced the small jennies, and mills had to be built to house them. Sparsely supplied

---

8. A quantitative study of the marriage registers and enumerated censuses for the village of Auffay show no evidence of seasonal migration by adult men, and children, especially daughters, remained at home until they married (see Gullickson 1986).

with streams to power the new machines, the Caux was destined not to be the site of factory spinning, although a few mills were built on the plateau in the early years when mills were quite small. As the machines increased in size, however, manufacturers sought rapidly running water for power, and spinning moved to the edges of the Caux, where its streams merged into small rivers and descended to the Seine River, leaving farmers, weavers, and unemployed spinners on the plateau.

By 1808, the mills were producing more yarn than male weavers could use, and the merchants began to hire unemployed and increasingly desperate spinners as weavers.[9] The hiring of women as weavers was a startling development in the region. For the first time, the cotton merchants' desire to increase production and hire cheap labor overrode their attachment to the traditional sexual division of labor, and they hired women to do men's jobs.

If women had been paid the same as male weavers, the sexual integration of weaving surely would have raised their economic and social status, but that did not happen. Although weaving was no longer strictly men's work, a new sexual division of labor within weaving was being established. Men continued to weave *siamoises*, while women were assigned to weave the new all-cotton calicos that the mechanization of spinning had made possible. Since demand for calicos was increasing at the expense of the demand for *siamoises*, this division of labor enabled women to dominate the craft. By mid-century, there were three times as many women as men weaving in the village of Auffay (fifty-four women versus seventeen men). In other villages, the predominance of women was even greater. In Totes, for instance, two hundred women and only forty men were weavers in 1851 (ADSM 6MP83). This new division of labor made it easy for merchants to pay women lower piece rates than they paid men and preserved the male-female hierarchy that the hiring of female weavers had threatened to overturn. Since men wove different fabric and were paid more than women, they could continue to think of themselves as more skilled (Noiret 1836, pp. 18–19).

The women who wove were the wives and daughters of men who worked at a variety of jobs—farming, artisan crafts, merchant businesses—and some of them, of course, were the wives and daughters of male weavers. Since the mills worked year-round and produced

---

9. A family reconstitution study of the village of Auffay from 1751 to 1850 makes it possible to follow individuals from one occupation to another in this period (see Gullickson 1986).

ever larger quantities of yarn, the putting-out merchants now pressured weavers (male and female) not to leave their looms during the harvest, and weaving became their sole source of income. In families where both parents wove, jobs were assigned on the basis of age rather than sex. Adults and older children wove, while younger children wound yarn onto bobbins for the shuttles, ran errands for the family, and assumed responsibility for the family's garden and any other land (Mars 1876; Sion 1909, p. 314).

Mechanical looms had a less profound impact on production than spinning machines and were introduced more slowly. Nevertheless, hand weaving was clearly doomed as a profession by the middle of the nineteenth century (ADSM L367, 6M83; Sion 1909, p. 317; Cauchois 1929, p. 15). The weavers struggled to compete with the new machines but eventually had to choose between factory work (which entailed leaving their villages) and farming. For a combination of reasons it was impossible for most weavers to resist migration to the mills: agriculture could not absorb all of the unemployed weavers because the availability of jobs in cottage industry had allowed the population of the region to exceed the labor needs of agriculture; weavers universally suffered from chest and neck ailments, varicose veins, and fatigue in the legs, which made it impossible for most of them to switch from weaving to heavy farm labor; and if male and female weavers could not find work in a factory, their children could, and at younger ages than in farming. Whether forced to move by unemployment or drawn to the new mills by curiosity and hope, considerable numbers of women and men migrated to the factories of Rouen from the 1840s on (Olphe-Galliard 1913, p. 30; Sion 1909, p. 441; Levainville 1911, pp. 58–59; Noiret 1836, pp. 17, 23–25, 30–31).

Mechanization and centralization of production had certain benefits for the merchant-manufacturers of Rouen. Machines helped stabilize quality in the industry; clustered factories eliminated the time and money spent on transporting goods in the proto-industrial era; and, in the long run, factory production gave manufacturers greater control over their work force. But in the short run the savings on transportation were offset by the expenditure on fixed costs (mainly buildings and machines), and workers did not easily give up control of the workplace (Reddy 1984, pp. 185–223). Moreover, the government and manufacturers of Rouen had long been worried about their ability to control textile workers if they were drawn into the city, and though Rouen workers would not be as rebellious as

Parisian workers, the manufacturers would eventually have to cope with the environmental and political problems created by rapid urban growth.

Although a few mills combined spinning and weaving under one roof, the three major processes—spinning, weaving, and dying—usually took place in separate establishments. All three types of mills existed in the city of Rouen, but far more of them were strung along the banks of streams on the city's outskirts. Small spinning and weaving villages became industrial suburbs.

Nineteenth- and early twentieth-century accounts of working-class life invariably trace a decline in living conditions from those of the rural *cauchois* weavers, whose houses "have a good appearance" and whose fields "are well tended," to those in the industrial suburbs, where the weavers, many of whom were still working at their own looms in their own houses well into the second half of the century, continued to raise part of their food in gardens behind their houses, to the city, where the lodgings of the workers were overwhelmingly grim. Standard descriptions of workers' living conditions in the city include narrow, pestilential alleys, open sewers, and dark, dangerous staircases leading to tiny rooms furnished with one or two cooking pots, a coverless mattress, and sacks of cinders where the children slept (Reybaud 1862, pp. 279–81).

As William Reddy's research has revealed, such descriptions cannot be taken at face value (1984, pp. 174–76). They are symbolically coded (the presence of only one bed raised the specter of incest, for instance), and their view of rural living conditions is as romanticized as their view of urban conditions is brutalized (Levainville 1913, p. 227; Reybaud 1862, p. 276; Cordier 1864, p. 38). Indeed, the goal of reformers who wrote such accounts appears to have been not to document actual conditions but to alarm the public and the government and impel them toward reform[10] (Reddy 1984, pp. 138–84).

Despite the flaws in the descriptions, it seems clear that living conditions did deteriorate as one approached the city. Even in the eighteenth century, merchants had had to pay higher piece rates to

---

10. Nineteenth-century reformers were far from accurate reporters of peasant and working-class life and work. Not only did they romanticize rural life and exaggerate the horrors of urban life, but they also were blind to the fact that the majority of hand weavers in the nineteenth century were women. Instead, they described the typical weaving family as one in which the man wove while his wife and children helped him by preparing the shuttles, greasing the machinery, and the like (see Levainville 1913, p. 227; Reybaud 1862, p. 276; Cordier 1864, p. 39).

urban workers because they had no access to garden plots as their rural counterparts did, and concerns about housing, open sewers, polluted drinking water, and other health hazards were too widespread in the nineteenth century to be unfounded (Reybaud 1862, pp. 282–96; Villermé 1840, 1:135–65; Pinkney 1958). Mill housing had not been planned and was not provided along with a job, and the tiny rooms workers found in the city appear to have borne little relationship to the small (and poor) houses of rural and suburban workers. There were no gardens, families lived piled up in apartments that were vacated during the day, and cheap cafeterias served meals to men and children while their wives and mothers worked in the mills (cooking as well as housekeeping were women's work) and to women who had neither the time, energy, nor inclination to cook after a day in the mills (Levainville 1913, p. 227).

THE PIEDMONT

Until the 1880s, the production of textiles was a minor part of the piedmont's economy despite the importance of the cotton crop in the South as a whole. Women did spin and weave cotton, linen, and wool for their family's clothing, and at least an occasional plantation owner taught his slaves to spin and weave, but the large putting-out textile industries that produced fabric for national and international markets in Normandy and other parts of western Europe in the nineteenth century did not develop in the South[11] (Mitchell 1921, p. 13; Newman 1978, pp. 219–20).

Early in the century, a few small mills appeared in the piedmont. They produced yarn that local women purchased either directly from the mills or from traveling porters. Like their eighteenth-century counterparts in the *pays de Caux*, hand weavers in the piedmont wove the machine-spun cotton with linen warps. Unlike the *cauchois* weavers, however, piedmont weavers in the eighteenth and nineteenth centuries were female, and they produced fabric for family use, not for sale. By midcentury, a few mills had installed power looms as well as spinning machines and were producing fabric for local markets, but such operations were rare at that time (Hall et al. 1987, pp. 19 n. 27, 25–26; Mitchell 1921, p. 18).

---

11. The putting-out system was not entirely unknown in the piedmont. In parts of North Carolina, women and children combined both farm work and mill work with the stringing of tobacco sacks for the tobacco warehouses (Newman 1978, pp. 219–20).

In the 1880s, a new group of manufacturers began to build cotton mills, which served as an alternative to farm work. With agriculture in decline, whole families, as well as single women and widows, left the farms on which they had been eking out a living and entered the mills. Some worked in the mills seasonally, rather like the proto-industrial workers in the *pays de Caux*, alternating planting, growing, and harvesting in the spring and summer with mill work in the winter. Others combined farm and factory work in more complex ways. The father of the family might work in a mill during the winter and be replaced at the loom by his wife in the summer so he could work in the fields. Or the women in a family might work in the mill while the husband/father continued to farm or do odd jobs for others (Hall et al. 1987, pp. 33, 39–40, 153).

Such labor patterns bear a closer resemblance to those of the proto-industrial cottage workers in the Caux than they do to those of French factory workers. Especially in the hand-spinning era, but also during the expansion of hand weaving that occurred in the early nineteenth century, Normand women were often the only members of the family who worked for the putting-out merchants. While wives and daughters spun or wove, their husbands, fathers, and brothers farmed, produced artisan goods that ranged from shoes to bricks, and toiled in merchant crafts such as baking or butchering. Once weaving moved into mills in Normandy, such combining of agriculture and manufacturing within the family became a thing of the past. Husbands and wives could not share mill work on a seasonal basis because men and women virtually never performed the same tasks. Similarly, the participation of men in farming while their wives and daughters worked in the textile mills was impossible for families who had moved into Rouen, and if it occurred in the industrial towns outside the city, it went unremarked by observers.

In the U.S. South the transition of farm families and farm women to the mills was eased somewhat by the rural setting of the piedmont mills, which made them more like the proto-industrial villages of the *pays de Caux* than like the industrial suburbs and the city of Rouen. Built in isolated areas with their own housing, stores, and school, mill houses were surrounded by garden plots and chicken coops, and more substantial amounts of farm and pasture land were available on the outskirts of the town. Indeed, aside from the presence of the mill and the absence of textile workers from their homes during the day, life in the piedmont mill villages bore a striking resemblance to that in the proto-industrial villages of the Caux. Both groups of workers retained strong rural ties. They kept animals and planted gardens and summer crops. In the piedmont, older children led the family cow to the pasture before they went to work in the mill in the morning and led her back in the evening, and younger children who did not work in the mill helped their mothers with the same work they would have done on the farm—feeding chickens, gathering eggs, churning butter, baking bread, and weeding the garden, just as the children of weavers did in the Caux (Hall et al. 1987, pp. 115, 146, 151; Mars 1876, p. 33).

Living conditions in proto-industrial villages and mill towns were better than in the purely agricultural villages of Normandy or on many piedmont farms, but they should not be sentimentalized. A native son, who was proud enough of his hometown to write two books about it, described eighteenth-century Auffay as filled with "an irregular agglomeration of low, damp, unhealthful houses, mean and shabby in appearance and distributed without taste." Conditions improved in the nineteenth century as streets were widened, swampy land was drained, and thatched roofs were replaced with wood and tile, but streets remained unpaved, plumbing rudimentary, and weavers among the poorest rural groups (ADSM, Municipal Council Records, Auffay 1832–50; Mars 1857, pp. 228–29, 260–61; Mars 1876, pp. 3, 79–81). Similarly, while some piedmont mills provided services that would have been impossible earlier in the nineteenth century in either country, like electricity and indoor plumbing, both were rare until well into the twentieth century. Moreover, streets were unpaved; dirt, mud, and flies abounded in the spring and summer; and the lack of sewers in most villages meant that most workers had to rely on foul-smelling privies in the backyard (Newman 1980, p. 351; Carlton 1982, pp. 90–95; Hall et al. 1987, pp. 115–20).

Differences did exist between the *cauchois* proto-industrial villages and the piedmont mill towns, however. The mills owned the houses and determined the rules of residency. The general rule in North Carolina was that a family had to provide one mill operative for each room of the house or sometimes two operatives for a three-room house. Families without enough children or adults to fill the labor quota took in boarders, who also, of course, helped pay the rent (McHugh 1988, pp. 19–20; Newman 1978, p. 210; Hall et al. 1987, p. 102). Children over age twelve might be required to take jobs in the mill unless they were explicitly excused (Carlton 1982, p. 102). In all towns, a family faced eviction if it could not provide enough workers or if any member proved to be an unreliable or unmalleable employee. Quitting was the worker's ultimate means of regaining independence, but it carried a high price tag because mill owners hired families to work for them and if one person quit, the entire family would be evicted (Hargett 1979, p. 57, quoted in Hall et al. 1987, pp. 106–7).

Piedmont mill owners controlled more than the number of workers per household and the behavior of operatives on the job. They also controlled workers' off-the-job behavior. As one North Carolina worker put it, "You didn't have no private life at all" (Newman 1978, p. 212). The local government was in the hands of the company, which enforced its own regulations and paid the salary of the town marshal, who was nominally appointed by the governor but in fact worked for the company (Carlton 1982, pp. 90–95). The goal was to instill middle-class values (especially thrift and diligence) in the workers. In one town, even women's dress was regulated, and workers faced eviction for disturbing the peace of their neighbors or for persistent drinking; less serious offenses (like riding a mule into a store) could result in temporary suspension from the mill. Pregnancy outside of marriage entailed immediate banishment from the village if the rest of the family wished to retain its home and jobs (Newman 1980, p. 351).

The control exercised by the mills was tempered to a certain extent by the extension of favors to employees. Women might be allowed to leave the mill to care for a sick child; a young couple might receive a loan to buy furniture; doctors' bills could be regulated and lowered for loyal employees with large families; and nurseries and schools were provided for children (Hall et al. 1987, pp. 122, 134). But the favors of paternalism came at the cost of freedom.

The Caux lacked both the control and the services of the piedmont mill owners. The proto-industrial merchants might own their weavers' looms as time went on, but they did not own their housing or even live in the same village with them. As a result, they could exercise little control over their workers' lives. Nor did nineteenth-century industrialists exercise such control over their workers, although they surely would have liked to, for they agonized over what they regarded as the workers' lack of decency and morality. In 1837, one group of Rouen manufacturers complained that workers allowed male children to go to cabarets, where they learned "lessons of precocious immorality" (AN F12 4705), and it was not uncommon in the nineteenth century for young, unmarried female mill workers to bear children (Fuchs 1984). French employers could fine or fire workers who did not show up for work on Mondays (a common problem in the early years of industrialization when workers were still accustomed to the more flexible work pace of cottage industry), failed to perform their jobs properly, or engaged in organizing or strike activities, but they could not control their leisure activities, as their counterparts in the piedmont were able to do later in the century, nor did they extend favors.

Mill Work

MIGRATION

Although the semirural nature of the piedmont mill towns paralleled living conditions in the proto-industrial villages of the Caux in many ways, work in the piedmont mills bore a far stronger resemblance to work in the Rouen mills than it did to work in proto-industry. In Normandy, mill building occurred in two waves in response to mechanization. Spinning mills appeared rapidly at the close of the eighteenth century; weaving factories, far more slowly as the nineteenth century progressed. The unemployment that resulted from both waves of mechanization forced young adults and sometimes entire families to migrate to Rouen because neither male nor female wages in the Caux were high enough to support a married couple, much less a family. Even the entry of women into hand weaving (and correlatively into garment making) in the early 1800s did not stem the drift to Rouen, however, because less work was available in weaving and sewing than had been the case in spinning. Nor were the weaving jobs permanent. Mechanical looms would eliminate them later in the century, resulting in a massive population shift from the countryside to the city.

By the time spinning was mechanized, a century of readily available jobs in cottage industry had accustomed families to keeping their daughters at home until they married, and the idea of sending young, unmarried girls to work in the mills near Rouen was not an attractive prospect to most parents. Daughters who did leave for the mills retained strong ties to their families and often infuriated mill owners by leaving at the approach of the harvest.

In addition to the resistance that stemmed from the break with habit and cultural tradition that occurred when unmarried daughters left home to work in the mills, parents may also have resisted out of fear that young women who lived and worked away from home would be more vulnerable to sexual exploitation than daughters who remained at home, a fear historians have demonstrated was based in reality (Hufton 1975, pp. 8–10; Tilly, Scott, and Cohen

1976, pp. 463–67; DePauw 1976, pp. 162–65, 188–91). Moreover, most peasants regarded factories and cities alike as dens of immorality. One articulate weaver in the 1830s argued, for instance, that women should not work in factories unless they were accompanied by a male relative whose presence would prevent "familiarities" (Noiret 1836, p. 19). Married women may have faced fewer dangers in moving to the new mill towns or the city, but the move could easily mean that the family had only reversed its unemployment problem because the early mills used small machines and continued to identify spinning as women's work. Migrating meant the women might be employed and the men unemployed. Such a prospect hardly made desirable the break with family and community entailed by work in the mills, and families preferred to stick things out in their home villages if they could. Some mill owners found it so difficult to recruit workers that they tried to hire state orphans on essentially indentured servant contracts (Evrard 1947, pp. 345–46, 351). The transition to factory spinning continued, however, despite the reluctance of the *cauchois* peasants to move.

Like the spinners before them, hand weavers struggled to compete with mechanical looms, holding out as long as they could at their hand looms, and when they did succumb to mill work, they preferred walking long distances to work in the few local mills to moving to Rouen and its industrial suburbs. Eventually, however, weavers had to make one of two choices—migration and factory work or agricultural day laboring. Most chose migration (Olphe-Galliard 1913, p. 30; Sion 1909, p. 441; Levainville 1911, pp. 58–59). As the size of the machines increased, men, as well as women and children, found employment in the mills. By midcentury there were 17,448 workers in the spinning mills in or near Rouen, split almost evenly among men, women, and children (see table 3.1).

In the piedmont, some women and men moved readily and eagerly to the mills, abandoning poor farms and lives of heavy labor for work they thought would be easier and the new houses being built by the mills. Others moved only to discover they could not bear to work in the mills, while still others remained on the farms. Throughout the late nineteenth and early twentieth centuries, widows, households headed by females, young single women, and landless farm laborers dominated the movement from the farms to the mills, partially because their economic prospects in farming were poor and partially because piedmont mills, like the early Rouen spinning mills and the later weaving factories, offered more jobs for women than for men (Levainville 1913, pp. 33, 37; Newman 1980,

TABLE 3.1. Employment Figures for the Mechanized Textile Industry in Upper Normandy,[a] 1847–1848

	Men		Women		Children		Total	
Industry	No.	%	No.	%	No.	%	No.	%
Spinning	6,224	54	5,628	53	5,596	71	17,448	58
Calico printing	3,880	34	1,180	11	1,940	25	7,000	23
Weaving	1,390	12	3,906	36	307	4	5,603	19
Total	11,494	100	10,714	100	7,843	100	30,051	100

Sources: ADSM 6M1100; AN F12 4476C.
[a] The arrondissements of Rouen, Dieppe, and LeHavre.

pp. 7, 41; McHugh 1988, pp. 3, 78). As one man reported, when his father died in 1913, leaving his mother with three young children, no matter how hard she worked, "She just couldn't make the going." Like many other widows, she moved her family to a mill town where she and her children, as they grew older, worked in the mill (Hardin 1980, pp. 2–3, quoted in Hall et al. 1987, pp. 37–38).

WORKING

Work in the mills was different but not necessarily easier than farm work. As the authors of *Like a Family* succinctly put it, "Mill hands rose early in the morning, still tired from the day before. For ten, eleven, or twelve hours they walked, stretched, leaned, and pulled at their machines. Noise, heat, and humidity engulfed them. The lint that settled on their hair and skin marked them as mill workers, and the cotton dust that silently entered their lungs would eventually cripple or kill them. At best, mill work was a wrenching change [from farming]" (Hall et al. 1987, p. 53).

Mill work also differed from cottage manufacturing in significant ways. One of the hallmarks of the proto-industrial system was the control spinners and weavers exercised over their work time and work space. Such control was lost when work moved into factories, where machines set the pace of work and supervisors and managers observed workers. Workers struggled to retain as much control over their environment and work as they could, organizing walkouts and strikes and quitting when they felt the assault on their dignity or independence was too great, but the gradual loss of control could not be reversed (Reddy 1984, pp. 87–137; Hall et al. 1987, pp. 90–105, 212–36). In addition, just as mill workers in the piedmont would be, Normand workers were now surrounded by noisy, dirty, dangerous machinery, a far cry from the spinning wheels, hand looms, and small spinning jennies of the proto-industrial era.

In both Normandy and the piedmont, labor was divided by age and sex, and in both regions mills employed more women and children than adult men (see table 3.1). In the Rouen mills, men operated large spinning mules that required strength as well as skill, while women operated power looms (Reddy 1984, p. 241; Reybaud 1862, p. 276). Children were employed as assistants in all branches of the industry, but the majority worked in the spinning mills, piecing broken threads and replacing full bobbins with empty ones (Reddy 1984, pp. 76–82). In some cases entire families worked in the same mill, but the division of production processes into different mills meant that husbands and wives as well as parents and children frequently worked in separate mills.

In the piedmont mills, the use of ring rather than mule spinning eliminated the need for strength and extensive training, and women and girls rather than men operated the machines. Weaving, which required more skill than spinning, was the only mill job men and women performed side by side. In addition, men carded raw cotton, made rovings, and did drawing in (Newman 1980, p. 349; Frankel 1984, p. 42; Hall et al. 1987, pp. 67–69). As in Normandy, children performed more tasks connected to spinning than to weaving. Girls worked as spinners, splicers, and winders, while their brothers usually entered the mills to doff bobbins, haul yarn, and run the machines in the carding room. In both countries, children began to work in the mills at young ages, and families and employers alike frequently ignored minimum age legislation that was designed to prevent the employment of children.[12] Some parents, especially widows, in both countries needed the money their children could earn, and in Normandy, at least, some parents thought their children were safer if they were in the mills than if they were left to fend for themselves while their parents worked (Reddy 1984, p. 238). In the piedmont, workers recalled that as children they had often found

---

12. In 1841, France passed its first minimum age law for factories. The law prohibited the employment of children under the age of eight in large textile mills. This part of the law appears to have been generally followed, but its provisions for older children were ignored. In 1874, a new law raised the minimum age to twelve and further reduced the work hours of older children (see *Le Travail et l'enfant au XIXᵉ siècle* 1978). By 1913, North Carolina, South Carolina, Alabama, and Georgia had passed laws that prohibited the employment of children under the age of twelve. As in Normandy, such laws were poorly enforced, however, and children continued to work in the mills until passage of the federal Fair Labor Standards Act of 1938, which established sixteen as the minimum age (see Hall et al. 1987, pp. 58–61).

mill work more interesting than school or play, and their parents had accepted their help even when they were not formally employed by the mills because it eased their work and increased their take-home pay (Hall et al. 1987, pp. 60–61).

Children and adults worked a staggering number of hours in spinning mills and weaving factories. In Normandy in the mid-nineteenth century, the standard workday was thirteen and a half hours of work plus one and a half hours for meals, amounting to fifteen hours spent inside the factory. In the summer the workday went from 5:00 A.M. to 8:00 P.M. In the winter, work began at dawn and continued until fifteen hours later, usually around 10:00 P.M. In addition, of course, workers had to walk to and from the factory, and for many of them the distance was two to three kilometers each way (AN F12 4705). These hours were tolerable only because neither the machinery nor the employees worked constantly. Judging from production figures, spinning machines ran less than half the time that workers were in the factory, and some mill owners reported that children worked only four hours a day and spent the rest of the time napping behind the machinery and playing in the mill's courtyard (Reddy 1984, pp. 111, 238).

A similar situation existed in the piedmont. In the late nineteenth century, the mills operated twelve hours a day, six days a week. Work usually began at 6:00 A.M. and ended at 6:00 P.M. As in the Rouen mills, breakdowns, cotton shortages, and even low water levels could result in break time for the workers. Before the 1920s, the machines ran slowly, and it was easy for operatives to watch each other's machines so they could rest, smoke, play pranks, talk to their friends, and engage in courting. Among the children, bobbin doffers had the most break time. They spent about half of each day resting or playing (Hall et al. 1987, pp. 77, 87–89).

In both countries, wages varied by age and sex. Children earned the least of all workers, followed by women in more skilled positions, and finally by men, who occupied the top of the gender hierarchy regardless of the work they did. Adolescent girls often earned more than adolescent boys because they performed the same work as older women, but by the time they reached age sixteen or eighteen, they had reached their earning ceiling. No matter how much longer they worked in the mills, they would never earn more because they were excluded from supervisory and other lucrative positions like machine repairing and mule spinning. Boys, however, could aspire to supervisory or machine shop jobs and in Normandy to mule spinning jobs, all of which paid well compared to the jobs held by women and children. On the average, women's wages were about 60 percent of men's in both countries (AN F12 4705; Hall et al. 1987, p. 67).

Gender Roles and Assumptions

The age and sexual divisions of labor that existed in the Rouen and piedmont mills were based on cultural assumptions about the proper relationship between the sexes and their "natural" abilities. These imagined differences in abilities were both a product of long-standing sexual divisions of labor and a rationale for the creation of new divisions.[13] In both countries, men were assigned jobs that re-quired strength (mule spinning and carding), skill (weaving, mule spinning, and carding), authority (supervisory positions), or an inti-mate knowledge of machinery (machine repairing). Women were as-signed jobs that required little strength and skill (ring spinning), nimble fingers (weaving and ring spinning), and patience. Only in rare cases, such as mechanical weaving in the piedmont, did other gender values like the desire to provide jobs for men as well as for women (because it was "unnatural" for the men in a family to be economically dependent on the women) take precedence over the sexual segregation of tasks and lead to sexually integrated work.

The confinement of women to low-skilled positions was buttressed by the assumption that they were only temporary employees, des-tined to leave the labor force when they married or when the family had passed some financial crisis. This assumption became increas-ingly untrue in both countries when the passage of child labor laws eliminated young girls and boys from the labor force. In the forma-tive years of mill building in both countries, the typical female worker was either a young girl or a widow forced into the mill by economic necessity. By the mid-twentieth century, children no longer worked in the mills, and married women predominated as the industry relied increasingly on female labor (Tilly and Scott 1978, pp. 195–97; Frankel 1984, p. 41). Such women were usually in the labor force for life. Confining women to less-skilled work meant that they received less satisfaction as well as less pay than many men and reinforced the desire of many women to drop out of the mill labor force when they could.

---

13. As Valerie Oppenheimer's research (1970, p. 102) has shown, people rarely perceive sexual divisions of labor as mutable, assuming instead that the current divi-sions have always existed, are based on natural differences between the sexes, and, consequently, are economically rational. Also see Lloyd (1975).

The belief that skills were sex-linked was so embedded in both cultures that neither workers nor employers challenged the sexual division of labor, despite clear evidence that at least some women were as strong as men, as knowledgeable about machinery, and as capable of exercising authority. Women played prominent roles in the early years of labor organizing in the United States textile and garment industries (Dublin 1979; Kessler-Harris 1982), traditionally performed agricultural tasks like butter and cheese making that required at least as much strength as men's jobs (Pinchbeck 1969), and on occasion demonstrated considerable knowledge of machinery. Two separate labor markets existed, however, and women were never considered for machinist, supervisory, or other positions held by men. Nor is there any evidence that women requested such jobs (Hall et al. 1987, p. 72). This is not to say that women never did "men's" work, only that they were never hired to do it. Few men knew more about machinery than Eula Durham, for instance, but her skills would never lead directly to a job, as her account of how a young supervisor ignored her advice about what was wrong with her machine illustrates. "After he went home," she recounted, "I stopped the frame off and went in the basement and got me a chain and come back and put it on. Started the frame up and it run just as pretty as you ever seen. I told them I've been down there forty-five years: I know when anything was running right and when it weren't. Cause weren't a frame in that mill I hadn't tore down and put back together. I know exactly what's the matter with them" (Durham and Durham 1978, pp. 11–12, quoted in Hall et al. 1987, pp. 71–72).

With the possible exception of mule spinning in Normandy, none of the jobs in the Normand or piedmont textile industries required physical or technical skills that were beyond the reach of most women. Occasionally a specific physical characteristic like height made a job easier (e.g., tall weavers could reach over their looms to repair broken threads, whereas short ones had to walk around to the back), but such characteristics were not prerequisites for specific jobs, nor were they sex-linked. In general, girls as well as boys could have worked as doffers, boys could have done splicing and winding, women could have repaired machines and supervised work, and men could have done ring spinning in the piedmont and power weaving in Normandy. That none of these things happened was a result of gender assumptions, not of innate sex-linked skills.

Reaction to the rare attempt by employers to break the sexual division of labor demonstrates how entrenched the conceptualization of male and female skills was in nineteenth-century Western culture. When the Rouen merchants hired women as hand weavers in the early 1800s, they posed an immediate threat to the assumption that women could not weave as well as men. To ward off the possibility that the old assumption was wrong, a new sexual division of labor based on the fiber used for warp threads was established, which shored up the old assumptions about the natural abilities of the two sexes and, coincidentally, facilitated the payment of lower piece rates to female weavers. Charles Noiret, a Rouen weaver, probably spoke for most male weavers when he explained that women "make the articles that are the most easily made and consequently are the least lucrative, because they are more suited to their [weaker] physical strength and their inferior intelligence." Men, by contrast, were "*naturally* inclined toward the articles whose construction is more laborious and difficult [i.e., *siamoises*] because they procure higher benefits" (1836, pp. 18–19). Noiret's logic is somewhat difficult to follow, but it is clear that he believed men were stronger, more skilled, and more intelligent than women. That this sexual division of labor was based on cultural rather than physical distinctions is nicely demonstrated by the fact that the fabric whose manufacture he regarded as being beyond women's strength and intelligence was the very fabric women wove at home in the piedmont.

Other reversals in the sexual division of labor also existed. In Normandy, spinning machines were operated by men; in the piedmont, men would not touch them. In the piedmont, both men and women operated power looms; in Normandy, this was women's work (Reddy 1984, pp. 162–65, 240–41; Reybaud 1862, p. 276; Hall et al. 1987, p. 67). Even when the demand for workers was great and men were clearly able to do the work, men strenuously resisted doing women's work. In the Normand hand-spinning era, for instance, able-bodied adult men never worked as spinners (except perhaps behind closed doors), even though most men had learned to spin as children and eight to ten spinners were needed for every weaver.

In both cultures, gender assumptions extended beyond job assignments. In addition to being thought to be physically weak, nonmechanical, and incapable of exercising authority, women were assumed to be the natural caretakers of children and families. As a result, adult women and young girls who worked in the mills had less leisure time than men and boys because they were responsible for cooking, cleaning, sewing, childrearing, and related activities. Indeed, the favors that mill owners extended to workers in the piedmont were also gender-based. Women were allowed to leave the mills to fix meals, nurse a baby, care for a sick child, and so forth. Men were allowed to leave for more "masculine" activities such as ball games (Frankel 1984, p. 46; Hall et al. 1987, pp. 135–36, 139, 158).

In both cultures, nineteenth-century critics of the mill system also became critics of the employment of female labor, viewing it as interfering with women's performance of their natural duties. Hugh Wilson, editor of the Abbeville, South Carolina, *Press and Banner*, argued in 1883, for instance, that mill work prevented girls from learning "the duties and work of a womanly life—the life which nature and the laws of our civilization intended that she should live" (quoted in Carlton 1982, p. 123). Jules Simon in France went so far as to argue that "the woman, become a worker, is no longer a woman." Separated from her children and husband for long hours every day, the female factory worker abandoned her children to wet nurses, left young children to fend for themselves on the street, failed to prepare meals, and allowed the family's clothes to fall into tatters, all of which Simon regarded as unnatural (1861, pp. i–iv). Neither reformer would have understood a woman like Carrie Gerringer, who "would rather be at work than be at the house anytime," including when her children were "little and growing up" (1979, pp. 21–22; Hall et al. 1987, p. 155).

The conflicts that could arise between reformers and working women are illustrated in a case cited by William Reddy involving Lille, another textile city in northern France. In 1858, a young widow claimed that all of her three children were over the age of twelve (the minimum age for full-time work), although the youngest clearly was not, so they could work with her in the mill. She had no money to pay for baby-sitting and was new in the city so she had no friends to turn to for help. Far from an uncaring act, taking her children into the mill seemed to this mother to be safer than leaving them alone while she worked. The factory inspector did not agree, however, and both the widow and her children were fired. The police agent who recorded the incident used it as an illustration of the "cynical willingness of parents to exploit their own children" (Archives Départementales du Nord M613/16, Oct. 1858, cited in Reddy 1984, p. 238).

Gender assumptions applied to unmarried women as well. In nineteenth-century France, the term *femmes isolées* was applied both to clandestine prostitutes (those who were not registered with the police) and to women wage earners living alone in furnished rooms, implying, of course, that one could easily become the other (Scott 1988, pp. 142–43). Most stigmatized of all were female factory operatives who worked away from home in the company of men. French reformers worried repeatedly about the morality of girls who worked in factories along with men,[14] and Dale Newman has recounted the case of a young piedmont mill worker who was told by his parents, "If you marry that woman from the cotton mill, don't ever come to our house again. Don't come home no more" (1978, p. 207). Male mill workers also experienced discrimination, but only women bore the double stigma of being mill workers and being out of their proper sphere—the home.

Both the Normand and piedmont industries were highly dependent on the labor of women and children, and though mill owners shared the reformers' opinions that women and at least female children belonged at home rather than in the mill, they were not willing to lose their inexpensive child and female employees. Accordingly, they opposed the passage of any but the mildest protective legislation; ignored the laws that were passed; and, when legislation finally did reduce the availability of children, encouraged married women to stay in the labor force (AN F12 4713; AN F12 4755, 4722, 4719; Hall et al. 1987, pp. 58–61).

Conclusions

Comparing the experiences of the proto-industrial and industrial Normand and piedmont textile workers raises at least two questions about the picture historians have traditionally drawn of the transition from farming to manufacturing and about the relationship among technology, culture, and the organization of work. These questions cannot be fully answered on the basis of this study, but they deserve more exploration, and further comparative research may change some of our views of industrialization.

First, the Normand and piedmont cases challenge the traditional, and oversimplified, view of peasants and farmers as entering an alien urban world in which virtually everything was unfamiliar and disorienting when they moved from the countryside to mill towns and cities. The piedmont mill village and the Normand proto-industrial system eased workers' transition from a rural to an urban society. The proto-industrial system did so by introducing peasants to the vagaries of national and international markets and the demands of unknown employers long before they set foot in a factory;

---

14. Jules Michelet found even the word *l'ouvriére* (female worker) to be "impious and sordid" (1860, p. 22).

the piedmont mill town by providing the familiar solace of general farm work (gardening, animal husbandry) for people while they worked in the mills.

Indeed, if one looks for the continuities as well as the discontinuities in textile workers' experiences, it appears in many cases that the transition to factory work was not as abrupt and probably not as psychologically disorienting as historians have supposed. To cite a third example, the young women who worked in the Lowell, Massachusetts, mills in the early nineteenth century retained no daily link to the chores and rhythms of the farm, but the boardinghouses in which they lived eased the transition from the farm to the factory by providing a surrogate family (Dublin 1979, p. 79).

In none of these cases did the manufacturers consciously choose to ease the transition to factory manufacturing for their labor force. After all, the eighteenth-century Rouen putting-out merchants could not have foreseen the Industrial Revolution and the building of factories; the entrepreneurs of the piedmont built their mills in rural areas, not to make mill work more attractive, although they needed to attract workers, but to take economic advantage of the fall line; and the Lowell manufacturers built boardinghouses not to satisfy the needs of their workers but to convince Yankee farmers that it would be safe to send their daughters to Lowell.

Nevertheless, all three groups of manufacturers did create a buffer zone between the rural farm and the urban factory, thereby easing the transition to factory work. At the very least, then, we need to introduce some variations into the standard picture of industrialization, and, if the transition experiences of the Normandy and piedmont workers turn out to have been more typical than atypical of textile workers, we need to redraw that picture altogether.

Second, the sexual divisions of labor that existed in both textile industries demonstrate that culture played at least as large a role as technology in the employment and training of the labor force. Technological developments did, of course, have profound effects on the production of textiles. As machines increased in size, for instance, it was not feasible to put them in workers' homes, and as a result the factory was born. In addition, machines increased the subdivision of production into small tasks. But gender assumptions were far more important in the sex-typing of jobs than were technological developments.

Even though technology sometimes eliminated the need for physical strength (as in ring spinning) and other times demanded it (as in mule spinning and carding), gender assumptions and not tech-

nology turned divisions of labor based on particular physical attributes into divisions of labor based on sex and age. Although the
designation of particular jobs as appropriate work for men or for
women varied between the countries, the assumptions that underlay
the assignments and the consequences of those assumptions were
the same. In both countries, men were assumed to be naturally au-
thoritative, mechanical, and easily trained. Women were assumed to
be submissive, nonmechanical, and good at repetitive tasks. Men
were also regarded as the heads of families and the major breadwin-
ners, whereas women's first obligation was to bear and rear children. These values made it appropriate to divide jobs by sex, to pay
men more than women, and, because men were assumed to be in
the work force for life, to train men and not women for skilled positions. In contrast, women were assumed to be temporary workers
(their proper place was the home, not the factory) and thus training
them to hold skilled jobs, even though they could be paid less than
skilled men, was perceived as economically unsound. The textile industries simply followed the gender assumptions of their respective
societies, delineating jobs and pay according to sex and age and for-
going the advantages of assigning work solely on the basis of ability,
experience, and reliability. Far from a consequence of mechanization or capitalism, preexisting conceptualizations of men's and wom-
en's skills and of the appropriate hierarchical relationships between
the sexes appear to have determined the divisions of labor in these
industries.

Ironically, then, it is the similarities and not the differences in the
textile workers' experiences in Normandy and the piedmont that
may tell us the most about the relationships between culture and
technology, men and women, and the transition from cottage to factory work.

4

Determinants of Industrialization
on the North American "Periphery"

Phillip J. Wood

Since the emergence of the first capitalist factories in eighteenth-century England, the role of textile production in the industrialization of formerly "peripheral" areas of the world economy has been replayed on numerous occasions. A recent study identifies twenty discrete regional or national textile "industries" as early as 1910, many of them outside the most advanced areas of capitalist production (Clark 1987). It should come as no surprise, therefore, that the textile industry figures prominently in a variety of theoretical and historical discussions of the transition to capitalism and the determinants of peripheral capital accumulation (see chapter 1 in this volume). Nor should it come as a surprise, given the diversity of case studies and theoretical approaches involved, that firm conclusions remain elusive.

Studies of the textile industry and of the industrialization of the American South are similarly inconclusive. A variety of factors have been identified as potentially significant determinants of the southern pattern of capital accumulation. They include, in no particular order, a shortage of capital (Woodward 1971; Carlton 1982; Cobb 1984); the poverty, illiteracy, and relative lack of skills among the southern labor force and its isolation from national labor market influences (Danhof 1964; Woodward 1971; Wright 1986); high levels of white community integration in a "traditional" society (Mitchell 1921; Blauner 1964); a system of coercive production relations rooted in the antebellum plantation system and the postwar dominance of planters and their values (Wiener 1978; Mandle 1978; Billings 1979; Billings and Blee 1986); social, economic, and political rigidities resulting from the racial element in the South's social structure (Nicholls 1960; Naylor and Clotfelter 1964, Maddox 1967, Key 1949); discriminatory freight rates (Tindall 1967; Woodward 1971); and dependence on external capital, markets, and commission agents (Woodward 1971; Wiener 1978; Billings 1979).

Though by no means comprehensive, this list indicates the diversity of thinking on the textile industry and the transition to industrial capitalism in the South. A review of the literature will also provide a sense of the unresolved questions confronting those who try to understand the southern historical experience: how to find a reliable way of distinguishing the crucial historical determinants of peripheral industrialization from the not so crucial; how to establish patterns of historical determination; and how to assess the relative merits of particular theoretical approaches so as to generate coherent explanations of historical reality.

One way of tackling these problems, though not the only one, is by means of the comparative method. Comparative analysis is present in most treatments of southern textile industrialization but usually is in a secondary role in which it is dominated by the assumptions and conceptual apparatuses of particular theoretical models. The logic and parameters of these comparisons are usually implicit rather than explicit, and they rarely make a major contribution to understanding beyond that provided by the model itself. Thus neoclassical competitive models usually involve not only an image of the traditional barriers to these processes in the South but also an implicit but equally schematic barrier-free explanation of growth and modernization in other regions (Higgs 1971; Williamson 1965). Moreover, social historians and historical sociologists, the most numerous recent dissenters against the free-market hegemony, have duplicated this situation in their contrasting images of "coercive" southern production relations and supposedly "free" collective bargaining between capital and labor elsewhere (Wiener 1978; Mandle 1978; Billings 1979). In both models, the comparative benchmark is industrial America, despite a variety of other temporal, locational, political, and economic differences that are not systematically addressed.

This essay is a comparative study of the roughly simultaneous experiences of textile industrialization in the Carolinas and Maritime Canada. The comparative method is used to clarify the historical factors that facilitate peripheral industrialization and to identify a series of parallels in the two industrialization processes: first in the logic of textile industrialization for regional capital; second in the constraints facing newly industrializing regions within larger capitalist economies; and third in the social and organizational forms taken by the industrialization process. Despite these similarities, however, the outcomes of these attempts at peripheral industrialization were very different. After flourishing briefly in the 1880s, the Maritime cotton mills stagnated, were swallowed by their central Canadian competitors, and eventually disappeared. By the Depression of the 1930s, the region's other secondary manufacturing industries had met much the same fate. In contrast, textile capital in the Carolinas overcame its constraints and went on to create and preserve the socioeconomic basis for long-term, expanded capital accumulation. Why were these outcomes so different?

Although the analysis presented here is by no means conclusive, it suggests that a potentially important determinant may be the differences in productive relations in the two regions. As has been argued elsewhere (Woodman 1977, 1979; Wood 1986, chap. 2), the crucial factors in the capitalist development of the Carolinas in the postbellum period were the gradual creation of the southern system of wage relations in cotton agriculture and the potential provided by the resulting pool of impoverished "free" wage labor for the creation and preservation of long-term locational advantages in the production of surplus value in industry. In contrast, agricultural production in the Maritimes in the late nineteenth century was overwhelmingly carried out not by wage earners but by farmers who owned their land. Continued ownership of the means of production by the direct producers and the continuing viability of petty commodity production within a framework of occupational pluralism impeded the creation of industrial locational advantages and prevented the Maritime textile industry from seriously challenging its competitors in central Canada.

Textile Industrialization in the Carolinas and the Maritimes, 1870–1930

The last quarter of the nineteenth century was a particularly difficult transitional period for capitalists in both the Carolinas and the Maritimes. The structures of social relations and of expectations upon which regional accumulation strategies had been founded had been seriously destabilized and destroyed, respectively, by the decline of the British market for lumber and wooden ships during the depression of the 1870s and by the Civil War and emancipation. Subsequently, as a result of the National Policy and the end of Reconstruction, both the Carolinas and the Maritimes were incorporated, as peripheral regions, into larger, already industrializing economies on disadvantageous terms with respect to population size and density, available resources, markets, labor power, and capital. In their search for new, practical means of self-preservation and accumulation, many capitalists in both regions turned to cotton textile production, even though that meant facing competition already established in other regions.

The "bets" made by the new regional industrialists were not completely blind, however. Textile production had existed in both regions in the past (Wright 1986, pp. 125–28; Wood 1986, pp. 31–33; Acheson 1985, p. 181), and capitalists in both regions had the examples of Great Britain and New England on which to build their hopes that textile production could eventually become the basis for expanded and diversified industrialization. Moreover, falling raw cotton prices throughout the late nineteenth century and protected markets in both countries also reduced risks and increased the margins for profitable production (Lemert 1933, p. 27; DeLottinville 1979, p. 4; Fite and Reese 1965, pp. 468–69; Vatter 1975, pp. 50–51).

Nevertheless, there were important difficulties in making this transition. They can be considered under three broad categories. First was the problem of mobilizing sufficient capital to construct, equip, and operate modern factories. Second was the complex of problems involved in mobilizing and maintaining, at competitive prices, a sufficiently large labor force with an appropriate distribution of physical attributes and skills and maintaining a competitive rate of exploitation. Finally, there was the complex of problems associated with peripheral location: dependence on external markets and the problem of transportation.

Textile production was chosen as one of the bases of accumulation strategies in both regions at least in part to deal with the first two problems. Even by the standards of the late nineteenth century, it was a relatively labor-intensive industry with modest fixed capital costs of entry. Moreover, despite innovations such as the ring spindle, the industry was technologically relatively stable. In combination, these characteristics imposed limits on capital accumulation as a means to increase productivity and on the competitive advantages associated with size and agglomeration. Since the capacity for increased machine speeds or work intensity was limited, adding new capital usually meant adding extra workers rather than shedding existing ones. Thus, with relatively constant returns to scale, small southern and Maritime mills promised to be only somewhat less efficient than their large competitors. Minor organizational or other difficulties could be offset by the common practice of ignoring depreciation costs (Carlton 1982, p. 60).

These characteristics only minimized the scale of the transitional problems, however; they did not eliminate them. Relatively significant amounts of capital had to be raised, and even though the problem of capital shortage was more serious in the South, the funds were raised in similar ways in each region. Mill-building campaigns were the result of collective rather than individual efforts, based on appeals to local loyalties, civic pride, and regional solidarity, and were associated with the building of towns and communities in interior areas. In both cases, however, the community was that of local businessmen, merchants, lawyers, landowners, and other professionals, whose common interest lay in increasing real estate values, demand for locally produced raw materials, and population and in expanding commercial and industrial activities (Acheson 1985, pp. 177, 180; McCann 1981, p. 64; DeLottinville 1979, pp. 40–42; Wood 1986, p. 35; Wright 1986, pp. 44–45; Carlton 1982, chap. 2).

Since capital was initially more scarce in the South, mill-building campaigns there involved larger numbers of smaller investors, and mills tended to be smaller (see table 4.1) than in the Maritimes. In the longer term, these differences in investment patterns and the scale of production tended to decline. In many cases, small-scale, local subscriptions were designed to demonstrate community support, to avoid charges of "Yankee" domination, and to provide seed money to test the viability of production in a given location. To the extent that these experiments were successful, small investors tended to decline in importance when the early mills were either taken over by larger investors or eclipsed by newer, larger mills (Wood 1986, p. 36; Carlton 1982, pp. 56–57.)

For the purposes of this study, however, the important point is that capital shortage in the South led initially to greater involvement by external investors than in Maritime Canada. With one exception, the Maritime mills seem to have been largely self-financed in all areas but working capital, which they obtained from the region's banks, particularly the Bank of Nova Scotia (Acheson 1985, p. 190; Frost 1982, pp. 13–14). In contrast, many of the southern mills were dependent on external sources for a variety of needs, including fixed capital. Typically, local subscriptions would provide enough capital to erect a building and company housing, and local tax con-

TABLE 4.1. Size of Cotton Mills in New Brunswick, Nova Scotia, and North Carolina, 1870 1890

Region	1870	1880	1890
New Brunswick			
Number of mills	2	2	5
Average number of employees per mill	64	172	350
Average value of capital per mill (thousands of dollars)[a]	–	–	486.6
Average value of products per mill (thousands of dollars)	80.3	138.1	350
Nova Scotia			
Number of mills	–	–	3
Average number of employees per mill	–	–	199
Average value of capital per mill (thousands of dollars)[a]	–	–	172
Average value of products per mill (thousands of dollars)	–	–	239
North Carolina			
Number of mills	33	49	91
Average number of employees per mill	44	66	94
Average value of capital per mill (thousands of dollars)[a]	31.2	58.3	81.4
Average value of products per mill (thousands of dollars)	40.8	52.1	105.1

Source: Wood 1989a, p. 14.
[a] For 1870 and 1880, capital refers to fixed and circulating capital. For 1890, capital includes only buildings, machinery, tools, and implements.

cessions would ease the early expenses. New England textile machinery manufacturers would provide credit for capital equipment in return for stock. Finally, because of the limited regional banking system, textile capitalists frequently turned to commission agents in New York, Boston, Baltimore, or Philadelphia for working capital, sometimes in return for stock but more often in return for a contract to become the mill's exclusive selling agent.

Machinery manufacturers tended to liquidate stock as soon as possible so they could proceed with their own accumulation strategies in the highly competitive struggle for market share. In contrast, commission agents tended to be directly involved over the long term. According to David L. Carlton, by 1916, 28 percent of South Carolina mill stock was owned by external investors, many of whom were undoubtedly associated with commission houses (1982, p. 57). These houses frequently used their control of marketing to maximize their volume-based commissions, which tended to exacerbate the industry's chronic problems of overproduction and low prices (Wood 1986, pp. 35–37). Paradoxically, it seems possible that the fragmented relationship between producers and commission agents (with its origins in capital shortage and the fragmentation of textile production) may have been an important reason the acquisition of textile mills by commission agents, which occurred in Canada in the 1890s, was postponed in the United States until well into the twentieth century. Nevertheless, the southern industry, which began with more involvement of external capital, survived and prospered, whereas its more financially independent Maritime counterpart did not.

The problem of recruiting skilled, manual, and supervisory workers was minimal in both regions but not nonexistent. In the South, which was a "low-wage region in a high-wage country" (Wright 1986, p. 76), efforts to recruit skilled labor into the region failed, reinforcing tendencies toward small-scale production, local development of skills, spinning, and especially the ring spindle. Maritime textile capitalists were more fortunate in that they were able to recruit skilled labor from elsewhere, especially the United Kingdom, and were therefore able to begin operations on a larger scale. In contrast with the South, however, in the Maritimes there were no cultural, historical, economic, or other barriers to emigration, and it proved to be difficult to retain either native or imported workers as industrialization proceeded more extensively and intensively elsewhere in Canada and in the northeastern United States (DeLottinville 1979, p. 154; Canada 1885, pp. 85, 87, 93, 108).

To effect the transition from farm to factory in rural areas and small towns, capitalists in both regions again adopted similar strategies in the mill village or company town and its associated institutions—company stores, churches, schools, kitchen gardens, and other social services. It has become fashionable to see southern textile mill villages as a consequence of the persistence of planter influence, as peculiarly southern attempts to establish, in industry, a parallel form of the paternalism of the southern slave plantation (Billings 1979, chap. 6.) When examined in a comparative light, however, some of this distinctiveness disappears. Mill villages (or company towns) have been a common form of social organization in the transition from nonindustrial to industrial production in North

America and elsewhere. In particular, they have played a role in mobilizing an adequate supply of labor power in rural areas before the availability of cheap mass transportation; in stabilizing, disciplining, and socializing a labor force which in the early years of industrialization tends to see factory work as temporary relief rather than a way of life; and in reassuring local populations that the new industrial proletariat poses no threat to established interests or life-styles (Braverman 1974, p. 67; Ware 1964, chap. 5; Woodman 1977, p. 549; Wood 1986, pp. 37–43; Carlton 1982, chap. 3; Wright 1986, pp. 138, 188; McHugh 1988).

Thus, when Maritime textile industrialists had to confront the same transitional problems as their southern counterparts, they responded in roughly similar ways. The two largest and most isolated Maritime mills, at Milltown and Marysville, New Brunswick, provided housing, required family labor, and paid employees on a monthly basis to maximize dependence and discourage sudden resignations. The Marysville mill also operated a company store (which deducted store bills and rents), a church, and a school and provided free land for kitchen gardens and pasturage and free firewood (Canada 1885, pp. 100–101; Kealey 1973, pp. 352–60, 364–65; De-Lottinville 1979, chap. 3).

Mill village paternalism was thus by no means a peculiarly southern phenomenon. Mill villages in both regions were to some extent practical responses to labor market problems, as Gavin Wright (1986, p. 138) suggests. But we should beware of accepting Wright's "market" definition of exploitation (wages lower than the going market rate) too readily and of concluding that therefore the mill village could not have been part of a strategy of exploitation. In practice, the nature and role of mill villages have been quite variable. Just as the Rhode Island system surpassed the more benign Waltham system as competitive pressures increased in the nineteenth century (Ware 1964, chap. 5), so it may be possible that paternalism in southern mill villages was more harsh and exploitative than its Maritime counterpart. But if this was the case, it cannot be explained simply in terms of the forms and institutions of the mill towns themselves, which were present in both regions.

If the choice of textile production eased the problems of capital shortage and labor recruitment, it could not provide answers to the problems of transportation and markets that were implicit in peripheral industrialization. The first occurs whenever production and consumption of commodities are spatially distinct and the transportation industry can be considered directly productive in the sense that it sells a value-enhancing change of location of the commodity. It also affects the speed of the circulation process and the turnover time of capital and can therefore have a significant impact on productivity (Marx 1978, pp. 227–29, 326–28; Harvey 1982). It is thus always a major factor in the possibility of peripheral capital accumulation.

In regionally fragmented federal states like Canada and the United States, political struggles often obscure technical questions of routing, speed, volume, "back-hauls," and so on. Nevertheless, it is possible to draw some tentative and rough conclusions about the role of transportation in our two cases. The textile industry in the Carolinas was somewhat closer to its markets in the northeastern and midwestern United States than Maritime producers were to theirs, chiefly in Ontario. Most southern capitalists suffered from disadvantageous freight rates until after 1945 (when the Interstate Commerce Commission announced its intention to eliminate freight rate discrimination), whereas the transportation costs of Maritime producers were subsidized until 1920, when a system of flat mileage rates was introduced. Up to that time, moreover, a differential rate on eastbound and westbound traffic constituted, in effect, a measure of protection for the Maritime producers (Potter 1947; Hoover and Ratchford 1951, pp. 78–84; Woodward 1971, pp. 312–17; Tindall 1967, pp. 599–604; Hearden 1982, pp. 94–95, 148; Forbes 1977). Nevertheless, capital accumulation in the southern textile industry continued to expand, whereas the Maritime industry went into relative decline long before it lost its freight rate advantages.

The problem of markets was also of concern in both regions and was at least partly a function of the logic of textile industrialization in peripheral regions, where skilled labor was scarce and technologies had to be chosen so that they fit with the size and skills of the available labor force. In both the Carolinas and the Maritimes in the late nineteenth century, this logic created pressure toward ring spinning rather than mule spinning. For both regions, the drawback of the latter, which could be used to produce higher-count, finer cloth with higher value added, was that it required skilled, usually male workers, whose skills provided them with the potential to resist managerial strategies of cost cutting and intensification. The ring spindle, in contrast, was faster, required less supervision, and could be operated by cheaper female and child workers, who were more available in predominantly rural areas (Wright 1986, pp. 138–40) and therefore more easily replaced and less capable of resistance. Female and child labor was largely unregulated in both regions. It was also one of their most significant competitive advantages over the New England industry, which not only competed with the South but also continued to export goods to Canada, despite Canadian tariffs (*Dominion Annual Register and Review* 1883, pp. 346–47; Wood 1989c, p. 57). Consequently, the ring spindle promised both more efficient use of the available labor power in the two regions and an important locational advantage in production. Its negative consequence was that its speed initially limited its use to the production of coarse gray goods. Only gradually did the necessary adaptations occur to permit the use of the ring spindle in higher-count production.

Overspecialization in coarse gray goods and the problem of markets thus were a function more of competitive necessity than of choice, and capitalists in both regions were constrained in their response. With more potential for importing skilled labor, Maritime mills could, and did, attempt to diversify into higher-count production. But the difficulty of keeping those workers made this a risky business. Production costs could be reduced, within technological and human limits, by the intensification of labor or by wage reductions. Alternatively, production could be limited to raise prices. Finally, new markets for coarse gray goods could be found. The second option, rationalization, was attempted in both regions in the mid-1880s but failed, partly because of the unwillingness of the owners of the larger mills to restrict themselves so as to protect their less efficient competitors and partly because competition in both countries assumed a sectional form (Acheson 1985, pp. 188–91; Hearden 1982, pp. 59–60). As a result, open class conflict emerged in both regions as managers and workers were at odds over attempts at intensification and wage reductions (DeLottinville 1979, chap. 4; Wood 1986, pp. 53–55; Hearden 1982, pp. 48–49). Finally, textile executives in both Canada and the United States recognized that the problem of excessive concentration in gray goods production provided no short-term solution in production itself and so tried to deal with it at the marketing end (Hearden 1982, pp. 48–65 and chap. 4). On average, American exports, chiefly to Canada, the Far East, and the Caribbean, averaged only about 8 percent of sales, but they were important for some individual firms (Wright 1986, p. 288 n. 19). Similarly, by 1892 four Canadian mills, including the one at Moncton, New Brunswick, were thought to be producing goods entirely for the China market ("Cotton Manufactures" 1892).

Locational Advantages in Textile Production

The points made above suggest that textile capitalists in the Carolinas and the Maritimes not only faced similar problems but also

TABLE 4.2. Rates of Exploitation and Profit[a] in Cotton Textile Production, Massachusetts and North Carolina, 1870–1939 (in thousands of dollars)

State	Year	1 Salaries	2 Wages	3 Cost of materials[b]	4 Value of products	5 Value added (4–3)
Massachusetts	1870	—	13,612.9	37,575.7	59,679.2	22,103.5
	1880	—	16,240.9	37,542.7	74,780.8	37,238.1
	1890	1,112.3	25,118.4	56,586.4	100,202.9	43,616.6
	1900	2,013.9	32,327.4	54,068.0	110,478.3	56,410.3
	1909	2,949.8	45,117.1	105,156.8	186,462.3	81,305.5
	1919	9,351.6	109,902.5	359,675.3	596,687.4	237,012.2
	1939	2,686.5	31,645.9	47,689.9	99,335.2	51,645.3
North Carolina	1870	—	183.9	963.8	1,345.1	381.3
	1880	—	439.7	1,463.6	2,554.5	1,090.9
	1890	170.3	1,475.9	6,239.9	9,563.4	3,323.5
	1900	586.7	5,127.1	17,386.6	28,372.8	10,986.2
	1909	1,609.8	12,130.6	48,687.6	72,680.4	23,992.8
	1919	5,644.9	49,134.5	186,779.7	318,368.2	131,588.5
	1939	5,226.5	74,981.8	158,352.8	324,208.2	165,855.4

Sources: Data for columns 1 to 4 taken from U.S. Department of the Interior, Census Office, *Ninth Census of the U.S.*, Vol. 3 (Washington, D.C.: U.S. Government Printing Office, 1872), pp. 529, 534; *Report on the Manufactures of the United States at the Tenth Census, 1880* (Washington, D.C.: U.S. Government Printing Office, 1883), pp. 131, 160; *Report on the Manufacturing Industries in the United States at the Eleventh Census, 1890*, pt. 1 (Washington, D.C.: U.S. Government Printing Office, 1895), pp. 454–55, 538–39; *Twelfth Census of the United States, 1900*, Vol. 8, pt. 2 (Washington, D.C.: U.S. Government Printing Office, 1902), pp. 366–67, 666–67; U.S. Department of Commerce and Labor, Bureau of the Census, *Thirteenth Census of the United States, 1910*, Vol. 9 (Washington, D.C.: U.S. Government Printing Office, 1912), pp. 532–33, 914–15; *Fourteenth Census of the United States, 1919*, Vol. 9 (Washington, D.C.: U.S. Government Printing Office, 1922), pp. 638–39, 1120–21; *Sixteenth Census of the United States, 1939*, "Manufactures," Vol. 3 (Washington, D.C.: U.S. Government Printing Office, 1942), pp. 424–25, 748–49.

[a] For a discussion of the method of calculating the rate of exploitation, see Wood 1986, Appendix.

[b] Includes energy costs 1900–1939 inclusive.

adopted similar strategies and organizational forms in their efforts to overcome them. Some of these problems, such as the shortages of capital and skilled labor, dependence on external capital, and high transportation costs, appear to have been more severe in the Carolinas than in the Maritimes. Yet the former region continued to accumulate textile (and other) capital, but the latter did not. Bearing in mind the range of technical, institutional, and organizational fac-

6 Productive salaries (1×0.5)	7 Depreciation (5×0.05)	8 Surplus value (5−(2+6+7))	9 Variable capital (2+6)	10 Rate of exploitation (8/9)(%)	11 Rate of profit (8/(3+7+9))(%)
—	1,105.2	7,385.4	13,612.9	54	14
—	1,861.9	19,135.3	16,240.9	118	34
556.2	2,180.8	15.761.3	25,674.5	61	19
1,007.0	2,820.5	20,255.4	33,334.4	61	22
1,474.9	4,065.3	30,648.3	46,592.0	66	20
4,675.8	11,850.6	110,583.3	114,578.3	97	23
1,343.2	2,582.3	16,074.0	32,989.1	49	19
—	19.1	179.2	183.0	98	15
—	54.5	596.6	439.7	136	30
85.1	166.2	1,596.3	1,561.1	102	20
293.4	549.3	5,016.4	5,420.5	93	21
804.9	1,199.6	9,857.7	12,935.5	76	16
2,822.4	6,579.4	73,052.1	51,596.9	141	30
2,613.2	8,292.8	79,967.6	77,595.0	103	33

tors eliminated above and the ambiguities inherent in comparative analysis (Mill 1925, pp. 253–67, 285–99), where might we look for an explanation of this apparently paradoxical situation?

As I have argued elsewhere, one possible explanation is to be found in the regional patterns of productive relations in the two countries and, more specifically, in regional capacities to produce surplus value (Wood 1986, passim; see also Cobb 1984, p. 158 and passim). Tables 4.2 and 4.3 present calculations of rates of exploitation and profit, using Census of Manufactures data in the two countries, which seem to provide some support for such a hypothesis. They reveal a contrast between the ability of peripheral textile capital in North Carolina to overcome the various disadvantages of its peripheral location and achieve higher rates of exploitation and the failure of Maritime textile capital to do likewise within the Canadian context. They also indicate the contrasting results of these patterns: the tendency for textile capital in the United States to be drawn toward the South and the tendency of the Canadian industry to concentrate in central Canada.

The Nova Scotia industry, which produced high rates of both exploitation and profit in 1890, appears to be the major exception to

Table 4.3. Regional Variations in Rates of Exploitation and Profit in Cotton Textile Production, Canada, 1870–1930 (in thousands of dollars)

Province	Year	1 Salaries	2 Wages	3 Cost of materials	4 Value of products	5 Value added (4–3)
New Brunswick	1870	—	22.5	105.0	160.6	55.6
	1880	—	40.1	168.3	276.2	107.9
	1890	—	498.0	901.2	1,750.0	848.8
	1900	57.8	600.6	1,062.7	2,228.2	1,165.5
	1910	39.2	673.4	1,443.4	2,673.2	1,229.8
	1915	23.6	616.4	1,058.0	2,189.0	1,131.0
	1930	43.3	828.2	1,228.2	2,159.0	930.8
Nova Scotia	1870	—	—	—	—	—
	1880	—	—	—	—	—
	1890	—	130.8	410.8	716.9	306.1
	1900	10.0	206.3	442.1	747.3	305.2
	1910	12.0	205.3	604.7	1,035.8	431.1
	1915	—	—	—	—	—
	1930	—	—	—	—	—
Ontario	1870	—	86.5	276.0	485.0	209.0
	1880	—	380.9	995.6	1,872.8	877.2
	1890	—	699.2	1,246.6	2,618.7	1,372.1
	1900	20.8	649.7	1,363.9	2,907.9	1,544.0
	1910	47.4	825.1	2,189.5	4,134.5	1,945.0
	1915	69.8	1,042.4	2,218.3	4,831.1	2,612.8
	1930	420.1	3,317.3	6,761.9	12,821.3	6,059.4
Quebec	1870	—	19.5	77.0	129.0	54.0
	1880	—	280.6	791.8	1,568.7	776.9
	1890	—	814.7	1,849.7	3,656.2	1,372.1
	1900	106.7	1,895.8	2,958.6	6,149.7	3,191.1
	1910	168.6	2,857.4	9,743.1	16,741.4	6,998.3
	1915	277.1	2,861.9	6,847.3	12,539.0	5,691.7
	1930	889.3	8,266.8	22,016.7	38,126.8	16,110.1

Sources: Data for columns 1 to 4 were taken from Canada, Office of the Census, *First Census of Canada, 1870–1,* Vol. 3 (Ottawa, 1873), table 53; *Second Census of Canada, 1880–1,* Vol. 3 (Ottawa, 1883), table 54; *Third Census of Canada, 1890–1,* Vol. 3, (Ottawa, 1894), pp. 120–21; *Fourth Census of Canada, 1901,* Vol. 3 (Ottawa, 1905), table 14; *Census of Canada, 1911,* Vol. 3 (Ottawa, 1912), table 1; Canada, Census and Statistics Office, *Census of Manufactures, 1916* (Ottawa, 1917), tables 5 and 7; Department of Trade and Commerce, Dominion Bureau of Statistics, *Manufacturing Statistics of the Maritime Provinces, 1930* (Ottawa, 1932), pp. 29–30; *Manufacturing Statistics of the Province of Ontario, 1930* (Ottawa, 1932), pp. 9–10; *Manufacturing Industries of the Province of Quebec, 1930* (Ottawa, 1932), pp. 10–11.

6 Productive salaries (1×0.5)	7 Depre- ciation (5×0.05)	8 Surplus value (5−(2+6+7))	9 Variable capital (2+6)	10 Rate of exploitation (8/9)(%)	11 Rate of profit (8/(3+7+9))(%)
—	2.8	30.3	22.5	135	23
—	5.4	62.4	40.1	156	29
—	42.4	308.4	498.0	62	21
28.9	56.5	479.5	629.5	76	17
19.6	58.3	478.5	693.0	69	22
11.8	54.2	448.6	628.2	71	26
39.2	43.3	20.1	867.4	2	1
—	—	—	—	—	—
—	—	—	—	—	—
—	15.3	160.0	130.8	122	29
5.0	15.3	78.6	211.3	37	12
6.0	21.6	198.2	211.3	94	24
—	—	—	—	—	—
—	—	—	—	—	—
—	10.5	112.1	86.5	130	30
—	43.9	452.4	380.9	119	32
—	68.6	604.3	699.2	86	30
10.4	77.2	806.7	660.1	122	38
23.7	97.3	998.9	848.8	118	32
34.9	130.6	1,404.9	1,077.3	130	41
210.1	303.0	2,229.0	3,527.4	63	21
—	2.6	29.9	19.5	153	30
—	38.8	457.5	280.6	163	41
—	90.3	901.5	814.7	111	33
53.4	159.6	1,082.3	1,949.2	56	21
84.3	349.9	3,706.7	2,941.7	126	28
138.6	284.6	2,406.6	3,000.5	80	24
444.7	805.5	6,593.1	8,711.5	76	21

these generalizations, but there are reasons to suggest that these numbers are not typical. First, disaggregation of the Nova Scotia data reveals that they are dominated by those of a single mill, the Nova Scotia Cotton Company of Halifax, whose rates of exploitation and profit were remarkably high in 1890, even by the standards of Quebec and North Carolina. It could be argued that, as a major port of entry to Canada, Halifax may have enjoyed a significant competitive advantage in recruiting skilled workers from Britain. Evidence from other sources suggests otherwise, however. According to James D. Frost (1982), the company was in difficulty throughout the 1880s, when it paid, on average, only 3 percent in dividends, a significantly lower return than the mills in New Brunswick and Quebec. At its annual general meeting in 1886, critics of the company among the shareholders expressed suspicions about incomplete financial statements and compared the mill's management to that of a charitable institution. The company had its worst year ever in 1889 and in 1890 was on the verge of bankruptcy, running on a three-day week for a large part of the year. In January 1891, ownership of the company passed to the Dominion Cotton Company of Montreal for 25 percent of its book value. The mill's production data for 1890 are therefore likely to be a function of the threat of bankruptcy and the precariousness of its employees' livelihoods, rather than a reflection of its ongoing competitive situation. The latter is probably better reflected by the provincial aggregates for 1900 and 1910. When the Scotia mill was destroyed in the Halifax explosion of 1917, it was not rebuilt (Frost 1982; Canada 1938, pp. 34–35; "Nova Scotia Cotton Company" 1886).

The calculations in tables 4.2 and 4.3 are not simply indicators of the results of such complex historical processes. They thus reflect not only the technical and organizational factors discussed above but a variety of social, political, historical, cultural, and other factors that determine regional variations in the "direct relationship of the owners of the conditions of production to the direct producers . . . which reveals the innermost secret, the hidden basis of the entire social structure" (Marx 1977, pp. 791–92). A discussion of all of the factors implicit in the historical and moral element in the determination of productive relations is beyond the scope of this essay, but it is feasible to pursue, albeit briefly, one potentially fruitful line of inquiry.

Without totally accepting the Brenner thesis—that the prior establishment of capitalist productive relations in agriculture alone provides the possibility of expanded capitalist development (Brenner 1977)—it can be recognized that preindustrial social structures are an important consideration in the path taken by capitalist development, alongside other technical, political, and natural factors. The clear contrast between the preindustrial class structures of the Carolinas and the Maritimes reinforces this conclusion.

In the South, the central preconditions for textile industrialization were the creation of a system of wage labor in cotton agriculture (Woodman 1977, 1979; Wood 1986, pp. 22–31) and the roughly simultaneous movement toward "enclosure," which gradually eliminated the common law tradition of open range and significantly increased the pressure on small livestock owners, whose independence had depended on the commons (Hahn 1982; King 1982; Kirby 1987, p. 29; Wright 1986, p. 49). These changes resulted from the long period of class conflict and organizational experimentation following the Civil War. When attempts to revive the gang-labor system characteristic of slave production failed, plantations were divided for purposes of cultivation into farms of thirty to fifty acres, operated by tenant farmers or sharecroppers and their families.

Based in theory on shares, which in some circumstances provide the possibility for capital accumulation, southern sharecropping was in reality a system of wage labor, operated largely at the discretion of those who owned the means of production (usually planters in black belt areas and country merchants elsewhere). Widespread illiteracy among croppers, together with a series of legal decisions in the 1870s which reduced their status to that of laborer or servant, placed control of accounts, crops, and marketing in the hands of those who furnished land and credit. Croppers lost control over what they produced and their incomes. Even though this form of sharecropping had its origins in antebellum agriculture (Bode and Ginter 1986; Applewhite 1954), its later expansion did not represent a return to traditional social relations but rather indicated that a process of proletarianization was revolutionizing the southern economy. Cotton cultivation spread into upland areas formerly dominated by independent farmers, drawing some of them into the process.

In this context, North Carolina can be distinguished from the rest of the South not only because it was the leading textile state but also because it was there that the proletarianization of white farmers and their families was probably most extensive (Wood 1986, chap. 2). Between 1837 and the mid-1870s, tenants' rights to crops grown under contract had been maintained, despite periodic attempts to place them in a legally inferior position similar to that of croppers or laborers. Legislation enacted in 1876–77, however, abolished the legal distinction between cropper and tenant, opening the way for the proletarianization of tenants as well as croppers. As cotton prices fell in the late nineteenth century and farm debt increased, the pool of impoverished farmers who no longer owned the means of production expanded. By 1910, when the size of North Carolina's textile labor force reached almost 50,000, there were over 107,000 tenants and croppers in the state, 42.3 percent of all farmers and more than twice as many as in 1880.

Throughout the period, a large majority (ranging from 60 percent in 1900 to 66 percent in 1940, with a low of 54.1 percent in the 1920s) of tenants and croppers in North Carolina were white (Wood 1986, p. 28). For these farmers, as well as for white owner-operators who were threatened with the loss of their land or whose location at or beyond the limits of the cotton belt made it difficult for them to obtain credit, the textile industry was an available, if not an attractive, option. At the cost of a significant loss of personal freedom, it held out the possibility of savings, which might later permit a return to the land. Few textile workers saw these hopes realized, however, because capital used the mechanisms of labor discipline and socialization inherent in the family labor system and the mill villages to generate rates of exploitation well above the national average for textiles while simultaneously maximizing the dependence of textile workers. In a context of widespread racial segregation, the promise of a textile industry dedicated to the salvation of the white family from racial competition partially legitimized this strategy of accumulation. The use of more direct racial blackmail, in the form of threats to use black labor in the mills should white labor discipline break down, helped to quell periodic rebellions (Wood 1986, pp. 37–43).

The specific historical links between agriculture and industry have yet to be uncovered. Estimates of mobility from farm to factory and back again vary, perhaps reflecting historical variations in agricultural profitability. Improving cotton prices in the first decade of the twentieth century, for instance, created a temporary obstacle to labor recruitment within the piedmont and required greater recruitment efforts in the mountain areas to the west of the region (Lemert 1933, p. 27; Hall et al. 1987, pp. 31–36). Similarly, it is not known with any certainty whether, or to what extent, the textile industry recruited former yeoman farmers who had lost title to their land or whether it simply took advantage of population growth in an already saturated cotton economy and recruited those who had never been able to gain title (Wright 1986, pp. 107–15). These questions, however, are secondary to the broad fact that textile industrialization occurred in a context in which proletarianization and impoverishment were taking place on a grand scale.

The southern textile industry was far better placed than its counterpart in New England, which faced stiff competition in the labor market from more productive capital. Wages, closely tied to those of black farm laborers until at least World War I (Wright 1986, pp. 69–70), were low, hours were long, the use of female and child labor went unregulated, and, in general, the ability of textile capitalists to extract surplus value were unfettered by all but the physical limits of workers. By the 1920s, when agricultural depression and surplus labor in the mill villages permitted massive increases in the intensity of work, it was estimated that the average southern competitive advantage over New England in the labor component of production costs exceeded 30 percent (Wood 1986, p. 81). By this time the destruction of the New England industry was virtually assured.

Small-scale, labor-intensive, unremunerative farming was as common in Maritime Canada as it was in the American South. In 1890, 49.9 percent of Nova Scotia farms and 35.9 percent of those in New Brunswick were units of fifty acres or less (Wood 1989a, p. 50). Many families, perhaps the majority, survived, as they had for decades, on the basis of occupational pluralism—some farming, either for subsistence or for the market, combined with wage work for larger farmers or in forestry or fishing or, where the opportunity presented itself, in mines or factories.

The most important difference between Maritime agriculture and its southern counterpart was not agricultural prosperity, however, but class structure, which in each region was the result of very different patterns of historical development: plantation production, dependence on world markets, slave labor, and only formal emancipation in the South; extensive property ownership, limited penetration by capital, and small-scale family farming and fishing, mostly for subsistence but with some petty commodity production, in the Maritimes. As a result, between 1870 and 1910, never less than 92 percent of all farm operators in New Brunswick were owners and 91.4 percent in Nova Scotia. And because there were fewer farms than in central Canada, tenant farmers and agricultural wage laborers were far more scarce in the Maritimes. In 1890, the number of tenant farmers and agricultural wage workers in the two Maritime provinces peaked at 7,557, compared with 61,000 in Ontario and over 20,000 in Quebec. Between 1890 and 1900, the total number of farm operators in Ontario fell by over 60,000; almost all were tenants or landholders on farms with fewer than ten acres. Quebec lost 25,000 with roughly the same profile, yet the two Maritime provinces together experienced a net loss of fewer than 12,000 (Wood 1989a, p. 51). According to the 1911 Canadian census, the average weekly cost of farm labor power in the peripheral Maritimes in 1901 and 1911 was higher than in Quebec and Ontario (Canada 1912, p. ix).

Workers in the fisheries were a potential second source of labor power for Maritime industries. But their geographic distribution did not always facilitate access to the region's factories and, like their counterparts in farming, most of them tended to be owners of the means of production within the complex of occupational pluralism and therefore also not free wage laborers in the classic sense.

Clearly, the process of large-scale proletarianization that occurred in southern cotton agriculture had no counterpart in Maritime Canada, where the pool of surplus labor freed from direct access to the means of production was severely restricted. In addition to this limitation, the situation in the Maritimes was exacerbated by two other factors. First, in the absence of strong social, cultural, or historical barriers to migration such as those operating in the postbellum South, patterns of emigration from the Maritimes to other, more rapidly growing regions of North America had become a feature of regional life (and had probably retarded regional industrialization) long before large-scale industrial growth occurred. Thus, even if some members of Maritime families left farming or fishing for other pursuits, there was no guarantee that Maritime industries would benefit.

Second, though the Maritime provinces were more successful in attracting new immigrant workers than was the South, they had great difficulty keeping them. This became increasingly problematic after the slump of the mid-1880s, when the differential between growth rates in the Maritimes and those elsewhere increased. Thus, like their southern counterparts, Maritime capitalists had to rely on the region's rural population to supply the bulk of their factory labor, but both its supply and cost were affected by continued access to productive property and by the loss of workers to other regions (Thornton 1986; Wright 1986, pp. 71–78; Wood 1989c, pp. 22–30).

The results of these contrasting situations for textile capital were clear. In the Carolinas, the costs of peripheral location were borne by the region's textile workers. Adrift in a sea of surplus rural labor power, they always failed in their repeated attempts to resist deskilling and intensification and to improve their conditions of life and work (Wood 1986, chaps. 2 and 3). In contrast, textile capitalists in the Maritimes were unable to impose the added costs of its peripheral location on their workers. In 1890, the last full year of independent operation for most of the Maritime mills, the mills in New Brunswick, which employed about 85 percent of the cotton mill workers in the region, paid the highest average annual wage ($284) of the four provinces (Wood 1989a, p. 53). In the same year, the St. Croix mill at Milltown, New Brunswick, had the highest average annual wage ($332.80) of all the Canadian cotton mills (Wood 1989a, p. 52); its management had failed in an attempt in 1886 to impose the costs of the crisis of that period on its workers.

Not the least of the problems management faced in its attempt to increase work loads and cut wages was the ability of many employees to return to their family farms or to follow already established migratory patterns in search of other work. After the 1886 strike was settled in a compromise, the managers announced that one-third of the workers would be fired and replaced, but no local replacements could be found and a hundred Scottish workers had to be imported to fill some of the vacancies. Community hostility persuaded many of these workers to leave as well, and in the following year, one of the strikers' central demands—for a ten-hour day—had to be conceded (DeLottinville 1979, chap. 4). The impact on the mill's competitiveness is apparent from the 1890 census. In that year, the Montreal Cotton Company employed about 65 percent more workers than the St. Croix mill (1,040 to 631), paid an aggregate wage bill that was 8.5 percent smaller ($192,000 compared to $210,000), and produced a mass of surplus value over four times as large ($337,000 to $75,000) (Wood 1989a, p. 53).

Conclusion

The virtue of the comparative method is that by placing explanatory hypotheses in comparative perspective it can help to identify the most crucial variables. In the present case, it suggests, first, that some of the historical and social variables that have dominated discussions of southern industrialization may not be as crucial as had been thought. The textile industries of the Carolinas and the Maritimes were both confronted by a range of problems typical of attempts at peripheral industrialization: shortages of capital and skilled labor, transportation disadvantages, and dependence on external capital, markets, and wholesalers. It appears that these problems may have been more severe for the southern producers than for their Maritime counterparts.

Second, textile capitalists in both regions developed a similar range of social institutions and practices in an attempt to compensate for these problems and to facilitate the transition from farm to factory. Yet the textile industry in the Maritimes stagnated and collapsed, while its southern counterpart continued to grow, to produce above average rates of exploitation and profit, and gradually to overwhelm its New England competition. We may thus conclude, with Woodward (1971, p. 317) and against a variety of social historians and dependency theorists, that capital shortage, external dependence, and transportation difficulties were not insuperable barriers to capitalist industrialization and that the institutions of the mill village were not by themselves crucial in facilitating that process. What seems more important, both as a potential solution to the comparative puzzle discussed above and as an avenue for future research, is the context of class relations and class resources in which these problems were experienced and which determined the efficacy of regional strategies of exploitation.

If this comparative discussion eliminates several causal variables, it does not, however, eliminate all of them. A number of possibilities remain to qualify the interpretation presented here. The most important of these is race, which is sometimes interpreted as an obstacle to capitalist development but can just as easily be seen as a device used to raise rates of exploitation among whites and thus increase the rate of accumulation (Billings 1979, p. 113; Reich 1981). But racial blackmail qualifies the present interpretation; it does not destroy it. For the threat of replacing white workers with black workers to be effective, the range of choices open to those replaced must have already been closed off. Like the threat of dismissal or denial of credit or loss of housing, the use of racial blackmail presupposes the prior creation of the social relations of capitalist production, in which workers are free in a twofold sense—from the various forms of precapitalist servitude and, most crucially, from direct or indirect access to other means of production and subsistence which are independent of capital. In the end, the activation of this process in the postwar South explains the region's painful yet successful industrialization, and its absence in Maritime Canada accounts for that region's industrial decline.

PART III

Paternalism and Worker Protest

5

Choosing between the Ham and the Union: Paternalism in the Cone Mills of Greensboro, 1925–1930

Bryant Simon

Paternalism was the label many observers stuck to the southern cotton mill world through the first third of the twentieth century. No firm epitomized this characterization more than the Cone mills of Greensboro, North Carolina. Indeed, "paternalistic" was the modifying adjective most often associated with the Cone industrial universe. In 1930, one student of the region's textile industry wrote of the mills: "The paternalistic policy of the company is one of the most complete and finished in the country" (Tippett 1931, pp. 198–99). Another commentator described the Cone factories as "highly paternalistic." Others dubbed the mill owners "noblemen," "models of modernness . . . [and] . . . industrial virtue" and the "patron saints of Greensboro." Cone paternalism, moreover, won wide acclaim as a sturdy brake against labor militancy, which seemed to some to be tearing apart many industrial areas ("Cone Group" 1928, p. 397; "A Town in America" 1929).

Despite the centrality of paternalism at the Cone enterprises and in the entire southern textile belt, the study of industrial paternalism has languished. Scholars have stretched the term so thin that it now has little clear meaning. Southern cotton mill paternalism has been defined as everything from kind fatherly stewardship (Mitchell 1921), to the complete control of rural industrial hamlets (McLaurin

1971), to the direct descendant of the Old South's master-slave relationship (Cash 1941; Billings 1979). This chapter examines the formation and initial breakdown of the paternalistic regime at the Cone mills in an attempt to clarify the historical roots of paternalism and its role in southern industrial relations. The Cone example demonstrates that paternalism was never so benign as filial devotion nor merely a cynical management ploy. Instead it represented a complex relationship between owner and operative that changed over time and evolved into a blend of consent and force, accommodation and intimidation.

Two main pillars bolstered Cone paternalism. First, it rested on the Cones' material power. They controlled not only the means of production but also the mill villages and all of the nearby houses, schools, churches, stores, and even basketball courts. Second, blending symbols, gestures, and welfare programs, Cone paternalism developed into a managerial style that featured personal involvement and accessibility.

Based on these pillars of material power and style, Cone paternalism precariously balanced consent and force. Although consent and force always coexisted, varying with fluctuations in the market, shifts in the labor supply, the size of profit margins, and workers' protest, one or the other always predominated. The Cones sought consent, industrial relations in which employees refrained from collective assaults on management's legitimacy. Consent, however, came at a cost. To create such a climate, the Cones donned a public face of goodwill and largess. They portrayed their firm as striving not principally for profits but more for the general good, well-being, and advancement of the workers. Most important, though the threat of force always hung in the background, the drive for consent wove a web of reciprocal, yet unequal, duties around the relationship between workers and management. Violations of reciprocity often sparked conflict. Sometimes tensions were resolved through compromise and concession, but when the mill hands directly challenged management's authority, force replaced consent (Genovese 1976; Lears 1985).

Over the first quarter of the century, Cone paternalism proved fluid enough to engineer an era of consent. After 1925, however, when management introduced the stretch-out, the mill communities bristled with conflict. For the next five years, many workers urged the Cones to live up to their paternalistic image, while others covertly challenged the owners' legitimacy. Finally, in 1930, a United Textile Workers of America (UTW) unionization drive in Greensboro became the occasion for a referendum on paternalism. The campaign ultimately focused on an unlikely symbol, the Christmas ham, a gift given each year by the Cones to their employees.

The first section of this chapter will examine the origins of Cone paternalism and the era of consent. The second section will follow the slow and uneven breakdown of consent in the wake of the introduction of the stretch-out. The final portion will highlight the UTW drive as a critical episode in the paternalistic dialectic.

Paternalism

The Cones followed an entrepreneurial path to Greensboro and mill ownership. The family immigrated to the South from Germany in 1847. After a brief stay in Charleston, they settled in Jonesboro, Tennessee, where they operated a general store. At the close of the Civil War, the Cones headed north to Baltimore and opened a wholesale grocery enterprise. Small southern textile manufacturers, searching for goods to fill their company stores, formed the bulk of the new venture's customers. Acting as sales representatives, the second-generation Cones, Moses and Ceasar, traveled throughout the piedmont. The job provided an excellent vantage point from which to chart changes in the regional flow of business and take advantage of them. In 1890, Moses and Ceasar liquidated the Baltimore business and used the capital gained to set up the Cone Export and Commission House in New York City to peddle the wares of small southern textile firms on national and international markets.

After a failed attempt by Greensboro boosters to convert the city into the "Little Pittsburgh of the South," Moses and Ceasar Cone, in 1893, purchased the defunct Carolina Steel and Iron Company. Located on the eastern outskirts of the city, the property included an industrial plant, twenty miles of graded streets, and housing for hundreds of employees. The Cones converted the complex into a textile mill and christened the new enterprise Proximity Manufacturing Company because of its nearness to raw cotton (Balliett 1925; Tippett 1931, pp. 193–212; Hall et al. 1987, 30–31; Cone 1983; Cone and Cone 1981).

Four years after Proximity opened, the fledgling National Union of Textile Workers (NUTW) started organizing piedmont laborers. By 1900, 150 Cone operatives enrolled clandestinely in the union, but secrets were hard to keep in the mill village. Announcing that he would destroy the plant before bargaining with a union, Ceasar Cone lashed out against the NUTW. He slammed the mill gate shut and bolted the door of the company store, forcing mill hands to walk several miles for supplies. Cone also hired a squadron of watchmen, who paraded around the mill community in paramilitary fashion. When these acts of intimidation failed to break the union, Cone evicted dozens of families. The impoverished NUTW withered under management's onslaught. Within a week of the first eviction, the looms of Proximity ran again; erstwhile trade unionists either left Greensboro or wandered back to work under a yellow dog contract (Lahne 1944, pp. 186–87; McLaurin 1971, pp. 154–56).

The defeat of the NUTW signaled the start of a new era of financial prosperity and industrial peace at the Cone mills. Profits from the Proximity plant were reinvested into horizontal and vertical expansion. The Cones added two new factories and a print works to their physical plant. By 1910, the Proximity mill employed more than a thousand operatives, White Oak as many as twenty-five hundred, Revolution an additional thousand, and the print works another five hundred. The adjoining mill villages housed fifteen thousand men, women, and children. Unlike other mills that surrounded Greensboro, which produced plaids, checks, and stripes, the Cones manufactured flannels and especially denim. To sustain the firm's growth, the mill owners devised novel distribution schemes, including the development of their own brand names, such as Cone Blue Jeans. By 1925, the Cones boasted, without dispute, the largest denim complex in the world (Arnett 1955, pp. 171–75; Tindall 1967, p. 367; Chafe 1980, p. 30).

By this time paternalism had become as synonymous with the Cone enterprises as denim. The public acrimony of the NUTW strike had jarred the mill owners and temporarily tarnished their public image. Afterward, through what the Cones called "humanizing" mill life and others tagged paternalism, the managers took steps to build an industrial universe marked by consent, not force. Before they could construct this cooperative community, they had to destroy the foundation of the 1900 strike—worker solidarity. Thus, initially, paternalism sought to pull apart workers' bonds of unity and link them as grateful individuals to a benevolent and charitable employer. Fundamental to this project was the development of consent, or what the owners tabbed labor loyalty (Zahavi 1983, 1988).

Management calculated loyalty by several indices. The stability and productivity of the labor force was one of the company's loyalty barometers. They also graded fidelity by the level of labor unrest; loyal workers shunned trade unions and renounced public challenges to management's authority. All capitalist firms sought loyal operatives, but the intense and personal involvement of the owners in the quest for faithful hands distinguished paternalistic regimes. Using a variety of maneuvers, the Cones endeavored to tie individual workers to the firm through the establishment of a personal bond between the employee and employer. Revolt against paternalism would entail not only collective action but a worker's refusal to recognize a personal tie with the owner. Faithful hands, the Cones trusted, would simultaneously feel a sense of indebtedness toward the owners for their jobs and benefits and identify their interests as being in concert with those of the firm (Zahavi 1983; Reid 1985).

Moses and Ceasar Cone ruled over their mill villages: they lived near the factories, they insinuated themselves into the worlds of their workers, and they emphasized direct access to management for all hands. Often the Cones ambled through their industrial hamlets, greeting workers and family members by their first names, exchanging pleasantries, and chatting with them on their front porches. They appeared at church meetings, presented children with Christmas gifts, offered advice on gardening, and addressed the annual father-son banquet.[1]

Intervention did not stop with these casual encounters. Tobe Sullivan remembered how Ceasar Cone, after asking why her children had skipped school, gave her money for shoes so that her offspring could attend their lessons free from ridicule. Another employee recalled that when a neighbor suffered hard times, Bernard Cone summoned the beleaguered employee to his office and promised him a wage hike until his fortunes improved. Others entered the factory only after the mill owners' intercession and moral judgment. "Aren't you bad about drinking?" Ceasar Cone asked an operative in search of work. After the unemployed hand guaranteed the mill owner that "no man has seen me drunk," he was hired ("A Town in America" 1929; Marley 1930; Terrill and Hirsch 1978, p. 175; Westbrook Family n.d.).

Each year, the Cones staged elaborate celebrations of labor-management cooperation. The annual Fourth of July picnic, featuring string bands, softball, three-legged races, and enough fried chicken, barbecue, and salad to feed ten thousand, was the most spectacular of these events. At the 1913 Independence Day gala, Ceasar Cone delivered "a message of love and esteem to my people."

---

1. Nearly every issue of the *Greensboro Daily News* and the *Textorian* from 1910 to 1940 contained a list of welfare activities in the Cone mill villages and noted the owners' participation in these and other functions.

Reporters from around the Tar Heel State attended the festival and wrote effusive testimonials to the Cones' paternalistic style (Mitchell 1913; GDN,[2] July 5, 1925).

The Cones fashioned a public and personal ideology to fit their style of management. At the core of this identity rested the mill masters' self-professed devotion to their employees' well-being. They operated their mills not for the "lowly pursuit of the dollar," the Cones declared, but for the "moral and spiritual uplift of the region." In other industrial zones, the Greensboro mill owners opined, manufacturers left their workers at the mercy of the marketplace, paid poverty wages, ostracized the sick and the aged, and surrendered their towns to the noxious influences of socialism and anarchism. By contrast, the Cone mills were "communities not factories," staffed by loyal Anglo-Saxon labor and shepherded by benevolent and concerned men (Balliett 1925, pp. 1, 3, 9).

Paternalistic gestures were a prime tool used to attract and retain faithful operatives, but the mill owners employed other strategies as well. The Cones, for instance, pioneered southern welfare work. As early as 1903, the family hired Pearl Wyche, whom Harriet Herring believed to be the region's first welfare secretary. The status of mill hands as recent arrivals to industrial society colored initial notions of welfare work. Loyal workers could be molded, management believed, only by breaking them of the wild ways of the countryside and inculcating them with "civilization" in the form of schools, baby clinics, hygiene classes, cooking seminars, medical advice, model mill homes, orchestras, company-sponsored sports teams, ice cream socials, and beet-growing contests. Whatever all these programs accomplished, they did not remove the countryside from the mill village, as attested by the scores of chickens and goats that hid under company homes. But far more alarming to the Cones than stray farm animals, Wyche's welfare efforts failed to shape a stable and loyal labor force. As a result, while retaining some of its early features, welfare work changed after 1910 (Cone 1912, p. 4; Balliett 1925, pp. 23–24; Herring 1929, p. 113).

During the second decade of the century, as the Cone enterprises burgeoned, a confluence of factors led to a regionwide labor shortage. World War I exacerbated the situation, as denim orders poured into Greensboro and laborers streamed out of the mills into higher-

---

2. Newspapers and periodicals cited in this chapter are abbreviated as follows: *Greensboro Daily News—GDN*; *Greensboro Patriot—GP*; *New York Herald—NYH*; *New York Times—NYT*; *Raleigh News and Observer—RNO*; *Textile Worker—TW*; *Textorian—TXT*.

paying jobs and the armed services. Turnover rates soared as well. Like many large firms, the Cone mills responded to the crisis by expanding the scope of their welfare system. By offering higher benefits and fatter pay envelopes, the Cones sought to draw a stable crew of nonunionized laborers to their mill villages. All the while they reminded hands that these new programs were nontransferable and belonged to workers only as long as they remained with the firm (Reid 1985; Hall et al. 1987, pp. 105–13; McHugh 1988, pp. 22–27).

Company housing, for example, had long been a feature of mill life, but after 1910 the Cones began to spruce up their villages. They built sturdy new houses rimmed with shrubs set along neatly paved streets lined with shade trees. Each home included running water, indoor plumbing, and electricity, along with garden space in the rear, flower beds on the sides, and a large front porch. For rent, families paid four dollars per month. Management also erected a YMCA near each factory, donated money for the construction of new churches, added a movie theater to one of the villages, and modernized the schools. In 1915, the *New York Herald* proclaimed the Cone mill communities "the world's model" (*NYH*, Sept. 15, 1915; Balliett 1925; Cook 1925).

After 1910, the Cones also instituted a series of wage supplements. They distributed cut-rate coal and wood, and when no Greensboro firm would deliver milk to the villages, the mill owners opened a dairy. During the labor-starved war years, mill officials began to produce cream, butter, and flour and to slaughter locally reared animals for beef and pork, all of which were sold at company stores at prices below those charged at city shops. Salaries climbed with the introduction of a bonus system that management insisted shared company profits with employees. As the Cones' fortunes soared, bonuses climbed to a wartime peak of one dollar for each dollar dispensed in wages (*GP*, Sept. 15, 1916; Balliett 1925).

Moreover, as the mills mushroomed, openings for loom fixers and foremen, jobs which paid more than other positions, became available. In recruiting from their own ranks, mill managers searched not just for skilled men but for loyal employees, whom they pointed to as symbols of the rewards of labor-management cooperation. At night school classes—a prerequisite for advancement—instructors trained students in textile mathematics and the credo of paternalism. Delivering a commencement address, one supervisor warned graduates about union organizers, who aimed to destroy "the Christian brotherhood that prevails at the Cone mills," and reminded them, "We are all working together for our own good" (*GDN*, Jan. 7, March 21, 1930).

By the mill masters' measurements, paternalism worked. Between 1900 and 1925, Cone workers did not publicly challenge management's authority or paternalistic image through strikes, walkouts, or union organizing. And some hands, at least partially, did adopt the notion of owner beneficence and industrial partnership. More than a few first-generation operatives voiced a personal commitment to Ceasar Cone. "Ceasar Cone was a wonderful man," remarked a Revolution card room worker in retrospect. "I tell you we all just love Mr. Cone," declared another mill hand in 1906. "He is so good to all of his people." Paternalism and welfare programs also seemed to have aided in the recruitment of a stable work force. "Welfare work is a good investment," Ceasar Cone noted in a moment of candor, "few leave us and as a consequence there are few new comers among us" ("Welfare Work" 1916; Cone 1912).

Despite Cone's proclamation of success, consent and employee loyalty were complex mixes of approbation, dissimulation, and self-interest. During the years of industrial peace at the Greensboro mills, resentments simmered below the placid surface of harmony. Workers registered their discontent by slowing down on the job, skipping work, or packing up and moving to other mill towns (Rhyne 1930, pp. 105–21; Beatty 1984; McHugh 1988, pp. 22–27). These forms of resistance represent individual revolt rather than collective action seeking to counter management's authority, but they suggest the need to construct a view of labor loyalty and consent that captures the range of workers' reactions to paternalism (Scott 1985).

Cone operatives did not give away their loyalty and ask for nothing in return. Instead, they found a way to convert economic dependence into mutual exchange and hammered out an informal contract between themselves and management (Zahavi 1983). This agreement called for workers to remain with the firm, labor productively, and eschew trade unionism in exchange for wages and benefits that were better than those offered at most places in the industrial piedmont. Workers based their commitment to the Cones not solely on awe of authority or fear of force but on shrewd economic analysis. Through kin and friendship ties, Cone workers fabricated a regional information network. Mill hands knew, for instance, that operatives in Marion, North Carolina, lived in "packing boxes on stilts," with newspapers on the walls, whereas they dwelled in commodious and well-built homes. They knew that operatives in Danville, Virginia, earned higher wages, but they garnered a larger income through the company bonus system. They knew that when hard times forced other factories to shut, the Cone looms continued to clank. And they knew that as sure as Christmas would come, they would get a holiday ham. As a result, many judged the Cone mills a better deal than the competition, be it the farm or other firms. One longtime worker captured this sentiment: "The Cone mills was always a little bit better to their help" (Potwin 1927; Page 1929; Rhyne 1930; Tindall 1967, p. 325; Wright 1975). The loyalty of Cone workers thus stemmed from a combination of the economic benefits of paternalism and the ability of the Cones to define the cultural and economic universe of the mill hands. When the advantages of paternalism came into question, the cultural consensus began to fall apart.

The Stretch-out

Five years before the stock market crash, the Great Depression hit the piedmont. Before 1925, the owners, satisfied with existing profit levels, constrained by a labor shortage, and shackled by a dearth of advanced technology, geared production to a relatively relaxed pace. In the wake of the wartime boom, however, the demand for textiles plummeted, prices plunged, and the industry went into a tailspin. Declining fortunes forced many mills to shut down, while the companies still operating scrutinized cost sheets and searched for ways to maintain profit margins and increase production in frantic bids to grasp part of the dwindling market. At the same time, the collapse of cotton and tobacco prices pushed farmers off the land and toward the mill gate. The convergence of these two phenomena left southern textile magnates with a labor surplus and falling turnover rates. Unhindered by the fear of losing their work force, worried by business forecasts, and prompted by newly popularized modes of labor control, the Cones reorganized production within their massive denim mills. The repercussions triggered by the economic cataclysm and management's response shredded the informal contract that for twenty-five years had tied Cone workers to their bosses (Tindall 1967, pp. 111–42; Wood 1986, pp. 59–93; Hall et al. 1987, pp. 183–212).

In January 1925, stressing the need for austerity and increased productivity, the Cones laid off hundreds of hands, slashed piece rates, revved up equipment, and assigned each hand additional machines. Operatives found themselves doing much more work for less pay. "I used to run 6 frames and now I look at 10," complained one weaver. "I used to get to rest . . . so's you could bear the mill . . . now you got to keep a-running all the time." Workers dubbed this blitz the stretch-out (Hall et al. 1987, pp. 210–11).

"Hundreds of folks go to jail every year . . . for doing things not half so bad or harmful to their fellow man as the stretch-out," declared James Evans, a Cone employee for more than two decades. Many hands shared his sense of betrayal and outrage (Terrill and Hirsch 1978, p. 178). In June 1925, after management had doubled the work load of White Oak weavers for the second time in six months, they turned to Evans, who was also an indigenous religious leader. "We've heard you in prayer meeting, we've believed in you," cried out several desperate workers. "Surely there's something you can do for us." Evans urged his co-workers to transform their common anger into collective action. By midmonth, they backed his proposal for a protest against the stretch-out. On a Tuesday morning, two by two, weave room operatives marched out of the factory and into the mill yard, where they stood singing gospel hymns (Terrill and Hirsch 1978, p. 180).

Within minutes, J. E. Hardin, the mill's general manager, confronted the crowd. He ordered the operatives back to work. The mill hands refused to budge, and Evans stepped forward to deliver a statement of resolve: "We stand before you . . . with a awful determination to have adjustment made in our work so we'll again feel like humans living in a free country. We mean to stand here . . . until a promise of adjustment is made. Every man, woman, and child is pledged to defend his job at the cost of his life. We hate violence but we hate slavery worse." When Evans finished, "the crowd set to clapping and yelling." Hardin pleaded for understanding and told the excited workers that the textile depression was responsible for the wage cuts and increased work loads. Waving a copy of the *Greensboro Daily News*, Evans challenged Hardin's woeful diagnosis of the textile industry's health. "There's lots of things I don't understand," the weaver submitted, "but the little I do know comes from the newspapers." Evans continued: "I see according to the quotations of the New York market cotton has went down $5 a bale, and the price of denim has increased 2 percent." The crowd again burst into applause (Terrill and Hirsch 1978, p. 181).

Finally, convinced that the workers would not back down, Hardin proposed a settlement. If the weave room operatives finished out the workweek, the general manager vowed, the proper adjustments would be made. "We went back to work on Monday on the same schedule we'd had before the stretch-out," remembered Evans (Terrill and Hirsch 1978, p. 181; Simon, 1989).

Three months later, workers at White Oak erupted again. Forty card room operatives walked off the job to protest the reorganization of work and an attendant wage cut. "We've been stretched out enough," declared one card room worker. "We work for a song, an' do all the singin'," exclaimed another. The Cones met the challenge with force. They fired the forty striking employees and threatened them with eviction. More important, averring that the mill could not operate without the card room, they locked out the entire White Oak labor force of fifteen hundred (Marley 1930).

Once again the Cones denied culpability and cited the textile industry's depression as the catalyst for the introduction of the stretch-out to the card room. Employing the press as a weapon once more, workers turned management's assertions on their head. Several days before the lockout, the *Greensboro Daily News* printed a copy of the Cones' family and business tax returns. Enraged hands posted the article on mill village streets and above factory time clocks. While card room workers struggled to maintain a pay scale of $12 per week, it was learned, Bernard Cone, the mill president, paid the government over $150,000 in taxes. The staggering profits churned out by the mills and the personal income amassed by the owner dramatized to workers not industrial partnership but the stark inequalities of mill life. Moreover, it appears that the publication of the owners' tax returns solidified the support of the White Oak community behind the strikers (*GDN*, Sept. 3, 4, 1925; Marley 1930).

Without union backing, the workers' ranks held solid for a week. On the day the unrest began, leaders put forth their demands for a return to the pre-stretch-out regime. Each night of the walkout mill hands and their families gathered at the foot of the seventy-foot-high White Oak mill gate, and two thousand strong they affirmed their solidarity by singing gospel hymns. Seven days after it began, an aged physician on the company payroll settled the dispute through arbitration. Both workers and management made concessions (Marley 1930).

The strikes of 1925 sought to reclaim rights under the old labor-management contract, which workers felt the stretch-out violated, not generate new demands. Many operatives linked the slide in their working conditions to the death of Ceasar Cone ten years earlier. "After old man Ceasar died—why, I don't know," recalled Lacy Wright, "it seemed like the benefits . . . began to gradually drop off." During the September unrest, an observer overheard a group of hands expressing the wish that the mill's founders were still alive. "They never cheated us—we could trust them." Throughout the card room rift, rumors swirled around the mill community that Ceasar's widow, cloistered in her Blowing Rock estate, was speeding toward Greensboro to settle the deadlock (Marley 1930, p. 18; Mitchell 1931; Wright 1975).

Beneath the continued evocations of paternalism and preferences for the past, however, lurked harbingers of future industrial relations. The stretch-out of 1925 called into question the benefits of laboring at the Cone mills. Moreover, it engendered working-class solidarity and revealed the mill hands' willingness, absent during the previous two decades, to channel their anger into resistance to management's authority. In addition, operatives developed their own norms to legitimate collective action. As the nightly gatherings at the mill gate revealed, many workers shared notions of Protestantism that stressed values at odds with the reigning order in their communities (Pope 1942; Simon 1989).

Although the strikes won workers a temporary reprieve from the stretch-out, the Cones continued to push ahead with their strategy for increasing worker productivity. After 1925, however, the Cones switched tactics. Whereas before the protests, existing machinery was speeded up, now scientific management techniques were adopted. Not long after the summer strikes, James Evans recalled, a stream of strangers—"mostly from the North"—descended upon the mill (Terrill and Hirsch 1978, p. 182). With a stopwatch in one hand and a clipboard in the other, these industrial engineers shadowed mill hands around the factory, timed their every move, and made cryptic notations (Nelson 1975). Under their supervision, mill officials rearranged the shop floor's geography, introduced faster and more efficient machines, and further intensified the pace of work. As one hand remarked, between 1925 and 1930, "just a little bit now and then," conditions "kept getting worse and worse." In the words of another operative, the Cones "stretched-out the stretch-out" ("Cone Group" 1928; Tippett 1931; Martin n.d.).

The new machines and the remapping of the shop floor were accompanied by changes in the firm's authority structures. After Ceasar Cone's death in 1917, his brother Bernard, a Johns Hopkins University graduate, took over the stewardship of the company. He prided himself on introducing a "new element of brains" to the firm, and he replaced men who had risen through the company ranks with college-trained supervisors and experienced New Englanders. In 1922, the mill owner hired the first of this new breed, a Clemson College graduate with a degree in textile engineering. Instead of the mechanical skills and personal relations on which their predecessors relied, the new managers gained their authority solely from the owners. No longer could the ambitious employee climb the company ladder to become a weave room supervisor. Thus, though managers gained greater control over the shop floor, they severed ties to the mill community and distanced themselves from workers (Hall et al. 1987, pp. 196–99; Cone 1983).

Nevertheless, the Cones did not abandon their paternalistic style or welfare practices with the introduction of new machinery and management techniques. Despite the size of the physical plant, the second generation of Greensboro mill owners still knew many of the hands on a first-name basis and remained immersed in the activities of the villages, cheering at sporting events, asking questions at gardening talks, visiting families, and stopping by the YMCA. Nor did the mill owners' image of themselves change; they continued to picture themselves as benevolent and selfless industrial leaders. Yet after 1925, these efforts yielded fewer results. Indeed, over the next half decade, the gulf between the Cones and their employees widened until it reached a climax in the schism of 1930.

Unionization

On March 12, 1929, operatives in Elizabethton, Tennessee, converted their anger over the worsening conditions of mill life into a revolt that reverberated into the piedmont. Before the year's end, Gastonia and Marion, North Carolina, also erupted with labor unrest. Both strikes gained national attention: Gastonia, for its Communist party leadership, along with the shooting deaths of a sheriff and a balladeer, and Marion, for the lawlessness of its deputies, who shot into a crowd, wounding twenty-five and killing six. Strike waves touched South Carolina as well (Bernstein 1960, pp. 1–43).

Although most observers expected rebellion from the strike zones, distinct rumblings could be heard in the Cone mill villages as well. "There is a sentiment for organization here," surmised a *Forward* reporter from New York in the fall of 1929 after a trip to the Cone factories. The owners, the journalist opined, would not stand opposed to the union "with an absolute 'No' " ("A Town in America" 1929). The Cones proved their visitor wrong. When the union came, they wielded their formidable power to crush the aspirations of some of their workers, all the while holding up the public armor of paternalism.

In response to the working-class unrest of the previous year, in early 1930 Bernard Cone proclaimed in a paternalistic idiom: "Labor unions have come into our state with the avowed purpose of unionizing our labor which heretofore has been happy and content and living on terms of confidence and friendship with its employers."

The impetus for unionization thus arose not from southern workers, Cone explained, but from the "outsider . . . the professional agitator, dependent for his living upon fomenting strife between employer and employee." Because of the textile depression, the mill owner concluded, "the unions can do nothing for the . . . laborer . . . it cannot increase his wages, because there is nothing out of which to pay increased wages" (*GDN*, Feb. 5, 1930; Tippett 1931, pp. 323–24).

Five days after Bernard Cone's diatribe against unions, William Green, president of the American Federation of Labor (AFL), spoke to a throng of Greensboro workers. Throughout the spring of 1930, the AFL chief addressed similar rallies across the region as part of the Southern Organizing Campaign, a regional unionization drive set up in the wake of the previous year's strike wave (Marshall 1967, pp. 122–32; Tippett 1931, pp. 173–209). In Greensboro, as elsewhere, Green extended his hand to business interests and local civic backers by assailing communism and stressing the AFL's mainstream values. "Mill riots would not have occurred had the federation been in Marion and Gastonia," he told the Chamber of Commerce, "the 5,000,000 members of the federation cannot be called agitators." Later, at a mass meeting, Green swore that the AFL sought "better manhood and womanhood, not class rule." After the rally, Green and the Southern Organizing Campaign packed up and moved on, leaving behind none of the machinery necessary for a local unionization drive (*GDN*, Feb. 26, 1930; *NYT*, Feb. 27, 1930; Tippett 1931, pp. 195–96).

Undeterred, a group of Cone workers approached the Greensboro Central Union for help. The craft federation greeted the industrial laborers' request with trepidation and counseled the operatives to forgo creating a union until the economic forecast brightened (*RNO*, July 7, 1930). But having already endured a long winter of depression and several seasons of managerial attacks, some Cone workers felt they had waited long enough. The prounion cadre, led by Evans and his son Percy, pestered the Central Union until it caved in and agreed to aid in a local unionization drive. For the next six months prounion operatives, with the help of their local allies and the UTW's national leadership, tried to win their fellow mill hands to the position that only a union could stop the erosion of their working conditions. It would be a tough fight (Terrill and Hirsch 1978, p. 183).

In May 1930, fifteen hundred Cone workers trekked out to a fallow potato patch in McAdoo Heights on the outskirts of town for the first union rally. Mill hands curious about the UTW had to walk to this spot because not a single Greensboro grocer, merchant, or minister dared allow his premises to be used for union meetings for fear of retaliation from the Cones. For most operatives, attending the rally represented the most brazen attack upon the Cone system of management of their working lives. The impressive turnout, numbering one-third of the company's payroll, impugned Bernard Cone's public boasts of a "happy and contented" work force (*GDN*, May 24, 1930; *RNO*, May 24, 1930; Tippett 1931, p. 196; Leary 1987, p. 50).

On June 11, the UTW staged another mass rally. A crowd of fifteen hundred gathered around a rickety wooden podium as UTW vice-president Francis Gorman beseeched them to join the union. Only the UTW, he proclaimed, would provide workers with the responsible weapon they needed to fight the stretch-out. These words struck a responsive chord. After the rally, five hundred Cone workers signed union membership cards. Within a week the national union sent them back a charter, and Local 1695 of the United Textile Workers of America was born (*GDN*, June 12, 1930; *TW*, June, July 1930; Tippett 1931, pp. 202–3).

After the formation of the local, the Cone management struck back. To be sure, the owners had exerted pressure on their work force before June, sending second hands and overseers to the McAdoo Heights meetings, where they stood conspicuously on the edges and taunted would-be unionists. Mill preachers warned workers against the devil and his serpentlike union and reiterated the oft-quoted biblical passage, "Servants, obey your masters." In addition, teachers admonished their students against "anarchists, communists, socialists and ne'er do wells" (*GDN*, March 21, 1930; Terrill and Hirsch 1978, pp. 162, 178, 182–83). But with Local 1695's birth, the Cone management unleashed its most brutal weapon—the eviction.

On July 10, just days before another scheduled meeting at McAdoo Heights, the sheriff of the Revolution mill village served thirty-six families with immediate eviction notices. As the law officers dumped the families' possessions onto the streets, a crowd formed. Many were stunned by the stark limits of paternalism. Forty-five years later, Lacy Wright still remembered the severity of the evictions: "The feeling . . . I had then was that was about as bad a wrong as I ever saw done." "We didn't think the Cones would do it," an onlooker told a reporter. Another less shocked worker said with more than a touch of irony: "We hope you see now how kind Mr. Cone is to his millhands" (*GDN*, July 11, 1930; *RNO*, July 13, 1930; *TW*, July 1930; Tippett 1931, pp. 202–3; Wright 1975; Martin n.d.).

The evictions shifted the focus of the unionization drive. Before July, the UTW had decried the stretch-out, emphasized the industrial benefits of trade unionism, and highlighted the AFL's respectability as outlined by Green and Gorman. Paternalism had remained in the background. But afterward, the Cones' style of management and material power moved to the foreground to emerge as the contested terrain of the campaign. Indeed, the unionization drive took the shape of an ideological struggle as the Cones and the union battled over the appropriation of symbols and information and how the past and present in the mill communities should be understood (Scott 1985).

In response to the changed tenor of the campaign, Bernard Cone appealed to his workers. He reminded the operatives of their shared pasts within the mill community and urged them to ignore the strangers in their midst and remain loyal to the firm. Recalling the crusading rhetoric of New South boosterism, he portrayed the mill as a buffer against the plight of rural poverty. Mill owners, he asked his employees to believe, constructed and maintained their citadels of the modern South not out of avarice but for the economic and moral salvation of the region. Published in the mill newspaper, the *Textorian*, Cone's appeal to his employees captures his picture of paternalism and loyalty: "Who are these strangers coming into our midst and trying to turn our people against us? . . . Have any of them spent sleepless nights, wrestling with our difficulties and trying to work out our mutual salvation? I want to say right here that the whole bunch of them have not as much real thought and interest and consideration for the good and welfare of our people in their whole bodies and souls as I have in my little finger." In return for the family's long-term benevolence, Cone asked his employees to demonstrate their steadfastness and to expunge the odious taint of unionism from the mill villages (*TXT*, June 6, July 25, Aug. 1, 1930).

Despite Cone's appeal for consent, the mill managers continued to use force to break the union. In August, they evicted another dozen families. This time the wrath of the company came down on workers for the double sin of belonging to the UTW and reading the "liberal" *Raleigh News and Observer*, the only newspaper in the piedmont that followed the events unfolding in the Cone mill villages.[3] After the latest evictions, Local 1695 moved to set up a

---

3. The *Greensboro Daily News'* coverage of the unionization campaign was spotty. Indeed, it is not unreasonable to assume that the Cones' influence stretched into the paper's editorial rooms. On May 31, 1930, the *Daily News* admitted that it had been

tent city for homeless workers to dramatize the Cones' cruelty and win community support, but the city council, on which Herman Cone sat, blocked the union's plans. "Uptown they couldn't seem to figger out a law on it [the tent city]," mocked Frank Martin, recalling the incident, "but they got the health doctor to come out and declare the right sanitation won't be carried out" (*RNO*, Aug. 6, 29, 1930; *TW*, Aug. 1930; Martin n.d.).

Meanwhile, the union leaders pounded away at the callousness of the Cones' actions and the bankruptcy of the old labor-management contract. The evictions, they charged, stripped the Cones of the gloss of paternalism and revealed the pernicious side of their leadership. Trade unionists, moreover, reinterpreted broadly shared religious and national tenets to sanction their movement. At a rally just after the initial evictions, Paul Fuller, AFL education director, delivered a sermon entitled "Christianity and the Mills." Fuller, a former minister of the gospel, told the mill hands that he had left the church pulpit for the union podium to do God's work, which was, he claimed, the AFL's quest. Only the union, others pointed out, could secure for workers their full rights of American citizenship. By withholding "a living and just wage," Percy Evans told a McAdoo Heights crowd, the Cones robbed mill hands of an "American way of life." Collective bargaining, another member of Local 1695 professed, represented the "God given constitutional right of every American citizen." With this statement, he placed the mill masters in opposition to the values of both Christ and the nation's Founding Fathers. By identifying their fight for a union with Protestant and American values, members of Local 1695 undermined the legitimacy of the Cones' authority (*GDN*, Aug. 1, 10, 1930).

By August, the ideological warfare over paternalism moved to a new battlefield. The union and management began to fight over a rather unlikely symbol—the Christmas ham.[4] Like Independence Day, mill officials cast the December holiday as a celebration of paternalism. "Christmas is the time when industrial peace and good will shine forth," commented a social worker in 1910 after visiting the Cone communities. Management billed Christmas as the time to acknowledge "a long year of hard work, unbeset by labor agitation

pressured into reprinting a speech by Bernard Cone impugning the motives of union organizers. See *GDN*, May 31, 1930, and Leary 1987, p. 51.

4. The ham as a metaphor was somewhat ironic in that the Cones were Jewish. Although there is no direct evidence, it is possible that the mill owners' religion became an unspoken, or whispered, dimension of the union campaign.

or grumbling or discontents" and rewarded loyal employees with a
ham (Vance 1910). As the unionization drive climaxed, the Christmas ham became a metaphor for paternalism. Workers were presented with a choice—they could select either the union and
working-class solidarity or the ham and loyalty.

Through the pages of the *Textorian* and the *Greensboro Daily News*,
the Cones, armed with the ham, attacked Local 1695 and its leaders.
Cartoons in the mill paper lampooned the union, charging that it
could not deliver the Christmas goods to each and every worker
(*TXT*, Aug. 1, 10, 1930). In pieces in the *Daily News*, the company
used devoted operatives to defame outsiders and applaud paternalism. Addressing a northeastern union organizer who had lambasted
the Cones, a "Night Employee" wrote: "If you had been here Christmas you might have gotten a smell of that nice ham every family
had given them as a gift by the company." Several weeks later, "A
Loyal Worker" echoed the sentiments of his nocturnal colleague.
Only the devil, she wrote, could be so evil as to send a union into
Greensboro to destroy the harmony of the Cone communities and
take away the holiday feast. Predicting that the union would stumble
in its malevolent mission, this faithful servant concluded: "We hope
we eat ham next Christmas" (*GDN*, June 20, July 16, 1930).

Prounion workers were quick to respond. "I have worked in the
cotton mills for over 15 years and I have sniffed the odor of fatback
so often that ham would puzzle me," Charles Schoolfield retorted.
He asked of the Christmas gifts: "Are they worth the price of being
dependent on baronial charity and the graces of the mill owner?"
Though less strident in his denunciation of paternalism, Mandant
Westbrook's view of the ham and the value of labor offers a view of
the processes of changing consciousness: "The first thought I had is
'I appreciate it' because they didn't have to give it to me! The other
thought is, 'By God they ought to give me a ham.' I've earned it and
it belongs to me without any body havin' to make a present of it." As
the assault on paternalism intensified, the worldview of many Cone
workers underwent a similar transformation. Instead of looking on
Christmas hams, and for that matter bonuses, picnics, and company-
churned butter, as gifts from benevolent masters, many workers began to recognize that their labor created the Cones' wealth, prestige,
and power. "They hate to have it said any company is giving them a
thing when it's their labor that produces what the company itself has,"
said Mandant's father, Wes, to explain some workers' attitudes toward
company benefits (*GDN*, June 24, 1930; Westbrook Family n.d.).

Under a blistering August sun, more than two thousand Cone
workers, the largest crowd of the campaign, gathered to hear Fran-

cis Gorman again. He abandoned his earlier rhetoric about the general values of trade unionism and took aim at Cone paternalism. At the close of his speech, he presented mill hands with a seemingly simple decision. "We can't ride two horses," he cried out. "We must make our choice and ride one, either the union or the ham" (*GDN*, Aug. 1, 1930; *TW*, Aug. 1930).

On the surface, the ham appeared to outlast the union. Just one month after Gorman's speech, Local 1695 was nearly defunct. But the UTW did not falter because Cone workers made the simple choice of the ham over the union; instead, a legion of factors led to its ruin. The textile depression and the larger economic climate, for instance, left mill hands with few ways to pressure management. The UTW, moreover, lacked the resolve, acumen, and financial resources required to challenge the Cones. When the unionization drive reached its decisive moment, just after the first wave of evictions, the national union pulled most of its organizational machinery out of Greensboro and deployed it instead in Danville, Virginia, where a strike had recently erupted (Smith 1960).

Management repression also battered Local 1695. Perhaps foremost, the evictions robbed the fledgling workers' movement of its most competent indigenous leaders. Many of these homeless trade unionists stayed on and continued to organize, living with friends or in isolated tents on the outskirts of the city, but by fall the chilly air and hunger drove most of them out of Greensboro in search of work. Even more crucial to the local's undoing than economics, poor trade union strategy, or company-backed subterfuge were the choices of workers.

Many did indeed pick the ham over the union, but only a few did so on Bernard Cone's terms, as docile and deferential employees. Some workers, to be sure, chose to bask in the glow of the Cones' paternalistic image and repudiated the UTW because they were grateful to have employers who were so kind and benevolent as to give them a Christmas ham each year. Yet most mill hands rejected the union for many of the same reasons that they had remained loyal to the firm in the past—shrewd and rational calculations. They recognized that by enlisting with the union they risked their jobs and bringing the full thrust of force down upon themselves and their families. Therefore, despite the stretch-out and the firm's vicious attack on the union, in 1930 large numbers of operatives continued to look upon the Cone mills as the best total package available.

Although a host of factors doomed the Greensboro textile union, the contentious tone of the unionization drive stretched the bonds of paternalism. After 1930, Cone operatives were not as loyal as they had once been, and they consented to management's authority only grudgingly. During the New Deal and war years, aided by new federal labor protections, they exhibited a determined zeal for collective action, a willingness to question the edicts of management, and the drive to build permanent union structures. Repeatedly through the 1930s and 1940s, Cone workers attacked the legitimacy of management's authority. Finally, as workers intensified their assault on the Cones' control and paternalism, consent waned and force predominated. Eventually, after World War II, the Cones abandoned paternalism. They sold off the mill homes, cut off welfare benefits, and introduced a depersonalized system of labor control. The mill owners' shift away from paternalism had its origins in the struggles waged between 1925 and 1930 and in the transformation, however uneven, of Cone workers' consciousness during that half decade.

6

"Jesus Leads Us, Cooper Needs Us, the Union Feeds Us": The 1958 Harriet-Henderson Textile Strike

Linda Frankel

From the postbellum era through the twentieth century, textile industrialization succeeded in the southern piedmont through a combination of strategies. Central to these were recruitment of a low-wage labor force composed of multiple family members—including high proportions of children and then women—adoption and uneven abandonment of paternalistic ideology and practices, and a fierce antiunion stance on the part of mill owners, bolstered by state support. The face of economic and political power worn by textile interests has helped mask struggles beneath a seemingly undisturbed veneer.

Confronted with these monolithic images, scholarship, popular mythology, and the media have presented southern textile workers as passive and acquiescent. They have attributed these characteristics either to the workers' investment in a paternalistic relationship with the mill owner or to the belief that the particularly invasive southern variant of textile industrial relations did not allow the workers any autonomous social space in which to develop an oppositional culture (Boyte 1972). Until relatively recently, the story that was told about life in the mill villages took one of two forms: it was either a story of poverty, fear, and failure or one of paternalistic benevolence and salvation, depending on whose perspective was represented. Paternalistic ideology and practices cast a long shadow that obscured the fuller dimensions of life and culture created by mill workers on the shop floor and in the villages (Hall et al. 1987, pp. xvi–xvii).

The failure of unionization in the southern mill villages has also long been a topic of dispute. In scholarship and in public discourse, structural barriers have tended to be submerged in psychological explanations that hinged on the disinterest, ignorance, and "traditionalism" of the mill hands. The high proportion of women working in the mills further reinforced these images because women were not viewed as "real" workers. Lack of interest in collective organization was interpreted as a sign of inhibited class or workers' consciousness rather than as a comment on the sanctions employed by mill owners or the inadequacies of the labor movement (e.g., Blauner 1964). Within this framework, labor conflict was often unexpected and viewed as a childish outburst, not an outgrowth of resistance. This portrait lingered even after an increase in unionization during the New Deal period. It was resurrected in the conservative postwar era of the 1950s and survives to this day, despite a growing body of evidence that disputes it.

One cannot deny that southern textile workers faced (and continue to face) tremendous constraints in their attempts to evade or challenge management control. Yet the very strategies owners and managers used to maintain control—a mixture of paternalistic, coercive, and bureaucratic techniques that changed over time—also evoked protest on the part of mill hands (Hall 1986; Hall et al. 1987; Marshall 1967; McLaurin 1971; Pope 1942; Tippett 1931). Recent studies based on oral histories from mill hands, analyses of archival materials, and closer examinations of labor conflict have begun to provide us with a more complex understanding of both the culture of mill communities and the systems of control and domination imposed by those who ran the mills. What emerges is a more dynamic picture of the relationship between workers and mill owners and managers (Hall et al. 1987; Janiewski 1985; Frankel 1986; Clark 1989). By these accounts, workers sought to grasp new opportunities, preserve accustomed ways of life, and evade the more odious constraints of work and life in the mill village. At the same time, owners and managers remained committed to getting out production, enforcing the necessary discipline within and beyond the mill gates, and preserving their prerogative to make decisions based on ownership of what was most often the town's, as well as the region's, major economic enterprise.

A significant, relatively contemporary example of this complex labor-management relationship is provided by the Harriet-Henderson textile strike of 1958–61. In November 1958, one thousand textile workers in Henderson, North Carolina, initiated a strike aimed at preserving a fourteen-year-old collective bargaining agreement with the Harriet-Henderson cotton mills. The Henderson workers sustained the strike for over two years in the face of the company's lockout and recruitment of strikebreakers, deployment of the Highway Patrol and National Guard, and conviction of national and local union leaders on charges of conspiracy to dynamite the plant. The Harriet-Henderson strike was the largest struggle of Textile Workers Union of America (TWUA) members and the most serious conflict involving southern textile workers in the post–World War II, pre-civil-rights era. But for the participants it was more personal. It was "something which brought us together," an expression growing out of generations of struggle to define for themselves the conditions of their life and labor, a vision of themselves as representatives of a broader movement of workers, a personally catalyzing event for the participants and for the town, and finally a turning point for a particular way of life in the mill villages.

Despite its importance, the strike has received only passing reference in the standard literature on southern textiles. This chapter aims to fill this gap by examining the roots of the 1958 conflict in the relationship of generations of white textile workers to the Harriet-Henderson mills. By focusing on the transformation of unfulfilled paternalistic promises into a collective bargaining framework, I argue that resistance to the mill owners' ultimate breach of faith—cancellation of the contract and lockout of the unionized workers—was rooted in a communally based and generationally transmitted worker culture. I will use the strike as a means of examining the link between the culture of the mill workers, collective organization, and resistance to management's attempts at control. From this case, one can better understand the relationship of unionism in the South to the culture of the mill village and to the political and economic power of southern textile interests.[1]

---

1. Material for this essay was drawn from a larger work, based on oral history interviews and archival research, which explored class and gender dynamics in the Henderson mill communities over a sixty-year period. For a more detailed account of labor relations, protest, and particularly the roles of women in the mills, families, and union, see Frankel 1984 and 1986. The dissertation will be published in revised form by the University of Illinois Press.

British historian E. P. Thompson (1963) and American historian Herbert Gutman (1977) focused on working-class culture in their efforts to get beyond the institutional and formal organizational history of labor and reveal the sometimes informal but nevertheless important activities, interactions, strategies, and networks through which groups of workers resisted erosion of their rights and customs under capitalist industrialization. Historians and anthropologists studying women workers have expanded this focus by uncovering the patterns of women's work culture across a variety of occupations. Based on her study of female department store clerks, Susan Porter Benson defines the concept of work culture as "the ideology and practice with which workers stake out a relatively autonomous sphere of action on the job. . . . A realm of informal, customary values and rules mediates the formal authority structure of the workplace and distances workers from its impact . . . work culture embodies workers' own definition of a good day's work, their own sense of satisfying and useful labor" (1988, p. 228).

This framework emphasizes the dynamic aspects of work culture—whether it results in adaptation or resistance—and the overlap of forces inside and outside the workplace which shape the behavior and outlook of all workers, male and female (Bookman and Morgen 1988; Lamphere 1987; Sacks 1988). It was precisely a relatively autonomous work culture, articulated in shop-floor conflicts and sustained by overlapping networks of kinship, neighborhoods, religion, and union, that the Harriet-Henderson management aimed to destroy. The 1958 strike represented the culmination of management's efforts.

From Paternalism to Unionism

The town of Henderson, North Carolina, lies near the Virginia border at the northern end of an arc stretching all the way from Georgia, where the primary concentration of southern textile mills can be found. Henderson has been a textile town since just before the turn of the century, when members of the Cooper family, already prominent in business (agricultural supplies and tobacco warehouses) and politics built two mill complexes at the northern and southern outskirts of town. These mills, the Harriet mill in South Henderson and the Henderson mill in North Henderson, with several expansions, have continued to produce yarn or sheeting under the same ownership up to the present.

During the sixty years preceding the 1958 conflict, several generations of an almost exclusively white work force experienced changes in the organization of work inside the factory gates as well as in the patterns of life in the mill villages of North and South Henderson. Although the town had a few other industries, the combined Harriet and Henderson mills constituted the largest single employer of working-class white families. Furthermore, the men who owned the mills, or their predecessors, also served at different times in a variety of other capacities in the economic and political power structures of the community, as mayor, county commissioner, trustee of the city schools, school superintendent, director of local banks and railroads, director of the telephone and telegraph company and the hospital, and leaders in the Democratic party. Female members of the family were active in the churches and in social and charitable organizations.

Textiles dominated the economy, the politics of the community, and the lives of the workers. The company transformed the strategies it used to attract, retain, and mold a productive work force to meet different needs, constraints, and challenges. These strategies were shaped by the social composition of the mill hands and the forms of resistance they could mount to management's definition of appropriate patterns of work and leisure. The company maintained a variable mix of coercion and co-optation; the workers had to balance survival, accommodation, and resistance.

Changes in the composition of the work force influenced managerial strategy and workers' resistance during these years. In the early decades, workers were recruited to the mills from the hard-pressed tenant farm families in the surrounding countryside. Age and sex divisions were critical in the construction of the mill work force. Young women figured prominently in the transition to industrial employment, constituting two-thirds of the work force in the earlier years, but all skilled and supervisory positions were held by men. Low wages and company policy required that families supply multiple wage earners to the mills, though mothers with many working children or with husbands in better-paying positions frequently were able to do paid and unpaid domestic work at home. Later, adult men and married women dominated the work force and together formed a couple-based family work unit (*Henderson City Directory* 1902; North Carolina Bureau of Labor and Printing 1900–1907; North Carolina Department of Labor and Printing 1910–26). By 1958, approximately 60 percent of the mills' employees were mature women, many of whom had entered the mills in their teens. By the time of the strike they had worked there for thirty or forty years and had witnessed major transformations in work process and labor relations.

Before the rigid systematization of work routines and the unionization that followed, all daily and long-term negotiations between the mill hands and management were based on informal manipulation of a system infused with paternalistic practices and traditions. Paternalism denotes the provision of nonwage goods and services, an ideology of beneficence, and the cultivation of deferential relations between the company and its employees. Paternalism promoted deferential relations through the employment of families and young children. Feelings of obligation on the workers' part were bolstered by management's control of access to housing, education, and jobs; a hierarchical work organization that gave a great deal of power to bosses and supervisors; and the use of religion and charity to legitimize the mill owners' authority.

This relationship flourished in southern mill communities for several reasons. First, mills were usually located in isolated rural areas or, as in Henderson, outside the town limits. In Henderson, like other mill towns, the company provided and controlled access to the housing, provided or supported schools and churches, arranged for the services of a doctor, supplied coal for heating, and thus had a hand in many aspects of daily life. Gratitude and fear were understandable responses to such pervasive control. Second, the company recruited particularly those families most in need of employment and already in some position of dependency: failing tenant farmers, widows, and youngsters with few other opportunities were among those sought out and attracted by the mills. Third, within the mills a hierarchy coordinated with age and gender divisions let the mill owner or "big daddy" appear benevolent while the supervisors and bosses down the line could manipulate family loyalties and take punitive measures. Fourth, an ideology of opportunity to belong to a privileged white mill "family" that excluded blacks had some appeal for poor whites experiencing hardship in the rural South. All of these forces led many to view mill villages as seamless webs of mutual interest, quiescent and conflict-free. But this picture does not hold for Henderson or for other mill communities whose struggles have been recounted in oral histories.

What were the elements of accommodation, survival, and resistance that coexisted in the culture of the working community? Workers brought from their rural backgrounds alternative customs and habits of work as well as kin-based networks of sharing, obligation, and sociability. Such activities as gardening, animal husbandry, fishing, and hunting supplemented mill wages, provided an undergirding of subsistence, and created a measure of independence for the village communities. Mutual assistance—nursing the sick, attending at births, caring for children, which were largely dependent on women's activities and ties—held the community together and provided a safety net of their own devising (Leloudis 1986). These responsibilities put a heavy burden on women, particularly those whose work stretched across the two sides of the mill gates. In the early decades, the boundary was more permeable as management allowed workers to leave the mills when their work was caught up. For youth, this flexibility provided some time for leisure pursuits such as courting or fishing; it gave married women time for family responsibilities such as nursing babies or fixing supper (Frankel 1986).

Conflict was not eradicated within the paternalistic framework but channeled into individualistic rather than collective forms. Frequent moves and irregular work habits attested to the mill hands' individual resistance to the imposition of industrial discipline. Grievances tended to be privatized and personalized, finding collective expression only periodically. In some cases, deferential relations encouraged by a paternalistic hierarchy combined with low wages and family dependency to reduce workers' capacity to take risks. Yet early strikes and attempts at unionization, though often unsuccessful, indicate that workers expected and demanded better treatment. Their expectations, though partly spawned by paternalistic promises, provided a seedbed for resistance when the mill owners sought to tighten production and increase efficiency.

Such was the case in Henderson in 1924, when management rescinded a 12.5 percent bonus that had been instituted to encourage steady attendance at work. In response to this wage cut, 250 workers in the Harriet number 1 mill walked out. After eight days they returned to work with the understanding that mill president Sidney Cooper would restore the cut wages when business conditions improved. Following this incident, the company erected a high-grade fence around the perimeter of the mills. The fence served a dual purpose: it prevented the hands from slipping out during working hours, and it protected mill property during future labor conflicts (company records, Oct. 15, 1924, in Clark 1989, p. 34).

In 1927, when Cooper's promise remained unmet, workers on the day shift in the Harriet mills walked out. They were followed by several hundred workers in all sections. Although the wage issue served as a rallying point, workers' complaints revealed dissatisfaction with mill discipline. They objected in particular to the locking of the mill gates, which prevented them from leaving work to attend to chores. They protested, "We are not a class of people to be locked in." Other issues included the poor working conditions, increased speed of the machinery, and overuse of the "spare-hand system," which resulted in insufficient work for too many hands. In a "peaceful" and "respectful" manner, hundreds of workers picketed the mills and attended mass meetings, which mixed social, religious, and union purposes. Speakers included the pastor of the Pentecostal Holiness churches in the mill villages, the superintendent of the Sunday school at the Baptist church, who was also the village barber, an overseer in the card room, and numerous workers. Purportedly to forestall the threat of violence, company officials, through their lawyer, asked the governor to call out the National Guard. The troops were withdrawn almost immediately when no violence materialized (*Henderson Daily Dispatch* [abbreviated hereafter as *HDD*], Aug. 1927).

Management offered to consider any personal grievances presented to the office, but the strikers adamantly refused this offer and sought recognition of the justice of their collective demands. When labor organizer Alfred Hoffmann arrived to offer the assistance of the labor movement, several hundred workers signed cards for the United Textile Workers; one source quoted in the *Henderson Daily Dispatch* estimated that there were seven hundred signers in South Henderson and three hundred in North Henderson. The union solicited funds from labor groups across the state and helped distribute provisions to fourteen hundred members of strikers' families. Village gardens and supplies from local farmers and merchants also sustained the protesters. But the strikers were never able to persuade workers at the mill in North Henderson to join them and close down that plant. After six weeks, management broke the strike by threatening nine key strikers with eviction from company-owned dwellings (*HDD*, Aug. 1927).

In the wake of the strike the company resorted to a familiar blend of philanthropy and punishment to restore the status quo and reassert control. Management simultaneously donated schoolbooks to the children of employees and fired a group of about one hundred carefully selected workers, increased surveillance in the mills, and began a card file system to keep track of all employees (company records, Oct. 19, 1927, in Clark 1989, p. 47).

In the late 1930s the company, responding to the effects of economic instability and depression in the industry and hoping to regain a competitive edge, implemented a modernization program that imposed more rigid constraints on the work process while retaining the arbitrariness and favoritism characteristic of earlier work relations. Along with the installation of new machinery, textile engineers and time study experts began to play prominent roles on the shop floor. Older workers and former bosses who had risen through the ranks were demoted or fired when new college-trained engineers and supervisory personnel were brought in from outside. The new system of production relied on piece rates, increased work loads, and closer monitoring of the performance of individual workers to meet company-defined standards of efficiency. Workers expressed the feeling that relations had moved from a familylike atmosphere to one that was impersonal and businesslike. At the same time, favoritism, family connections, and personal grudges continued to influence access to jobs and desirable shifts. Discrimination was not eradicated but subordinated to the more stringently defined efficiency goals of management. These changes had a particularly acute effect on the young mothers who remained in the work force as part of married, two-paycheck couples or as female heads of households. These women and their families needed to be able to coordinate shifts or take leaves for pregnancy without risking the loss of their jobs (Frankel 1986).

Thus when conditions more favorable to unionization arose during World War II, a younger generation of workers reacted to the intensification of work and erosion of flexibility by responding positively to an organizing campaign in the plants; following a vote favoring representation, two locals, 578 (South Henderson) and 584 (North Henderson), of the Textile Workers Union of America were formed. Following the establishment of a joint contract with the mills, these two locals achieved over 90 percent membership despite the state's right-to-work law (TWUA holdings, Wisconsin State Historical Society). The union campaign was based on informal discussions among small groups of workers. Social gatherings with singing and dancing, held at the village store, which had served as the headquarters of the 1927 strike, provided opportunities for those committed to collective organization to convince their neighbors and fellow workers of the benefits to be gained by voting for representation. The substantial support that the union received gave it the ability to negotiate a contract and formally protect the rights and respect to which the workers felt they were entitled.

The Henderson workers were somewhat distinctive in achieving collective organization. Only 10 percent of southern workers were unionized during this period (Marshall 1967). A major reason for their success was the relatively benign attitude of the company, which did not mount an extensive campaign against the union chiefly because the mills' lawyer persuaded the president that unionization could be part of a more modern, bureaucratized mode of labor relations (Clark 1989, pp. 88–89). Although workers could not talk about the union inside the mill gates, they were free to do so outside the gates and in the homes they had purchased from the company. Sales of company-owned housing to employees cemented the ties between the workers and the community while divesting management of an economic burden. It also eliminated the chance that troublemakers would be evicted and thus helped reduce fears about union talk.

Unionization changed the climate of worker-management relations as well as the attitudes and capacities of union members. For the mill workers, organization brought greater job security, predictability, and self-respect, both in the workplace and in the community. As in other industries, the collective bargaining process and the grievance procedure provided formal mechanisms for mediating conflict over wages and working conditions. The national and regional offices of the TWUA provided technical assistance and organizational resources. In addition, unionization increased the political power of these textile workers, enabling them to join with other organized workers, including members of the United Automobile Workers (UAW) at the local truck factory, to influence the outcome of local elections.

Nevertheless, some aspects of the paternalistic framework still infused the relationship between the union, the workers, and the mills. For example, some workers transferred their expectation of personalized treatment from the bosses to the union leader. Further, although men and women participated together in union activities, gender hierarchies rooted in domestic and factory relations were not directly challenged. Ironically, the contract gave renewed credence to the paternalistic notion of mutual expectations and obligations. Reshaped in a more democratic form, mutual respect and cooperation toward shared goals were reemphasized as legitimating and motivating factors in the labor-management bargain.

Union members hoped the rules would preserve the "family feelings" by making everybody get along, that is, by providing a check on management's prerogatives to control work. Workers hoped unionization would provide greater "order" and rules, which "compelled the bossmen to be good and to help you see where you could get along." Management, however, found the rules useful only to the extent that they supported the "businesslike" trend toward increased managerial control over production, including increases or decreases in operations, changes in work-load assignments, disciplining of workers, and so forth. These divergent interests and interpretations of the contract inevitably produced conflict, especially over the regularity and intensity of work. Management tried to limit absenteeism, while workers sought continued flexibility to meet the pressures of work, the demands of home and family, and the need for physical recuperation and relaxation, all of which influenced variations in work habits. Management also tried to increase workers' output by requiring each to tend more machines, but workers fought this threat to their safety, socializing, and satisfaction.

The company defended these changes by citing the need for more efficient production. The union resisted through grievances, negotiation, and, ultimately, a brief strike in 1954. When the company refused to adhere to negotiated settlements of these issues, the union was forced to use the grievance system to seek redress, which often proved time-consuming, and successes were mainly defensive. Even so, these disputes slowed or impeded managerial goals enough to anger mill officials, who preferred to set priorities without interference (Clark 1989; interview with Luther Jackson).

The 1958 Strike: Solidarity in Defeat

Labor conflict came to a head in 1958, when management refused to renew the expiring contract and instead proposed a series of drastic changes which undercut the basic premises of the union agreement.[2] At the heart of management's proposals was the elimination of arbitration, which in the words of the local union presidents Luther Jackson (584 North) and Charlie Raines (578 South) left "no way for orderly, peaceful redress of employee grievances" (*HDD*, Jackson and Raines 1958). The company clearly knew that its stance would provoke a strong response. The company president, J. D. Cooper, Jr., expressed a willingness to risk temporary disruption to pave the way for greater control over workers on the job: "Within the past two years, there have been radical changes in the operation of a textile plant. . . . If we are going to operate these plants successfully we must have a contract which will enable us to take advantage of these advances" ("The Henderson Story" 1960, p. 9).

---

2. Material on the strike comes from TWUA holdings in the Wisconsin State Historical Society, the *HDD*, Amalgamated Clothing and Textile Workers Union (ACTWU) files, and extensive oral history interviews I conducted from 1978 to 1980 with twenty-one former Harriet-Henderson workers. For this essay interviews with Edith Adams, Luther Jackson, Arieta Martin, Esther Roberson, Ethel Rogers, Lois Wilder, and Lucille Wilder were especially useful.

Both the company and the union saw this strike as a test case for the viability of collective bargaining in a period marked by the erosion of gains made during Franklin Roosevelt's presidency. With an impending presidential election that could potentially shift national politics once again in a more liberal direction, southern industrialists may have encouraged management to take a firm stand in Henderson so as to weaken an important union stronghold and thus reaffirm the antiunion position of the South. The strategy pursued by the Harriet-Henderson company followed a pattern numerous other textile firms had successfully employed to weaken or destroy existing unions. In most of these cases, either short, unsuccessful strikes ensued or the workers capitulated to management demands. In Henderson, however, union members voted unanimously to go on strike rather than continue to work without an effective contract. The conflict shows the difficulties of sustaining organization in a hostile environment but also a high degree of working-class solidarity not usually attributed to southern textile workers.

Following the vote to strike on November 16, 1958, picket lines were set up, and by early December commissaries were opened in the two union halls to distribute food to the striking workers. The mills remained closed for three months. Following a series of futile negotiations during which the mill president vowed never to change one comma of his proposals, the company reopened the plants in February with labor recruited from the surrounding counties. After provoking a confrontation at the North Henderson mill picket line over delivery of cotton, the company obtained a restraining order which severely limited the number of picketers and imposed restrictions on their behavior. At the urging of the mill president, the police chief and sheriff claimed that they did not have adequate personnel to handle potential unrest and thus requested that the governor send in state troops. A large contingent of Highway Patrol officers escorted the strikebreakers as they drove through the mill gates.

The reopening precipitated picket line violence and other incidents. Large numbers of strikers were arrested for disorderly conduct, assault, damaging personal property, and violating the restraining order. Violence against strikers and union representatives by armed strikebreakers and others was ignored. Strikers were arrested solely on the basis of identification by mill officials and foremen watching from the mills, but scabs found to be carrying weapons or using their cars as weapons against pickets were typically not arrested. Those few who were arrested received light charges or dismissals, but arrested strikers received heavy fines and were often sentenced to prison or road work. As the strike progressed, the issue of violence on the part of strikers, though provoked by managerial intransigence and resulting in only minor property damage, eclipsed the more important conflict over workers' rights.

As tensions increased, the governor of North Carolina, Luther Hodges, himself a former textile executive, finally began to take an active role in the strike, meeting with company and union officials. When a compromise was worked out involving union concessions, however, a new issue arose that undermined the resolution—the job rights of displaced strikers. In mid-April 1959 a tentative agreement was announced and strikers celebrated at special church services. Union members were to begin to fill a new second shift on April 20, with a third shift soon to follow; strikebreakers were to remain on the first shift, but strikers were to be put on a preferential hiring list. With great relief and hope, union members reported their availability for work to their foremen. In what workers called the "Great Betrayal," the majority were informed that their jobs were no longer available because they had been permanently replaced by recently hired workers. Fewer than thirty former workers were called back to the first shift, and once there they were cursed and threatened by nonstrikers. A siege by angry union members at the Henderson mill kept most of the scabs in the plants all night. The governor was furious with mill president J. D. Cooper, Jr., for misrepresenting the number of jobs that remained open to the returning strikers and thereby personally embarrassing him, but he nevertheless quickly shifted his focus to the issue of violence and held TWUA representative Boyd Payton responsible for any incidents in response to the betrayal.

From this point on the mills operated with nonunion workers, and the strike turned into a lockout. A group of small businessmen and townspeople petitioned the governor to close the mills until the situation was resolved, but he wished to avoid challenging the mill owner and, when a third shift was announced, he returned to the familiar tactic of supplying protection to the mills. After an abandoned mill building (an old house formerly used as a nursery and community center) was demolished by an explosion, the National Guard was called in and a new restraining order was issued which further restricted the resumption of picketing (the state legislature had passed a bill giving the Guard arrest powers). A special term of the recorder's court was held to hear all cases against the strikers.

In June 1959, soon after the third shift went back into operation, a group of six local union leaders and national representatives was arrested on charges of conspiring to dynamite the mill. The trial was held in Henderson, the county seat, in July, with jurors drawn from the same areas from which scabs had been recruited. On the basis of testimony from a State Bureau of Investigation informant with a criminal record, the unionists were convicted and ultimately sentenced to lengthy prison terms.[3]

As the plant proceeded to full-capacity employment, the leadership of the union fought its legal appeals. The year-long active strike shifted into a different mode, mainly a public relations and support effort for the prisoners, kicked off by a large anniversary rally held in Henderson in November 1959. The day before the rally, Cooper strategically announced an expansion program of several thousand dollars for the mills. The union mobilized its members and embarked on a nationwide campaign to gain support for the striking workers and justice for the prisoners by publishing a weekly *Freedom Fighter* newsletter supported by ads from sympathetic tradespeople in town. At the same time, the national union undertook a lengthy process of tapering off relief and trying to place members in new jobs. With a great deal of disappointment and some resentment among members unwilling to concede defeat, the TWUA finally terminated the strike in June 1961, two and a half years after it had begun.

Unionized workers took a tremendous risk by standing up for their contract and continuing to resist while management refused to change its position and ultimately brought others in to take their jobs. Many of the workers had been in the Harriet and Henderson mills for twenty to thirty years; their parents and grandparents had also worked there. These were the only jobs they knew, and they had invested their lives in the work and in the community. Although the international union spent more than $1.5 million on the strike, set up an extensive relief effort on behalf of the strikers, provided legal assistance to those arrested, brought pressure to bear on state and federal officials to release food surpluses and secure jobs for some strikers in the public sector, and tried to keep the strikers' views alive in the media, on a daily level it was the determination and anger of the rank-and-file participants that fueled the strike.

Sources of Strike Imagery and Solidarity

The roots of resistance sprang from a mill village culture that had been transmuted into a union context. A popular slogan on the picket

---

3. Convicted unionists included TWUA representatives Boyd Payton, Lawrence Gore, and Charles Auslander and local union members Johnnie Martin, vice-president of Local 578, Warren Walker, Calvin Bay Pegram, Charles Abbott, and Michael Jarrel.

lines—"Jesus Leads Us, Cooper Needs Us, the Union Feeds Us"—
illustrated how the striking workers cast their expressions of solidarity
and justice using the interwoven imageries of religion, paternalism,
and unionism. These themes also echoed in the letters to the editor
of the local paper written by strikers to defend their position.

RELIGION: "JESUS LEADS US"

Religion provided one important axis of solidarity for the strikers;
religious sentiments and church-based connections undergirded cohesiveness in the villages. In earlier days, the mill owners had un-
derscored the importance of religion in providing an ideological
justification for "clean living" and hard work.

But the churches represented more than an avenue for mill-
dominated activity and beliefs. Mill workers had achieved a great degree of autonomy in their religious institutions. They belonged to a
range of denominations—Methodist, Baptist, Pentecostal, and many
smaller sects—that served as focal points for social activity and
moral life in the mill villages. Separated from the uptown branches
of the various denominations, the churches also nurtured a compet-
ing arena for workers' self-organization and sense of respectability.
The emergence of revivalism and the growth of the smaller Pentecostal sects made possible a class-based religious organization. As
workers' lives improved and they had more resources to invest in
their churches, they built organizations that served their social and
spiritual needs.

This cohesiveness was evident during both the strike in 1927 and
the 1958 conflict. As in the 1927 strike, support from religious leaders
lent legitimacy and moral weight to the 1958 strike cause. TWUA
representative Boyd Payton, who had wanted to be a preacher before
becoming attracted to the union cause, served as an inspirational
leader for the Henderson unionists, particularly through his weekly
Sunday radio broadcasts. In numerous letters to the editor of the *Henderson Daily Dispatch*, strikers drew a contrast between their own support of Christian values and the unchristian behavior of the scabs,
"Cooper-lovers," and "Money-lovers." One striker wrote accusingly of
Cooper, the mill owner, "If you love God, as much as you do your
money, Henderson wouldn't be in the shape it is in tonight" (*HDD*,
Hale 1959). Another linked respect for laboring people with God's
love: "The laboring people are the backbone of our nation, so should
be treated with respect. God must have loved them as He made so
many of them" (*HDD*, Forsythe 1959). For some, following God's guid-

ance was the only way to a solution: "I believe God is going to work this out because He said, 'If I be for you, who can be against you?' " (*HDD*, Hale 1959) and "If both parties were Christians, I sincerely believe a workable contract could be negotiated" (*HDD*, Wilder 1959).

PATERNALISM AND CLASS:
"COOPER NEEDS US"

Along with the religious theme, workers argued that they deserved consideration based on their years of loyal service to the mills and to the town. This view was expressed in two different but intertwining strands. The first was that workers' loyalty to their employers, whether based on a paternalistic or contractual bargain, should be acknowledged. As one union activist put it, "We've always given the mills our best efforts. If the reward for our long and loyal service is a public flogging, a brutal effort to starve us into submission, put us back to where we were 15 or 20 years ago, we'll have none of it . . . our pride and self-respect is not for sale" (*HDD*, E. Roberson 1959).

From an earlier emphasis on workers needing the jobs, services, and status derived from working in the mills, the focus shifted to what the workers had done for the mills. The labor of the striking women and men and their families had built the mills and the town. For their continuing loyal efforts, they argued, they deserved re-spect and fair treatment. Workers expressed a sense of pride over their role in building the prosperity of the mills and the town, cou-pled with the feeling that this effort and loyalty had been betrayed: "We have asked ourselves whatever gave us the idea that long years of loyal service would count for consideration at the hands of our employers? The Henderson we helped build, expand, is certainly not the place we thought it" (*HDD*, Langley 1959).

The second strand was a deepening awareness of the class-based power of the mill owner to dominate the town. One striking worker wrote, "People has said as far back as I can remember this town was run by the Coopers. I couldn't believe it at one time but now I know it is" (*HDD*, Turner 1959). Another wrote, "It makes me ashamed to know that one man (because of his money) can buy out a town like this one" (*HDD*, G. Roberson 1959). Workers on strike realized that the sentiment that "Cooper needs us" was wishful thinking.

THE UNION MAKES US STRONG:
"THE UNION FEEDS US"

Finally, the strikers voiced their gratitude to the union for extending to them the fair treatment, solidarity, and support the town and the mill management had failed to provide. When mill supporters attempted to cast the union representatives as outsiders, local members responded with a vigorous defense: "We feel fortunate in having friends who are interested in helping us workers get fair treatment even though they are from out of town, since those for whom we have worked for so many years have shown so clearly how little we mean to them except for labor in gaining them success" (*HDD*, Langley 1959).

Criticisms of union officials' "high salaries" and supposed influence over the mill workers were similarly met with disdain. Strikers vouched for the democratic basis of all union decisions, claiming, "We of locals 578 and 584 are not as some of you seem to believe poor, dumb sheep who blindly follow any leader, however 'persuasive' . . . no leader however inspired and inspiring could just talk us into going through what we've endured these past eighteen weeks." The irrelevancy of union officials' pay was contrasted with the aid the union provided to the strikers: "We don't care what Mr. Payton's salary is or any other union officials. They have really earned any amount they get. The union is taking good care of its members. We eat very well and get the best medical care and most of our bills are getting paid" (*HDD*, Journigan 1959).

An important dimension of conflict—ideological and practical—in mill communities, including Henderson, has been over the issue of "insiders versus outsiders." The mill owners have always argued that they should be left alone to tend to their own business without the "interference" of outside interests—unions. Through fourteen years of collective organization, the workers had redefined boundaries between the insiders and outsiders. Although they still saw themselves as part of a mill family, they no longer accepted management's version of membership, authority, and alliances. First, the union represented and defended the group of black workers who worked in the mill yard loading and hauling cotton. These workers also went on strike and received aid from the union along with their white co-workers. Second, through shop stewards and the grievance system, workers sought to share power in setting working conditions. Third, the union movement provided a broader network of "brother and sister" workers that spread beyond the village limits across the state, the region, and, ultimately, the nation.

The lives of the majority of members remained rooted in and confined by the daily activities of work, family, and church in Henderson, yet the improvement of their standard of living as well as the presence of the union on the shop floor played a critical role in a process whereby they redefined themselves as workers. During the strike this redefinition was enhanced both for those who had been union leaders before the strike and for those who became involved in and galvanized by the strike activities. The strike itself was a transformative event for many workers who had been only marginally involved with the union during quieter times. Picket line duty, work in the food distribution centers, and speaking tours to enlist money and support all centered strikers' lives around the conflict.

New roles and attitudes emerged from the strike and its aftermath. For example, maintaining solidarity during the strike required greater equalization of the roles of male and female union members than in less critical times. The energies of women in particular were more intensely harnessed during the strike than under normal circumstances. Women paraded militantly on the picket lines, often making up the majority. They shouted at the strikebreakers and taunted the troopers and were arrested along with men, although not in equal numbers. Union president Luther Jackson recounted the story of one union member who relieved a highway patrolman of his blackjack while pretending to flirt with him (North State Video n.d.).

Some women who had not been especially active in the union before the strike were drawn into more active roles, either on the picket lines or helping to manage the massive distribution of clothing, food, and other aid the union organized. Those who had been activists in the union before the strike maintained or increased their involvement. As the strike wore on and men were better able to get jobs elsewhere, women assumed the greatest burdens of strike activities. Women's labor provided the backbone for relief efforts; women took charge of clothing distribution and worked closely with international union representatives to administer the assistance programs. The devastating impact of the strike on their families made women powerful speakers on behalf of the strikers' needs. When they traveled to labor conventions and rallies in cities all over the East and Midwest, female union members in particular were given standing ovations and contributions in response to their heartfelt and fervent appeals for aid to the strikers in Henderson.

The extensive relief apparatus set up by the locals with the assistance of the international union was very important in sustaining solidarity among the workers and allowing them to continue the struggle over the long term. Yet, given the legacy of paternalism and the limited range of employment options available to the strikers—particularly older workers—union assistance, in addition to building morale, assumed an aspect of permanency that was difficult to dispel. Union representatives worked hard to secure other forms of assistance for the strikers—unemployment compensation (which became available only when the plant was back in full operation and strikers on all three shifts had been permanently replaced), federal food surpluses, Social Security and disability payments. They also brought pressure to bear on state officials to encourage the hiring of strikers on state construction projects or at the state mental hospital in a nearby town. The union provided assistance as well to members who enrolled in training programs or completed their high school equivalency work. Nevertheless, when the international union tapered off relief and finally decided to terminate the strike, tensions arose with local members who wanted to continue striking.

Aftermath of the Strike

The strike left a legacy of division and bitterness in the community that is still evident thirty years later. Family members and church members who supported opposite sides in the strike refused to speak to one another for many years after it ended. Yet union members remained strongly committed to their cause, and, although they no longer worked together, they maintained their personal connections after the strike ended. Strikers also remained active in the political arena, voting out of office the mayor who had opposed them, electing sympathetic county officials, and campaigning for the victory of a Democratic governor, Terry Sanford, whom they hoped would grant pardons or prison releases to the convicted union leaders (Luther Jackson interview).

The strongest identification for the defeated strikers remained with each other and with the knowledge that they acted properly in defending the rights of working people. Indeed, stories about the strike, some apocryphal, continue to be a mainstay of conversation when former strikers get together. Many individual strikers, particularly those who were able to receive additional education or training and thus secure nonfactory work, expressed the feeling that the strike was "the best thing that ever happened to me." Some found that their new service and clerical jobs—private duty nursing, bookkeeping, office receptionist, hairdressing, waitressing—allowed them to "get out with the public more" and broaden their horizons. Others who were either too old to secure new jobs or too young to receive Social Security did not fare so well. Regardless of personal outcomes, strikers expressed little regret about participating in a battle for the defense of their way of life that ended with such cataclysmic change (Esther Roberson, Edith Adams, Ethel Rogers interviews).

The loss of the strike and the lockout of the union, however, dealt a lethal blow to the connection between the longtime village residents and the mills. In the years following the strike, workers who replaced the strikers commuted to the mills from outside the villages. Later, new workers who were not connected to the former workers moved into the villages.

To this day, the plants remain unorganized. Yet the years of successful organization did leave an important legacy of union experience in the lives of the strikers as well as in the wider community. Union members in Henderson had strengthened their political influence, improved their economic status, and exerted a measure of control over their work lives. The union also provided an important arena within which women could "express their views and ideas just like men" (Lucille Wilder interview). Members viewed the union as a source of self-respect and security. Those who found work in other settings with unions or state employees' organizations remained active in the labor movement. Most passed on to their children an attitude of tolerance toward unions.

Unionizing attempts still face tremendous obstacles in the southern textile industry, particularly as multinational corporations relocate work to other countries with lower wage rates and authoritarian political regimes (Wright and Clark 1979). As the workers in Henderson learned all too clearly, maintaining collective bargaining agreements and representing workers' rights in the mills is a constant uphill battle; success can be eroded in the daily struggles on the shop floor, in the often frustrating grievance machinery, or, more decisively, in a forced strike, lockout, or plant shutdown. Solidarity among workers may be critical to staying in the battle, but it may not prove sufficient when mill owners can rely on an alternate labor supply and the support of the state to reinforce their power. Yet as the example of the Harriet-Henderson strike shows, when worker solidarity fuses long-term personal and cultural ties with the backing provided by collective organization, workers are prepared to go a long way to preserve the control and self-respect they have achieved.

7

The Brown Lung Association and Grass-Roots Organizing

Bennett M. Judkins and Bart Dredge

In October 1985, textile workers in the small community of Kannapolis, North Carolina, wrote another chapter in the long and difficult history of union organizing in the South. Cannon Mills had been sold in 1982 to Los Angeles financier David Murdock. The new owner's reputation for having a singular interest in profit contrasted with the Cannon family's paternalism. Officials of the union recognized the sale as an important opportunity to organize the mill workers, who were fearful of impending changes, especially an anticipated three thousand layoffs during the next three years. It was also a chance to improve the state's meager union participation rates: 12 percent of the textile workers and 5 percent of the manufacturing work force.

The Amalgamated Clothing and Textile Workers Union poured $150,000 into the Cannon campaign, brought in a dozen organizers from other union offices, and introduced such sophisticated organizing techniques as television commercials and computerized mailings. After "an often acrimonious 16 month campaign" (Ellis 1986, p. 12C), however, the workers rejected the union by a greater margin than in previous campaigns when the Cannon family had owned the mills (McIntosh 1985, p. 1C).

Following an increasingly common managerial strategy, Cannon officials had hired a law firm that specialized in antiunion campaigns. In addition, they had released letters, speeches, and videotapes to their employees and to the public to "drum home the message that a union's demands [would] weaken the company's competitive position" (Ellis and Olmos 1985, p. 10A). Finally, the company had appealed to workers' fears by threatening to sell Cannon Mills if the union was voted in. In one of the mills, company representatives displayed posters with a picture of a padlocked gate. Ironically, only weeks after using this threat successfully to defeat the union effort, Murdock sold 80 percent of Cannon to Fieldcrest Mills, a subsidiary of the Amoskeag Company of Boston.

The reasons for the overall failure of unionization in the South, particularly in the textile industry, have been a subject of debate for many years. Early explanations argued that southern textile workers are generally intransigent in their opposition to labor unions because of their basically docile character and their traditional acceptance of nonadversarial relationships at work (see Mitchell 1921 and Morland 1958). These explanations are based on the view that workers' attitudes and personality configurations remain stable over time and will not change to accept unionization. Melton A. McLaurin (1971) countered, however, that mill hands have actively sought organization and were not coerced to organize by outsiders. In the late 1800s, mill workers joined the Knights of Labor when there was no full-time organizer in the field primarily because they saw it as a means to obtain benefits. In some areas of the South, they organized their own chapters of the National Union of Textile Workers and then prevailed on the AFL to organize them into NUTW assemblies (McLaurin 1971, p. 203). In the late 1920s and early 1930s, southern textile workers became involved in a series of strikes that shook the foundations of the textile industry (see Marshall 1967 for an account of these strikes and Hall et al. 1987 on the great textile strike in 1934). More recent labor struggles centered on union representation elections in Henderson, North Carolina, in 1958 (Frankel 1986) and in Roanoke Rapids, North Carolina, in 1974 (Conway 1979).

Indeed, southern textile workers continue to seek unionization, despite contraction of the industry and sophisticated antiunion strategies on the part of management. In March 1987, for example, workers at a Firestone Mill in Gastonia, North Carolina, asked the union to organize their plant. Their issue was the stretch-out system, which required ever-increasing individual work loads and had prompted workers in the same mill to strike in 1929 (Pope 1942). The history of textile unionization efforts shows textile workers to be far from docile. We must look elsewhere than workers' attitudes for the reasons most of these efforts ultimately failed.

Many explanations for the lack of union success in the South focus on social psychological factors. Recent work in the sociology of social movements, however, suggests that such explanations are insufficient and that, in particular, the resources available for social movements are critical to their success or failure. The Brown Lung Association (BLA), an occupational health movement organized in the mid-1970s, provides key evidence of the importance of organizational resources to social protest by supposedly unorganizable southern textile workers.

The BLA succeeded in organizing workers but subsequently declined. Examination of the BLA helps provide the needed alternative explanations for textile unionization outcomes. The BLA's major focus is a disease called byssinosis, or brown lung, which mill workers contract by inhaling cotton dust into their lungs. At its peak in 1981 the BLA had fifteen chapters in five states, thousands of members, and hundreds of thousands of dollars in funding (see Judkins 1986, pp. 115–25).

Although small, even in comparison to the struggling southern textile unions, the BLA was instrumental in mobilizing an occupational health movement among southern textile workers, who had repeatedly resisted unionization attempts. Equally important, as Charles Levenstein et al. point out, the "Brown Lung Association was able to build links between progressive scientists and disabled workers and to demonstrate that . . . textile workers could grasp difficult issues and be a potent political force" (1987, p. 221).

This essay explores the history of the Brown Lung Association and the occupational health movement of which it was a part. It focuses on the similarities and differences in its formation and union organizing, particularly in the southern textile industry. It asks specifically why people joined the BLA, what environmental supports facilitated the development of the movement, what groups the BLA targeted, and the extent to which organizational structures and strategies facilitated the association's success or failure. Answers to these questions will arise from the broader context of social movement theory, based on a resource mobilization model. Rather than assuming worker docility, our approach suggests that successful mobilization of textile workers around health and safety issues may benefit southern textile unions and the labor movement in general.

Theoretical Explanations of Collective Organizational Behavior

The sociological literature on collective behavior and social movements attempts to "explain individual participation in anti-establishment activities" (Feree and Miller 1985, p. 38). The experiences of both the Brown Lung Association and southern textile labor organization can be understood in part by the application of social movement theory.

Until the 1970s, sociologists tried to answer questions about collective social action largely within the confines of social psychology. Traditionally, early collective behavior research took four major directions. First, collective action was explained by the psychopathology of the individual (Hoffer 1951). Next, collective action was tied to the social marginality of the individual (Feuer 1969). Third, many studies treated collective behavior as an expression of relative deprivation (Davies 1962; Gurr 1970; Gurney and Tierney 1982). Finally, Neil Smelser (1962) applied the structural-functional theories of Talcott Parsons (1961) by pointing to the "structural strain" in society as underlying episodes of collective action.

Although differing in many ways, all of the social psychological theories share several assumptions. They presuppose that participants in collective action are irrational in their understandings and actions. They base their analyses on individually perceived discontents that are transitory rather than structurally endemic. They treat collective action as deviant, aberrant, or criminal. Finally, they suggest that most participants somehow simultaneously derive the same conclusions from their individual experiences, that a group consciousness arises from extraordinary social conditions, and that this consciousness guides social action.

Following the social and political turmoil of the 1960s, social movement theorists began to move beyond the confines and limitations of traditional collective behavior models. The alternative explanation that has received the most attention is the resource mobilization perspective (e.g., Gamson 1975; McCarthy and Zald 1977; Tilly 1978). Although some have suggested that the resource mobilization perspective is really more a political sociology than a theory of collective behavior (Zald and Berger 1978), it continues to dominate theoretical discussions pertaining to transformative social movements, such as the Brown Lung Association.

The resource mobilization literature views social movement organizations as rationally organized activities that, far from being deviant, are a normal and often predictable part of political and social processes (Rush and Denisoff 1971). This perspective represents a shift from the traditional explanations of collective behavior. First, the individual participant and the movement itself are no longer condemned to social deviancy. Second, the unit of analysis is changed, in large measure, from the individual participant to the movement organization. This is not to suggest, of course, that resource mobilization presents a complete break with collective behavior theories. Efforts continue to integrate and synthesize both perspectives (e.g., Klandermans 1984; Gusfield 1970). Some writers (Perrow 1979) have even found a thread of earlier collective behavior analysis in the resource mobilization theories. The differences are important, however. Social movement organizations are described by various resource mobilization accounts as continuations, by disorderly means, of orderly political processes (Gamson 1968, 1975; Tilly 1978).

Most resource mobilization theorists include both orderly and disruptive collective action in a rational choice model of social change (McCarthy and Zald 1973, 1977; Oberschall 1973). It is this model that we will use for our analysis of the Brown Lung Association. Implicit throughout this rational choice model is the importance of incentives to ensure at least initial participation in the movement. Participation reflects an element of self-interest, not the appeal of ideology or a sense of relative deprivation, as in the rival social psychological theories. The BLA leadership provided a carefully planned menu of benefits for the organizational membership. Without such benefits, mobilization of members might have been impossible, reducing the potential of attaining any further organizational goals. Although all organizations provide some incentives for participation, we are limiting our analysis to a particular type of voluntary association: institutional change movements that attempt (1) to alter various "elements of social structure and/or the reward distribution of society" (McCarthy and Zald 1977, p. 1218); (2) to mobilize unorganized groups against institutional elites, as in the case of the BLA (Gamson 1975, pp. 16–18); or (3) to promote the interests of those individuals or groups typically excluded from effective political power (Jenkins and Perrow 1977; Tilly 1978).

Resource mobilization theorists argue that individual grievances are of secondary importance in the mobilization of social movement organizations. Several (Tilly 1978; Jenkins and Perrow 1977; Oberschall 1978) argue further that grievances, if not secondary, tend to be relatively constant and derive from "structural conflicts of interest built into social institutions" (Jenkins 1983, p. 530). Although important for group formation, grievances are explained by these structural conflicts of interest. The individual health and economic grievances of byssinosis victims are easily understood in these terms.

Instead of grievances, resource mobilization theory emphasizes the process "by which a group secures collective control over the resources needed for collective action" (Jenkins 1983, p. 532). Though different schemes focus on different resources of social movement organizations (see, e.g., McCarthy and Zald 1977; Tilly 1978, p. 69; Freeman 1979), we will restrict our discussion to money, facilities, labor, legitimacy, and technical expertise.

We will not, however, limit discussion of the efficacy of social movement organizations to a simple calculus in which the accumulation or mobilization of various resources becomes the sole determinant of the success or failure of a movement. Outcomes are best understood within the context of the existing "structure of political opportunity" generated by the social movement organization itself (Eisinger 1973). The mobilization of aggrieved populations, money, media exposure, technical expertise, and other potential resources is necessary for activity by the movement, but the resources themselves are insufficient as measures of a movement's success. Instead, the success or failure of the Brown Lung Association and other similarly organized groups is determined by the ultimate advantages and opportunities achieved within the political system at large.

Our understanding of the Brown Lung Association conforms to the model presented by William A. Gamson (1975) in which the success of a social movement organization is measured in two ways. First, the organization must establish favorable relations with the surrounding power elites. The group must develop "channels of access" to relevant government bodies as well as to the media. The organization must be accepted as a political actor and must be recognized as legitimately speaking for the constituency for which it claims to speak—in this case the victims of byssinosis. Second, the organization must enjoy some success in achieving previously established organizational goals. Specifically, these goals should reflect the preferences of previously unmobilized constituencies and generally target groups external to the membership of the association. In the case of the Brown Lung Association, the goals were education of workers to the hazards of cotton textile employment, success in filing and winning workers' compensation claims, and establishment of a federally mandated and monitored cotton dust standard for cleaner mills.

Mobilization of Participants in the BLA

Of particular significance to early efforts of the BLA was the mobilization of individual brown lung victims. We will describe mobilization as it worked to formulate the grievances of byssinosis victims, to establish leadership and membership patterns, and to establish an effective recruitment and commitment process (Perry and Pugh 1978). We will begin by looking at the approach to recruitment provided by Mancur Olson's (1965) theory of collective action. Olson argues that individuals cannot be mobilized simply by the prospect of benefits from the movement's success. "Rational, self-interested individuals will not act to achieve their common or group interests" but rather will attempt to take a free ride on the contributions of others to securing such common interests (1965, p. 2). To avoid this free-rider problem, movement organizations must provide some form of selective incentive (i.e., a benefit available only to those who contribute or participate) to initiate the mobilization of participants.

Selective incentives may simply take the form of economic rewards for participation "that have a monetary value or can easily be translated into ones that have" (Clark and Wilson 1961, p. 134). The organization does not have to be in a position to guarantee the selective reward for participation; it must only make promises of rewards and be able to increase the possibility of reward. Each member, then, will conduct a rational calculus of the "expected utility" of participation based on the perception of potential success (Zald and Jacobs 1978, p. 408). Although it was not able to guarantee monetary rewards for participation, the Brown Lung Association provided such an incentive by enhancing the potential of workers' compensation awards for individual members. Although this enhanced potential later accrued to textile workers not affiliated with the BLA, this selective incentive was crucial for mobilization in the association's early stages. Without it, the BLA would have had great difficulty mobilizing byssinosis victims to fight for such collective goals as the implementation of a federally enforced cotton dust standard.

Rather than targeting active workers, typically the focus of unionization attempts, organizers of the Brown Lung Association directed their mobilization efforts at retired and disabled textile workers. They patterned their strategy after the previous success of the Black Lung Association in the coal industry, a grass-roots effort to address the problem of black lung, or coal worker's pneumoconiosis. Retired and disabled coal miners and their supporters greatly influenced the passage of state and then federal legislation in the late 1960s and 1970s that provided substantial benefits to coal miners and their widows (see Denman 1974; Hopkins 1982; Judkins 1986; and Smith 1987 for varying accounts of this movement). Early organizers of the Brown Lung Association, some of whom had worked in previous labor conflicts in the coal fields, were aware of the miners' struggle and the relative success they had enjoyed. Representatives of the two organizations met in 1975 at the Highlander Center in Tennessee to compare goals and strategies.

Recruiting retired and disabled textile workers was an important and clever strategic move for the organizers. Unlike active workers, they did not fear losing their jobs or homes, which has often been the fate of workers who attempted to join a union. Mostly retired and living on fixed incomes reduced by substantial medical expenses, the disabled workers sought a way to supplement their meager incomes. Although many of the early recruits to the BLA had previous union experience, the majority of the members and leaders, like most southern textile workers, had little or no affiliation with unions, either present or past.

The early members fought for compensation in an environment completely opposed to monetary compensation for brown lung disease. Before the organizing efforts of the BLA in 1975, for example, only thirty-six claims for byssinosis had been awarded in North Carolina and none in South Carolina (Judkins 1986, pp. 129, 133). The Brown Lung Association provided the incentive for participation by a series of actions which convinced early members that their chances of recovering benefits were enhanced through membership in the association. One such action was the introduction of free screening clinics.

To facilitate and simplify efforts to locate potential brown lung victims and to initiate the process of obtaining compensation benefits, BLA organizers began in 1975 to set up screening clinics that provided free medical examinations for workers suspected of having brown lung disease. Initially, the clinics were devised to show byssinosis victims that brown lung disease itself was important and that a doctor or other qualified medical professional believed they had the disease. By demonstrating this interest on the part of experts, the early activists were able to create the pool that would become the core membership of the Brown Lung Association.

Although much of the initial work of the organizers was to educate people about cotton dust and compensation, the ultimate outcome of the screening clinics was an organization of retired and disabled textile workers who would themselves carry on the struggle. As one organizer later recalled, "People who wouldn't have come together for a meeting, because meetings would seem too foreign to them, had their first public experience in an event where they saw lots of other people there for the same reason, and that was an empowering experience" (Brody 1981). To garner support and active membership beyond the screening clinic, people who were thought to have byssinosis were asked to attend follow-up meetings to learn more about the process of filing for compensation. They became the core membership pool for the development of local chapters.

To encourage continued participation in the BLA and to develop the appeal of individual monetary compensation into collective action, the organizers implemented a follow-up strategy—the mass filing of compensation claims, often with more than one hundred applicants in attendance, many of whom also participated in highly visible demonstrations outside government offices. These actions reinforced the new sense of power among group members, many of whom were unaccustomed to collective action of any kind. Furthermore, the mass filings drew media attention to problems confronting the victims of byssinosis, which increased the members' perceptions that the BLA could enhance the potential for compensation rewards. Media exposure also generated both sympathetic responses from the public and more applicants for compensation.

Beyond the clinics and the follow-up meetings, the mass filings were the first effective event contributing to group awareness and solidarity. Although it was possible for individual members to consult lawyers and attempt to recover compensation awards on their own, the mass filings revealed to members the need for an association. As documents in the files of the BLA emphasized: "Do not let the lawyers just mail in people's forms. If you don't pull your people together to actively participate in this first event as a group, you may have lost them to the lawyers. The danger is that their cases will then become a matter between them and their lawyers and they won't see the need for the Association" (*Planning a Clinic* n.d., p. 2).

The mass filing of claims and accompanying demonstrations were revealing and educational experiences for BLA members. They communicated the significance of collective, as opposed to individual, action and taught lessons about the members' relationships with the environment outside the familiar textile world. These events began the transformation from passive to active participation in the movement. Documents in the association's files reinforce this point: "Every event that people participate in, every meeting is an educational experience and a group building experience. People don't learn from just being told or taught things, they have to *experience* things. And the experiences have to be repeated and they have to build on each other for people to really learn and understand" (*Planning a Clinic* n.d., p. 3).

As members became actively involved in their struggle for compensation, they encountered resistance from the medical and legal professions, government agencies, the insurance industry, and elected officials. Frequently, many of those whom BLA members naively assumed had been working on behalf of the mill workers' interests opposed the Brown Lung Association and its struggle. Doctors, for example, often disputed the very existence of the disease; the government seemed reluctant to assist in either compensation efforts or attempts to set a reasonable cotton dust exposure standard for the mills; lawyers sometimes used harassing or delaying tactics during the compensation process; and elected officials turned a deaf ear to the cries of the victims and their families.

Struggle against this resistance took a twofold approach. First, the BLA addressed an increased number of target groups. This helped maintain the vitality of the movement by increasing public awareness and diversifying BLA activities. Unlike the textile unions, whose primary target was the textile industry, the BLA was able to target the media, medical research facilities, state-level compensation commissions, federal occupational health agencies, and a host of other entities that either had or soon developed an interest in the problems of current and potential byssinosis victims. This varied exposure increased the range of potential sympathizers for the movement and allowed success in one area to compensate for temporary failure in another. Thus success hinged less on a particular activity than was the case for the textile union with its undiversified environment.

Second, struggle with these groups created a subjective perception in the BLA membership of enhanced power to effect political change, reinforced by objective successes. The experience of struggle transformed the consciousness of individuals and the political opportunities of the collective organization. Unlike textile unions, which have experienced few representation election victories and even fewer successful strikes, the Brown Lung Association enjoyed many small victories that kept the movement alive. Increased acceptance by the medical research community, the passage of a compensation bill in South Carolina, dramatic improvements in the North Carolina compensation system, several key compensation victories in the courts, the publication in 1980 of a Pulitzer prize–winning series on brown lung in the *Charlotte Observer*, and several hard-fought legal battles for the creation of a federal cotton dust standard in 1984 all contributed both to recruitment into the movement and to the continuing participation of early members.

Partly as a result of these successes, the Brown Lung Association grew rapidly in a short time. In its first four years, the BLA expanded into four states (North and South Carolina, Georgia, and Virginia), opening chapters in fifteen cities. It reported a membership of eight thousand retired and disabled textile workers, although less than one thousand were active at any one time. Funding and staff also expanded quickly. With funding from foundations, churches, and the federal government, the organization grew to a staff of forty by 1981 with an estimated budget exceeding $300,000. As the organization grew, its staff became more specialized, and this specialization was reflected in an organizational division of labor. At its peak, the BLA supported two full-time lawyers, a medical researcher, a professional fund-raiser, an accountant, at least one staff person for each chapter office, and several other people whose sole responsibility was working with active workers.

By 1981, the Brown Lung Association had become what some resource mobilization theorists have referred to as a "professional social movement" (McCarthy and Zald 1973). The group had been mobilized by active "social movement entrepreneurs," was mainly funded by external sources such as government and private foundation grants, and relied heavily on the media for exposure to potential sympathizers and contributors. Unlike labor unions, the BLA depended very little on its own membership for financial support.

Appraisal and Discussion

The Brown Lung Association was very successful in mobilizing the necessary resources—money, personnel, media coverage, and external support—to operate as a modern social movement. It was moderately successful in accomplishing its three major goals: educating workers and the public about brown lung, getting compensation for afflicted workers, and cleaning up the mills (see Zald and Ash 1966; Gamson 1975; and Marwell and Oliver 1984 for a discussion of movement successes and failures).

Increased media attention to the disease from 1975 through the early 1980s (see Judkins 1986, pp. 182–83; Hall 1978) suggests that the BLA made substantial information on brown lung available to people both in and out of the textile industry. Many southern textile workers, especially in North Carolina, were also successful in their claims for workers' compensation. By 1986, over $24 million had been awarded to sixteen hundred claimants in North Carolina. Only 51 percent of claimants were successful, however, and they represent less than 10 percent of the population in both North and South Carolina (where even fewer claims were successful) who are estimated to suffer from the disease (Conn and Covington 1980,

p. 11). The number of compensation cases peaked with an average of forty-eight per month in 1981 and then dropped to fewer than twelve per month in 1986, mirroring the general decline of the BLA after 1981.

The brown lung movement was also successful in obtaining a cotton dust standard to clean up the mills after winning the support of the Supreme Court in the 1981 case of *ATMI* v. *Donovan*. Many of the mills have reportedly met the standard, but a report by the Office of Technology Assessment raises some questions about enforcement. Inspections by Occupational Safety and Health Administration (OSHA) have been extremely rare, even in the most dangerous workplaces. The agency is able to inspect only about 4 percent of the nation's 4.6 million workplaces each year and only about 20 percent of the manufacturing establishments ("OTA Report" 1985). Furthermore, according to a letter in the BLA's files, the South Carolina OSHA office admits that it conducted site inspections for cotton dust violations in only two mills in all of 1986. In achieving the cotton dust standard, the association at best enjoyed what Sidney Tarrow (1981) termed a "shadow success."

Considering its success in mobilizing resources, and to some extent in accomplishing its goals, what does the brief history of the Brown Lung Association have to contribute to our understanding of the broader union struggle? The movement occurred at a time when many commentators predicted improved prospects for textile unionization as social change accelerated in the South (McLaurin 1971; Leiter 1982; Simpson 1981; McDonald and Clelland 1984). Union activity has remained stable at best, however, and some evidence suggests that it has declined. In 1984 and 1985, unions in North and South Carolina lost over 60 percent of elections (Ellis 1986). Slight improvement occurred in 1986, but the percentage of the total North Carolina work force belonging to unions dropped from a high of almost 8 percent in 1970 to a low of 4.8 percent in 1982 and has remained around that level (Ellis 1985). Of course, these figures must be put in perspective for the entire nation, which has experienced a substantial decline in overall union membership and activity in the last few years. From 1979 to 1987, union membership dropped from 24 to 17 percent ("Union Membership Declines" 1988). In 1985, unions reported the fewest number of strikes since the government began tracking labor struggles in 1946 ("Unions Report Fewest Strikes in 39 Years" 1986). Perhaps even more significant, in the 1980s American labor experienced the worst bargaining record since the 1920s (Moody 1990, p. 7).

The brown lung movement, in contrast, demonstrates that southern textile workers can be organized. Given the appropriate incentives, they can become active participants in the struggle for labor justice in the South. Most retired and disabled mill workers joined the BLA for a very personal incentive—workers' compensation—not unlike active workers who joined unions for monetary gain. Being a part of the BLA was very different, however, from being a member of a traditional union. First, achieving the monetary goal was not completely linked to the group's success, as it generally is with union struggles. At the same time, the successful compensation claim was a victory for all and encouraged many others to join the association.

Second, the activities of the BLA involved many different target groups (media, government, courts, state and federal agencies, and sometimes specific companies or their insurance carriers) and work on several levels (local, state, and regional meetings, as well as collective action on each level). All of this activity provided multiple opportunities for leadership and group building.

Third, both the resistance the members faced (often from parties traditionally perceived as protective of textile workers) and the support they received (also from unexpected sources) encouraged an expanded picture of organizing relationships beyond the traditional union posture of "labor versus management." The Brown Lung Association organized retired employees regardless of where they had been employed; the union typically focused on workers of a particular employer. Classwide appeals in organizing southern textile workers may avoid the intense opposition from employers often associated with organizing in specific companies. A classwide appeal may shift the free-rider problem from unions to employers: facing a classwide organizing effort, a particular employer may rationally decide to allow other employers to bear the costs of opposing organization (including work disruption) while enjoying the benefits of any success other employers experience.

The initial screening clinics brought mill workers together in a supportive environment where they could renew friendships and work associations. The mass filing of compensation claims provided a vehicle for collective action which not only put additional stress on the compensation system but taught an important positive lesson to workers unfamiliar with such organizational activities. Although union organizing efforts and strikes can have much the same effect, much more is at risk and there is a greater likelihood of failure. The BLA encouraged group actions that were educational and group-building experiences, as well as aimed at achieving more limited goals with several target groups. In turn, they reinforced the relationship of common goals to the accomplishment of individual goals.

The experience of the BLA also suggests that occupational health could, and should, be a more important union organizing issue, just as health and safety issues are likely to provide impetus for future movement organizations like the BLA. Mayer Zald and John D. McCarthy suggest that the future of social change will reflect the growth of movements that arc "reactive to the negative externalities of economic growth and the industrial production system" (1987, p. 322). Whether alone or in concert with reform organizations such as the BLA, labor unions need to confront issues of occupational health.

Unions have attempted to improve safety and health conditions since 1970 by amending law, expanding the application of exposure standards, and improving administrative practices (Goldsmith and Kerr 1982, p. 143). Also, many OSHA proposals are coordinated with collective bargaining agreements, which has made OSHA more responsive to trade union programs when determining its regulations and enforcement programs. At the same time, the complexity of occupational health and safety issues has resulted in more sophisticated language in writing contracts as workers have begun to use established forms of labor relations to address occupational hazards. A survey done before OSHA was formed, however, revealed that although unionized rank-and-file workers believed health and safety issues to be of top priority, union leaders focused their attention on salary and benefit disputes rather than working conditions. Similar studies have documented that employed persons in general stress the importance of health and safety conditions (Berman 1978, p. 119). The success of the BLA and these survey results suggest the potential of closer union attention to health and safety in the workplace.

Occupational health as an organizing issue points to the potential importance for the labor movement and the broader occupational health movement of linking active and retired workers. The basic tactic of the brown lung struggle, as well as many other grass-roots efforts to address occupational health issues, was to focus on compensation for diseases caused in the workplace. Generally, retired rather than active workers have been both the participants in and the direct beneficiaries of these movements. Although active workers have been recruited in these campaigns, few have participated, perhaps because filing a compensation claim could threaten their employment.

The underlying assumption of the compensation strategy was that the cost would force the companies to improve health conditions in the workplace, thereby benefiting active and future workers. Unfortunately, this plan has not enjoyed much success. According to Vicente Navarro, in the early twentieth century, compensation became an accepted alternative to cleaning up the workplace, and occupational medicine developed to define for management those damages that needed to be compensated (1983, p. 17). In addition, other societal institutions—governmental, educational, and scientific—all contributed their own interpretation to this definition, which means that any attempt to address the problem must take into account the power of these structures and the mechanisms through which they function. It is only through the democratization of these institutions, Navarro contends, that the majority of working populations can be transformed from passive subjects to active agents in a redefinition of society (p. 35). Barbara Ellen Smith, in writing about the black lung movement in the coal fields, echoes a similar sentiment by suggesting the need not only for a coalition of active and retired workers but also for greater worker power in the workplace: "A lasting and effective preventive campaign would have required a tighter alliance between working miners, disabled miners and widows, a much firmer conviction that black lung [was] not inevitable, and, at least eventually, a political vision of how miners might improve their occupational health by asserting more control over the workplace" (1983, p. 51).

One vision to emerge recently has centered on the concepts of workplace and economic democracy. The basic idea is to increase workers' participation in management as well as experiment with various forms of employee ownership. Although labor unions have generally reacted suspiciously to this trend, the potential for greater economic democracy to address problems of occupational health is evident. First, as Navarro points out, workers are becoming increasingly aware of the impact of demands for higher productivity, such as the textile stretch-out system, on their health and their lives. Only when workers are in decision-making positions can the proper balance between the economic health of the industry and the physical health of the workers be achieved (Navarro 1983, p. 13).

Second, because of rapidly advancing technology, workers will continue to be "guinea pigs" for new machinery and new chemicals in the workplace. In some cases, several years may elapse between development and detection of diseases. The long latency periods for many of these diseases necessitates effective health surveillance programs. The experiences of mill workers in the BLA suggest, however, that the knowledge workers themselves possess about their physical health and the work environment must be integrated into this process as well (see Judkins 1990).

Third, this struggle must include not only active and retired workers but consumer and worker groups to challenge the autonomy corporate directors have had over decisions affecting the health of workers and increasingly the communities around their plants. As Martin Carnoy and Derek Shearer point out, the thrust of this action will not be class consciousness but networks of mobilized citizens who recognize their mutual victimization by industrial hazards and waste (1980).

The struggle for workers' control in American industry has a long history (see, e.g., Montgomery 1979), but the nature of that struggle and the context of the control changed in the 1930s, when most trade unions conceded to management the right to administer the workplace. The Wagner Act of 1935 enabled workers and unions to place their faith in the process of collective bargaining (and the strike) to wrest concessions from management. Although major labor gains were achieved during the next few decades, waning union membership and weaker contracts suggest that alternative strategies should be considered. Although it is anticipated that union activity will continue to play an important role in advancing the cause of occupational health, we now know that those who have been able to organize effectively around safety and health issues have increasingly found that the fundamental requirement for social change is democracy in the workplace (Calavita 1983, p. 445).

The case of the Brown Lung Association shows that the explanations for success or failure of social movements, such as labor unions, must take organizational resources into account. Southern textile workers are not necessarily docile or quiescent. Their protest may be sporadic, but this is a function of their resources, not their attitudes.

The Brown Lung Association provides an important case history from which future labor struggles might benefit, particularly in the southern textile industry. It not only demonstrates that southern mill workers are not docile but that, with the appropriate incentive structures, they can form viable and effective organizations for social change. It also points to the importance of occupational health as an organizing strategy, as well as to the significance of linkages between active and retired workers in this struggle. Finally, it suggests the significance of mobilizing external resources in the community to achieve the economic democracy necessary to enhance the success of labor struggles in the future.

PART IV

Contemporary Problems

8

Employment Patterns in the British and U.S. Textile Industries: A Comparative Analysis of Recent Gender Changes

Roger Penn and Jeffrey Leiter

The textile industry in both Great Britain and the United States is undergoing restructuring. Though historically central to the process of industrialization in both countries and still important in the manufacturing sector of each, the textile industry has declined on both sides of the Atlantic. This decline has been characterized by sharply falling employment caused by severe import competition, technological modernization, and a general shift from manufacturing to service employment in both nations.

The British portion of this research was sponsored by the Economic and Social Research Council (Grant No. G13250011) as part of the Social Change and Economic Life Initiative. This initiative was funded by the ESRC and ran from 1985 to 1989. It involved an examination of social and economic change in six localities in Britain: Aberdeen, Coventry, Kirkcaldy, Northampton, Rochdale, and Swindon. We thank Richard Davies and John Hughes for their comments on an earlier draft of the section on Britain in this essay. We also thank Brian Francis and David Dawkins for their help with the graphics. Finally, we thank Michael Podgursky for making available data on U.S. displaced textile workers from the Current Population Survey. An earlier version of part of this essay was presented to the symposium "Social Impact of Technology: Perspectives on Change" at the Annual Meeting of the American Sociological Association in Chicago in 1987 under the title "Technical Change and Gender Relations in the British Textile Industry: Evidence from the Social Change and Economic Life Research Initiative." That paper is available from the Department of Sociology, Lancaster University, as Working Paper No. 13.

Although the processes of restructuring are similar, developments in the gender composition of the labor forces in the two nations have been very different. In Britain, textile employment has become increasingly male, while in the United States it has become increasingly female. This essay seeks to account for the differences and in the process to compare the operation of textile labor markets in the two societies. This comparison sheds light on how technological change, labor markets, and work force composition are intertwined in the context of restructuring within the textile sector. A comparative approach to the analysis of gender in textile employment is especially useful for distinguishing the effects of restructuring, which are basically the same in the two societies, from the effects of historical, cultural, and labor market context, which differ in some crucial ways.

Trends in the Size and Composition of the Textile Labor Force

In both Britain and the United States, textile employment shrank through the 1970s and 1980s. From 1971 to 1987, the number of textile employees in Britain fell by almost 50 percent (Office of Population Censuses and Surveys 1971, 1987). The decline was sharpest in northwestern Britain (over 60 percent), the historic center of British cotton textile manufacture since 1800 (Mathias 1969) and employer of about 16 percent of the textile labor force in the late 1980s. Rochdale, a city of two hundred thousand inhabitants in the traditional cotton textile belt of southeastern Lancashire and a major cotton mill town since the early nineteenth century (Penn 1985), saw a loss of about 75 percent of its textile employment between 1971 and 1987.[1] As the site of an Economic and Social Research Council project that has produced both firm- and individual-level data, Rochdale will be used as an exemplar for our analysis of change in the gender composition of textile employment in Britain.

Contemporary U.S. textile employment is overwhelmingly concentrated in the South with 72 percent of textile employees working in Alabama, Georgia, North Carolina, South Carolina, Tennessee, and Virginia (U.S. Department of Commerce 1982). Government statistics on national trends in textile employment, therefore, can be taken to apply to the South. After a decade of relative stability, U.S.

---

1. Comparisons across the 1970s and 1980s are complicated by a change in 1981 in the British census definition of the textile industry whereby the definition became more restrictive.

textile employment declined 26 percent in the decade from 1973, when it reached its peak, to 1983 (U.S. Department of Labor 1985).

Though differing in magnitude, the overall downward trajectories of British and U.S. textile employment are similar, but those of the gender compositions of the two labor forces are different. In Britain, the proportion of males has risen, especially in the cotton-manufacturing Northwest, from about 55 percent in 1971 to about 63 percent in 1987 (Office of Population Censuses and Surveys 1971, 1987). In the United States, the proportion of females has increased, from about 43 percent in 1960 to about 48 percent in 1983 (U.S. Department of Labor 1985). The proportions of men and women in both countries' textile labor forces are now somewhat similar, but the sex ratios are changing in opposite directions. These different trends in gender composition are related to changes within the industry and in the relationship between the textile labor market and the wider regional economy in each nation.

Hypotheses

The analytical problem of explaining where specific segments of the labor force work in the structure of industries and occupations can be approached from three major directions. The demands of the jobs, the capabilities and preferences of the workers, and the choices available to them are analytically distinct factors that may contribute simultaneously. As job, worker, and labor market characteristics change, the labor force composition of a particular industry in a particular local labor market can be expected to change. In this section, we lay out the potential impact these various factors may have on shifts in the gender composition of textile labor. In the subsequent sections, we introduce the peculiarities of British and U.S. history and social structure in the context of which textile employment patterns are changing.

TECHNOLOGICAL CHANGE AND REQUIREMENTS FOR SKILL AND DEPENDABILITY

Technological change, such as the introduction of microelectronics and more automated spinning and weaving, may change the skills required of textile workers. Consistent with the postindustrial society thesis (Bell 1974) and the skilling thesis associated with human capital theory (Penn and Scattergood 1985), some have argued that skill requirements in textiles are increasing (Berkstresser 1987; U.S.

Department of Labor 1974; Harwood 1985). Others have observed a long-term trend to implement textile technologies that reduce skill requirements (Hall et al. 1987; Newman 1980). The idea of deskilling is consistent with Harry Braverman's (1974) contention that capitalists reorganize and innovate technologically so as to diminish skill requirements, shrink labor costs, and assert greater control.

Skilled jobs in textiles fall into three categories: general machine maintenance (e.g., electricians), specialized machine maintenance (e.g., loom fixers), and skilled production work (e.g., mule spinners). Men have dominated skilled textile employment in both countries (Blauner 1964; Penn 1985; Turner 1962), although only in Britain have male-dominated craft unions controlled access to many positions via apprenticeship programs.

The effect of technological change on the gender composition of textile labor hinges on the interaction of skill requirements and the gender composition of skilled occupations. The greatest increase in the male proportion would derive from increasing skill requirements and continuing male domination of skilled work. The greatest increase in the female proportion would derive from decreasing skill requirements and diminished male domination of skilled work.

In addition to changing skill requirements, technological innovation toward more capital-intensive production may lead to a greater preference among employers for the most dependable workers to avoid costly down time (following here Blauner's [1964] observation that in highly automated plants responsibility has become more highly valued than skill). If employers perceive men as more dependable, they would express this preference by hiring an increasing proportion of males.

SUBSECTORAL CHANGE:
CONSUMER VERSUS INDUSTRIAL TEXTILES

The mix of products in each country's overall textile sector shifts over time. Since the gender composition of employment in the various textile subsectors varies, the shifting product mix may change the gender composition of the overall sector. For example, in Britain, production for industrial consumers such as the aerospace and vehicle industries has historically employed more males than the production of consumer textiles such as shirts and sheets. The combination of severe import competition in consumer markets (Lloyd and Shutt 1983) and increasing demand for sophisticated industrial inputs (e.g., carbon fibers and kevlar) (Penn and Scattergood 1987) may be partly responsible for the observed increase in the proportion of males employed in British textiles.

Subsectoral shifts may be at work in U.S. textiles as well. Increasing female employment, however, would require opposite trends from those in Britain: either industrial textiles must employ proportionately more women than consumer textiles, or consumer textile employment must be increasing relative to industrial textile employment (i.e., declining more slowly).

The technological change and subsectoral shift hypotheses may be combined. If technological change that requires gender-linked worker characteristics is concentrated in a sector that is expanding or contracting particularly quickly, changes in the overall gender composition of textile labor would be accelerated. In the British case, for instance, the relative expansion of industrial textiles with its faster rate of technological change can be expected to produce an overall masculinization of British textile employment.

WORK OPTIONS OUTSIDE TEXTILES

The growth in the local labor market of industries besides textiles can affect the gender composition of textile labor. The more females are employed in nontextile industries, the more male-dominated textiles should become. This would be the likely outcome of expanding service sector employment. In contrast, if manufacturing employment expands in other industries than textiles, we can expect textiles to become more dominated by females. Contraction in textile employment, such as that being experienced now, could reinforce either trend.

The effects of regional economic expansion outside textiles on the gender composition of textiles will be especially pronounced where nontextile employment is more desirable than textile employment, for example, if the earnings potential is better. Such a difference in workers' preferences for textile and nontextile employment should lead to a queue to enter the nontextile sector in which gender may be associated with the order of the queue (on relative position in job queues, see Thurow 1975). This has probably happened since World War II in the U.S. South, where expanding durable goods manufacturing employment (i.e., in SIC 28–30, 33–39) in the six primary textile-producing states was filled almost 68 percent by men in 1988 (Equal Employment Opportunity Commission 1988).

The effect of nontextile expansion on the gender composition of the textile labor force should be most pronounced when nontextile employment is more desirable to one gender than the other or when there are fewer gender barriers to advancement outside than inside textiles. As has been shown for Britain (Penn 1991), where textile production is becoming increasingly full time and inflexible, the growing service sector with its part-time and flexible work schedules may be especially attractive to women who have to balance work and domestic commitments. This account takes issue with the suggestion that hours of paid work in Britain are becoming universally more flexible (Atkinson and Meager 1986). It would help explain the increasing proportion of males in British textiles.

Great Britain

DATA

In the absence of data about the entire British economy, we use an intensive case study of Rochdale. Researchers at Lancaster University collected three types of data between 1985 and 1989. First, twenty-two textile firms, which employed 85 percent of Rochdale's textile workers and included all firms with fifty or more employees, responded to a 1986 mail questionnaire about changing employment and technology since 1980. Second, using a somewhat longer chronology, the research team interviewed managers, union leaders, and work force members at selected firms about changing forms of employment and the factors behind them. Finally, in the summer of 1986, 987 residents of Rochdale, ages twenty to sixty, provided work histories describing their movements among textile jobs, textile industries, and sectors in the local labor market.

Employment in the twenty-two-firm sample fell 31.4 percent from 1980 to 1986. Table 8.1 shows that Rochdale echoes the nationwide trend for textile employment to become more male-dominated. The proportion of males increased in nine firms but decreased in only one. This trend proved to be unrelated to whether the firm was a subsidiary of a larger firm, whether its overall employment had expanded or contracted, or whether it was unionized. We now turn to the three explanations outlined earlier to see which of them helps account for this increase in the proportion of males in the Rochdale textile labor force.

TECHNOLOGY AND SKILL

Table 8.1 shows that firms that introduced new microelectronics technology since 1980 were more likely to show an increase in the

TABLE 8.1. Changes in the Proportion of Males in Rochdale Textiles by Introduction of New Technology and Textile Subsector, 1980–1986

| | Percentage of Firms Where Proportion of Males | | | Total | |
	Decreased[a]	Was constant	Increased[a]	Firms	Employees
Total sample	6.5	54.5	40.9	22	3,273
Microelectronics					
Introduced	0.0	28.6	71.4	7	2,076
Not introduced	6.7	66.7	26.7	15	1,197
Subsector					
Consumer	0.0	33.3	66.7	6	732
Industrial	0.0	66.7	33.3	6	1,484
Both	11.1	55.6	33.3	9	987

[a] The criterion is change in proportion of male employment by at least 10 percent.

proportion of male employees than firms that did not adopt the new technology. This association cannot be accounted for, however, by the hypothesized requirement that the introduction of new technology would require the firm to hire more skilled workers in that the seven firms that introduced microelectronics did not report a significant shift to skilled manual workers. On this dimension, the technological innovators are similar to the entire twenty-two-firm sample, of which more than two-thirds reported no significant increase in the proportion of skilled workers in the manual work force.

Although the proportion of skilled workers is not increasing, both the mail survey and the subsequent case studies provide evidence that skilled textile work in Rochdale is becoming more skilled in its content. One-third of the firms reported that the skills of overlookers, technicians, and maintenance electricians had increased, but none reported that they had decreased. This finding is consistent with the views expressed by trade union officials and workers and with the considerable retraining of skilled workers in the sampled plants. The intensification of demands within the skilled segment is increasing the bifurcation of the manual work force. Because they decide collectively on the suitability of managerial candidates for apprenticeships, male textile craft workers can exclude women from apprenticeship programs and, therefore, from entry into much skilled textile work (Penn 1985, 1990). This leads to continuing male skilled employment. In the absence of expanding skilled employment, however, it does not explain the increasing proportion of male textile workers in Britain.

Although technological change does not increase the proportion of male employees by enlarging skilled employment, it may produce this effect by diminishing opportunities for part-time work. The movement toward full-time employment, though not pronounced in Rochdale, is concentrated in firms that have implemented microelectronics technology since 1980. Forty-three percent of the firms that had introduced microelectronics increased their full-time employment by more than 10 percent, but no firm that had not adopted this innovation had done so. Since nearly all part-time textile workers in Rochdale and all of Britain throughout the 1970s and 1980s were female (Elias 1989), the shift to full-time workers with the adoption of technological innovation helps account for the association of such innovation with a decreasing proportion of female workers.

SUBSECTORAL SHIFTS WITHIN TEXTILES

The shift in Rochdale from consumer to industrial textiles would account for the increasing proportion of males as long as industrial textile employment maintains its "male differential" over consumer textiles, 73.3 percent versus 56.7 percent in 1980. As table 8.1 shows, however, consumer textile firms exhibit the highest rate of increase in the proportion of male employment. By 1986, the male differential had shrunk to 75.9 percent versus 62.6 percent. Consumer textiles is converging with the traditional pattern of male dominance in industrial textiles. The specific subsector of textile production is, therefore, not a critical factor in the increasing proportion of male textile employment in Rochdale.

COMPETITION FROM NEW INDUSTRIES

Census of Employment data reported in table 8.2 show that the relatively stable aggregate amount of employment hides huge shifts in the industrial distribution of employment. The precipitous drop in textile employment and smaller losses in a few other industries are balanced by dramatic gains in public administration and defense, distributive trades, and insurance and banking, all of which lie outside manufacturing in the government and service sectors.

The rising proportion of males in textile employment may be explained by the rising number of females in these other industries in that the overall rates of male and female labor force participation in Rochdale have been approximately constant (in contrast to the

TABLE 8.2. Total and Female Employment in Selected Industries in Rochdale, 1971 and 1987

| | Total Employment[a] | | | Female Employment[a] | | | | | |
| | | | | 1971 | | 1987 | | | |
	1971	1987	% change	Number	% total	Number	% total	% change
Textiles	161	27	−83.2	69	42.7	8	31.4	−87.7
Metalworking	89	78	−12.4	16	18.1	15	19.6	−2.4
Transport and communication	15	31	106.7	2	14.5	6	18.6	164.7
Distributive trades	45	83	84.4	28	61.3	42	51.1	−53.7
Professional and scientific services	59	33	−44.1	43	73.0	27	82.6	−63.3
Public administration and defense	8	94	422.2	5	27.9	54	57.0	967.3
Insurance and banking	8	29	262.5	5	59.9	17	57.8	249.9
Miscellaneous services	25	20	−20.0	13	53.3	16	78.4	17 6
Total of selected industries	420	395	−6.0	181	43.1	185	46.9	2.4

Source: Census of Employment 1971, 1987.
[a] Numbers of employees are given in hundreds and rounded to the nearest hundred for reasons of confidentiality.

United States) in a context of approximately constant total employment. This means that changes in the absolute numbers of male and female textile workers derive only from a shifting of workers out of textiles into other industries, with females being shifted at a higher rate than males. The falling proportion of females in textiles can be explained by the rising employment of females in Rochdale's growing industries, notably public administration and defense, where the proportion as well as the magnitude of females rose, and distributive trades and banking and insurance, where the magnitude rose even though the proportion fell.

The shift of females out of textiles and into government and service sector industries can be explained in part as a preference among Rochdale women for part-time work. Similar to the relationship between technological innovation and shifts to full-time employment, industries differ in the amount of part-time work they offer. From 1971 to 1987, the percentage of women in part-time employment declined by more than 90 percent in textiles but increased by more than 70 percent in transport and communication, by almost 78 percent in distributive trades, by more than 39 percent in the sector including public administration and defense, and by more than 266 percent in insurance and banking.

Many textile firms have eliminated the swing shift that enabled women to work for three or four hours in the evening and increasingly offer only two full shifts, from 6 A.M. to 2 P.M. and from 2 A.M. to 10 P.M. The case study interviews demonstrated that these shifts are distinctly unattractive to many female workers, in part because these women perform much domestic work but also because of changing patterns of male work. Rochdale is now a major commercial distribution center and the headquarters of a national private bus company. Truck and bus drivers are away when children need to be delivered to school, when they return home, and during the early evening. Working mothers must accommodate these demands when seeking paid work. Government and service sector employers in Rochdale are adopting flexible hours both to suit their economic needs and to attract workers. This situation confirms Frank Pyke's (1987) analysis of household structures and paid work in Macclesfield.

Why have textile firms moved in the opposite direction toward increasingly inflexible and conventional forms of shift work? We have already noted the industry's desire to keep its new sophisticated and costly capital-intensive production processes running as much as possible. The firms have not been able to maintain production twenty-four hours a day because of the persistent economic uncertainties facing the industry and the replacement of the very large batch jobs of the past by shorter runs. Nonetheless, because of their large capital investments, managers place a high priority on dependability in the work force. It is not clear whether managers think males are more dependable and use inflexible shift arrangements to push out women or whether they find shift work more conducive to keeping production up, with the gender effect developing as a by-product.

The decline in the number of part-time female textile workers helps account for the rising proportion of males, but it does not explain the decline in the number of full-time female textile workers. Because there is no evidence to suggest a declining demand for full-time work by women in Rochdale, the central factor appears to be an increasing perception by women in the city that textile employment is less desirable than new types of employment. The work history analysis supports this conclusion but also allows us to refine it.

Figure 8.1 indicates the sectors in which Rochdale males and females held their first jobs in selected years between 1950 and 1986. In 1986 males were as likely to enter textiles after completing their education as they had been in the 1950s, whereas women no longer took their first job in textiles, although their rate of entry had been greater than men's in the 1950s. Nor are either female or male job changers in the 1980s nearly as likely to enter textiles from another industry as they were in earlier decades, as shown in figure 8.2. The work history data also show that in the 1980s many men and women moved from the job in textiles to another. If anything, women return to textiles in greater proportions than men, about 60 percent versus 40 percent in 1986. The female shift out of textiles and into the service sector, therefore, primarily involves young adults leaving school. The male segment of Rochdale's textile labor force is replenished by young adults leaving school, but the female segment gets few new members and declines by attrition.

CONCLUSIONS

Though Rochdale historically has been a center for female employment as a result of widespread textile production, the proportion of female employment in textiles had fallen to only 30 percent in 1987. We have rejected the theory that this is because of the shift from consumer textiles to the more male-dominated industrial textiles (employment patterns in consumer textiles are similar to those in the industrial sector) or that it is attributable to a higher demand for

FIGURE 8.1.   Females' First Job, Rochdale, 1950–1986

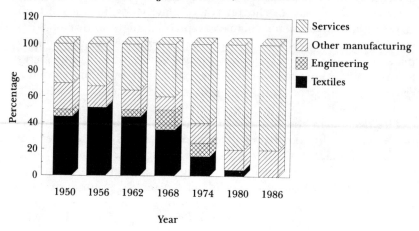

Males' First Job, Rochdale, 1950–1986

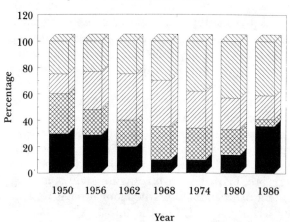

Source: SCELI "1000 Questionnaire" (Rochdale events only)

skilled workers because of technological change (the proportion doing skilled work has not increased).

We have found evidence that technological change toward more
capital-intensive production discourages the employment of part-
time workers, who usually are women. The change in the pattern of
work hours is a major factor in the elimination of women from textile employment. Seeking flexible and part-time jobs so they can

FIGURE 8.2. Percentage of Females Moving out of Specified Sectors into a New Job in Textiles, Rochdale, 1950–1986

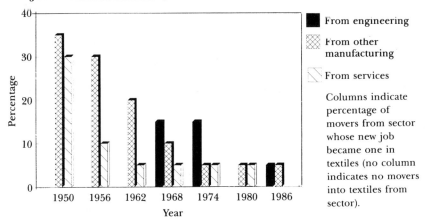

Percentage of Males Moving out of Specified Sectors into a New Job in Textiles, Rochdale, 1950–1986

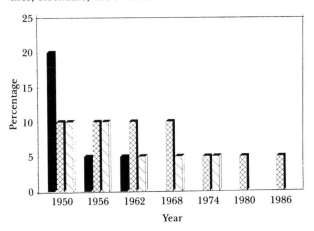

Source: SCELI "1000 Questionnaire" (Rochdale events only)

combine work with their domestic roles, women turn instead to the expanding government and service sectors. Ironically, these "modern" industries provide "traditional" employment options. The work history analysis shows, however, that this changing preference characterizes only new entrants into the labor force. We find no massive outflow of women from the industry once they have become established in it.

We now turn to a similar analysis of gender and employment in the U.S. textile industry. Overall, it, too, has faced steeply falling employment. The proportion of females, however, has risen slightly. We will apply the same theories, hypotheses, and explanations to the U.S. case as we did to the British one. Data sources do not include a survey or case studies of textile firms comparable to the Rochdale data, but they do include extensive government documents and a representative survey of displaced textile workers from whom we can learn about individual job shifts out of textiles.

The United States

HISTORICAL AND CONTEMPORARY TRENDS

Throughout its hundred-year history as an important employer, the southern U.S. textile industry has recruited women in very large numbers. At times there have been more female than male employees. In the nineteenth and early twentieth centuries, the family labor system, upon which the industry was founded, provided housing and mill employment for entire family units. In the earliest years, when the supply of experienced, skilled weavers was insufficient to meet the needs of the quickly expanding industry, weavers, usually male, could extract from mill owners cheap housing and employment for their wives and children (McHugh 1988). After World War I, the balance of power in the textile labor market shifted to mill owners partly because of the depression in farming, from which mill families were usually recruited, and partly because of technological changes that reduced the skill requirements of mill work (Hall et al. 1987). Mill owners began to erode the welfare benefits of the mill village, including the cheap housing, and to cut wages so that the family's subsistence required more than one individual's contribution. Thus women continued to work in the southern textile industry in large numbers, but the reasons changed when the balance of power between textile owners and workers shifted.

Though racial or ethnic minorities are not an important feature of the changing composition of the British textile labor force in the recent period, the increasing proportion of blacks is central to the U.S. analysis. Through most of southern textile history, blacks were largely excluded from mill work. Black employment hovered around 2 percent, never exceeding 4.5 percent, from 1900 to 1960 (Rowan 1970).

The few black textile workers were rarely assigned formally to production jobs, although some gained production experience by informal arrangements with white machine operators (Frederickson 1982).

In the mid-1960s, two factors combined to open up textile employment to blacks, especially in low-skill production jobs. The southern economy continued to diversify as it had following World War II, including into the higher-paying automotive, chemical, and electronics industries. The children of textile workers, especially the better educated among them, began to seek these more desirable jobs, thereby leaving unfilled labor demand in those years when the textile industry was not contracting.[2] Then the Civil Rights Act of 1964 provided the legal basis for a union-supported federal court challenge to racial exclusion in textiles (Hughes 1976). By the 1980s, over 20 percent and in some locations as many as 50 percent of southern U.S. textile workers were black (Leiter 1986).

The racial composition of the U.S. textile labor force has changed much more in the contemporary period than has the gender composition. The gradual trend toward changes in gender composition must, therefore, be disaggregated by race. From 1966 to 1987, the number of white textile workers, both male and female, declined absolutely and proportionally, though the decline for males was most pronounced. In contrast, employment of both male and female blacks increased absolutely and proportionally. The number of black female textile workers grew the most, almost fourfold in this period (Equal Employment Opportunity Commission 1966–81, 1985–88).[3] The modest increase in the proportion of females in textile employment is thus completely accounted for by the fast-growing employment of black females and actually hides the declining number and proportion of white female workers in this industry.

These data refine the questions to be posed when comparing textile labor force composition trends in Great Britain and the U.S.

---

2. The manufacturing industries that are new rather than traditional in the U.S. South are heavy employers of white men, in particular. In the six southern states that account for most textile employment, 51 percent of blue-collar workers in the chemical, petroleum, rubber, primary and fabricated metals, machinery, electronics, automobiles, and instruments industries were white men in 1988. This is not a particularly high figure in comparison to the United States as a whole, but it is high in comparison to textiles, in which only 35 percent of blue-collar workers were white men in 1987 (Equal Employment Opportunity Commission 1985–88; the EEOC reports exclude the smallest firms, which employ from 10 to 20 percent of textile workers).

3. For 1966 and 1987 total textile employment in the reporting firms was 779,620 and 528,258, respectively. The percentage of white males was 49.3 and 38.2; of black males, 5.9 and 10.9; of white females, 41.8 and 35.3; and of black females, 2.0 and 11.6.

South. Rather than accounting for the difference in aggregate trends for women, we need to understand the falling rate among women in Great Britain in contrast with the falling rate among whites (especially males) and the rising rate among blacks (especially females) in the U.S. South. Can these different developments be explained by similar social forces or are contextually specific explanations required? The basic explanations focus on changes in the organization of textile work and changes in the labor market in which textiles is one of several alternatives.

TECHNOLOGY AND SKILL

One important possibility is that requirements for skilled workers may have changed in such a way as to have changed the demand for workers of different races and genders. This would be especially likely if part of the employment contraction is the result of the replacement of many low-skilled machine operators by fewer high-skilled programmers and maintenance personnel. Because historically white males have monopolized the more skilled occupations in textiles (Penn 1990), a scenario in which the requirements increased for skilled workers in U.S. textiles is not consistent with the decline in the proportion of white males in textile employment.

The decline in the numbers of white males in textile employment is more consistent with the deskilling of the textile labor process. This explanation, however, finds no support from data on the number and composition of skilled craft workers in textiles from 1966 to 1987 (Equal Employment Opportunity Commission 1966–81, 1985–88). The number of craft workers has fallen at the same rate as has overall employment. Indeed, the proportion of skilled textile employees was identical in 1966 and 1987: 14.4 percent. The representation of the different race and gender groups in skilled textile jobs changed in a fashion similar to general changes in the total employment data; the numbers and proportions of both white male and female craft workers declined, while both the absolute numbers and the relative proportions of black males and females increased. Black male employment in these relatively high-status, high-paying jobs rose much faster than did black female employment, thereby reversing the trends for textile employment more generally. The decline among white males and the increase among black females in overall textile employment must be explained by other factors than changes in the skill requirements of textile work.

FIGURE 8.3.   Relationship between Percentage of Female Employees and Value of Machinery per Worker for Four-Digit U.S. Textile Industries, 1982

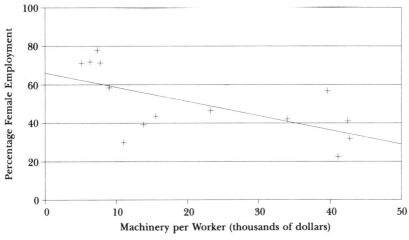

SUBSECTORAL CHANGES

Although skill requirements in textile employment appear not to have changed, employers' preferences in hiring may have shifted, and these preferences may have implications for the race and sex of those hired. The Rochdale analysis found an increasing similarity between industrial and consumer employment patterns. Textiles in Britain are increasingly manufactured through capital-intensive production processes. Larger fixed capital investments might have led to increased hiring of men, who are perhaps perceived to be more dependable than women and hence less likely to cause costly down time. But the case studies in Rochdale provided little empirical support for this interpretation. Rather, it was the lack of female applicants for textile jobs that was central to the gender change in employment patterns.

An analogous situation in the U.S. South would have been the disproportionate hiring of white males as a result of increasingly capital-intensive production (Rowan and Barr 1987). But white male employment in U.S. textiles is falling. This does not mean that the connection between capital intensity and hiring could not apply in the United States. It may exist in a weak form because the shift to capital-intensive production has occurred on a smaller scale than in Great Britain. Figure 8.3 presents the cross-sectional relationship between the percentage of female employees (U.S. Department of

Labor 1985) and the dollar value of machinery per worker (U.S. Department of Commerce 1982) across fourteen textile subindustries that vary considerably in capital intensity. Unfortunately, this source did not include data on racial composition of employment. Nevertheless, the predicted relationship is represented by the modest negative slope of the regression line: the higher the capital intensity, the lower the percentage of female employment.

This finding should be interpreted with caution for three reasons. First, we have no data on the causal link between capital intensity and female employment. In particular, we lack information on managerial hiring preferences based on differential perceptions of dependability by gender. Second, the observed relationship depends entirely on the cluster of four knitting subindustries depicted in the upper left corner of figure 8.3. Though these are major employers of textile labor (28.5 percent in 1982 [U.S. Department of Labor 1985]), without them the regression line would be flat, indicating no relationship. Therefore, percentage of female employment could be explained by some unexplored difference between knitting and all other textile subindustries. Finally, an examination of the somewhat limited time-series data available for individual textile subindustries reveals no regular relationship between change in capital intensity (measured this time by the inverse of payroll as a percentage of value added) (U.S. Department of Commerce 1982, 1989a) and the proportion of females in textile employment (U.S. Department of Labor 1985, 1988). Moreover, in the subindustry with the most pronounced increase in capital intensity for which a relatively full-time series was available (finishing, man-made fibers, silk), there was virtually no change in percentage of female employment, which indicates that capital intensification was associated with an absence of feminization in such plants.

If observed increases in black female employment are to be explained by variations in hiring preferences in textile subindustries that differ in capital intensity, it would have to be in the more labor-intensive subindustries in which employment shrank the most slowly. A comparison of 1982 machinery costs per worker with percentage employment change between 1977 and 1982 across fifteen textile subindustries shows that, to a modest extent, this is indeed the case. Although most of the subindustries show employment losses in a narrow band between zero and 20 percent, in the four subindustries that showed greater employment losses per capita, machinery costs were above the median, and the only subindustry with an employment gain had one of the smallest per capita machinery costs.

Available aggregate data, therefore, do not support the notion that changes in skill requirements explain falling rates of white male and rising rates of black female textile employment in the southern United States. Such data do, however, give some qualified support for the possibility that redistribution of textile employment into more labor-intensive subindustries may be contributing to the overall change in the race and gender distribution of textile employment.

COMPETITION FROM NEW INDUSTRIES

Aside from the restructuring of the textile industry, a different explanation involves the diversification of the regional economy, which increases employment options outside of textiles that some textile workers may prefer or new entrants to employment may choose over textiles. In Rochdale, where female employment in textiles has been falling, the data suggested that women were moving into service sector jobs because these jobs allow more flexibility in hours of work than the increasingly full-time, shift-based daytime textile jobs. Women declined to enter British textiles because their multiple roles led them to prefer the flexible working hours offered by other industries.

In the United States, where white male employment in textiles is falling, the same labor market approach requires different reasoning. White men in the U.S. South may be assumed to seek the best possible wages, which are not likely to be found in the relatively poorly paid service sector but in other, higher-paying industrial jobs. In the U.S. South, as in Rochdale, where textile employment has contracted greatly in recent years, it is unlikely that many textile workers leave their jobs voluntarily.

For this reason, data collected by the U.S. Census Bureau from "displaced workers" can help in understanding the reasons for the greater decline of white male and the greater growth of black female textile employment. The 1984, 1986, and 1988 January Current Population Surveys asked respondents if anyone in their households had lost a job during the past five years. Affirmative answers, which unfortunately excluded those who voluntarily left their jobs, triggered a supplementary questionnaire. The displaced workers identified in this way included 320 textile workers, who can be treated as representative of displaced textile workers from 1979 to 1988.

Table 8.3 presents the race and gender distributions of these displaced textile workers and their new jobs, if any, along with information about the wage changes they have experienced in finding

TABLE 8.3. Numbers of Displaced Textile Workers and Changes in Their Weekly Earnings by Industry or Sector in New Job, Race, and Sex

	Industry/Sector of New Job				Still unemployed	All displaced
	Textiles	Manufacturing[a]	Service	All reemployed[b]		
White males						
Number of workers	35	65	23	109	11	120
Row percent	32.1	59.6	21.1	100		
Column percent	37.6	41.1	25.6	39.2	26.2	37.5
Wage change—amount[c]	0.45	−32.57	−5.94	−29.25		
Proportional change[d]	.121	−.008	.062	−.003		
White females						
Number of workers	29	53	45	103	21	124
Row percent	28.2	51.5	43.7	100		
Column percent	31.2	33.5	50.0	37.1	50.0	38.8
Wage change—amount	−15.59	−21.22	−71.48	−42.54		
Proportional change	−.038	−.015	−.291	−.134		
Black males						
Number of workers	13	17	9	30	1	31
Row percent	43.3	56.7	30.0	100		
Column percent	14.0	10.8	10.0	10.8	2.4	9.7

Wage change—amount	-14.71	-37.03	-28.75	-34.02		
Proportional change	-.015	-.129	-.169	-.150		
Black females						
Number of workers	16	23	13	36	9	45
Row percent	44.4	63.9	36.1	100		
Column percent	17.2	14.6	14.4	12.9	21.4	14.1
Wage change—amount	-49.82	-41.45	-0.31	-20.88		
Proportional change	-.160	-.148	-.003	-.076		
All[e]						
Number of workers	93	158	90	278[f]	42	320
Row percent	33.5	56.8	32.4	100		
Wage change—amount	-12.21	-30.20	-39.29	-33.85		
Proportional	.020	-.037	-.147	-.077		

Source: 1984, 1986, and 1988 Displaced Worker Surveys, gathered by U.S. Census Bureau as supplements to the January Current Population Surveys.

[a] Includes those currently employed in textiles.

[b] Includes those in miscellaneous industries.

[c] Mean change in constant 1983 dollars from previous textile weekly earnings to weekly earnings in industry or sector of reemployment.

[d] Mean change in constant 1983 dollars from previous weekly earnings to weekly earnings in industry or sector of reemployment as a proportion of previous textile weekly earnings.

[e] Includes those missing on race and/or sex.

[f] Forty-two displaced textile workers, unemployed at time of survey, were not included here.

replacement jobs. The race and gender groups here (see "All Dis-placed" column) are distributed in much the same way as they are for the total population of textile workers in the 1980s. Women of both races are somewhat more likely to be displaced than would be expected from their overall proportions in the textile labor force. This trend may help explain the shrinking proportion of white fe-males, but it moves in the opposite direction from the trend for black females. In any case, these differences should not be overinterpreted because of the small size of the sample of displaced textile workers. Overall, the pattern of displacement does not in itself explain the changing race and gender distributions in textile employment.

Black males and females, however, are disproportionately likely to be rehired into textile jobs (compare "All Displaced" with "Textiles" columns). This echoes and may help explain the overall trend to-ward increasing black employment. If we can assume that displaced textile workers, regardless of race and gender, prefer to find new jobs in the textile industry, this tendency to rehire blacks out of pro-portion to their displacement may reflect a managerial preference for black textile workers with experience, probably because their wages tend to be lower (Leiter 1989). Consistent with this reasoning is the large wage loss that black females displaced from textiles ex-perienced on being rehired into this industry, which involved, on average, a reduction of 16 percent in their weekly wages. Rehired black males do not suffer as large a proportional wage loss.

In the Rochdale case, changes in the composition of the textile labor force were explained as the result of the preference of new female employees for flexible working hours that were increasingly met in certain parts of the service sector. The data on displaced workers do not rule out this explanation for the United States, but they make it unlikely. Reemployment in the service sector entails a greater wage loss than reemployment in textiles or in the manufac-turing sector as a whole, especially for displaced white female textile workers, a larger proportion of whom find reemployment in the service sector than any other race and gender group.

In the contracting U.S. textile industry, the personal impacts of shifting employment echo traditional power and privilege differen-tials in the labor force. White males displaced from textiles continue to find jobs at about the same wage rate, although large numbers of them must search for alternative employment. New textile jobs seem to be the best available for black males who have lost mill jobs; contraction of the industry is, therefore, very bad news for them. Black and white displaced females are especially heavily represented where they are paid most poorly: blacks in the manufacturing sector, whites in the service sector. Assuming a preference for replacement of wages, these findings contrast, except for white males, with the Rochdale scenario, in which employees' preferences are served by job shifts.[4]

Analyses of individual-level job shift data for British and U.S. textile workers suggest quite different dynamics. The declining proportion of women employed in British textiles appears to stem in part from the attraction of alternate employment in the context of rigid textile work schedules. In U.S. textiles, the declining proportion of white males also reflects attractive alternatives, but the increasing proportion of black females may also be the result of a competitive managerial strategy of seeking new sources of cheap labor. In Britain, the continuing strength of textile unions blocks this strategy and may contribute instead to heavy investment in new technology. The absence of strong textile unions in the United States permits southern firms to continue their long-standing cheap labor approach at the same time as the larger firms belatedly begin to modernize.

Conclusions

The analytic problem of this chapter has been to explain the differing directions of change in the gender composition of textile employment in Great Britain and the United States. The explanations that prove most useful show important contrasts, but the similarities are at least as striking. Such similarities are particularly notable for theory building when, as in this case, the phenomena to be explained contrast cross-nationally.

The first similarity in our findings is that the set of changes involving internal textile restructuring is not sufficient to account for the labor force composition trends in either country. We have investigated the effects of technological innovation, capital intensification, skill and dependability requirements, subsectoral shifts among different branches of textile production, and overall employment

---

4. The possibility that differential wage loss reflects differences in human capital can be investigated by including education in a multiple regression analysis. When wage in the new job is regressed on wage in the former textile job, dummy variables for the four race-gender groups, dummy variables for reemployment sector, and years of education, the basic findings from table 8.3 are confirmed. Although years of education has a statistically significant positive effect on wages in the new job, service sector reemployment continues to be costly, as does membership in any of the race-gender groups except that of white males.

contraction. These factors alone do not explain the observed trends in the composition of the labor force.

Instead, industrial restructuring must be considered in the context of shifts in regional economies and labor markets. In Britain, textile reorganization away from flexible and part-time work schedules may have diminished the attractiveness of work in textiles for women, but new women workers have stopped applying for textile jobs only in the context of a rapidly expanding service sector. Service sector employers have promoted flexible schedules to attract women who need to balance work with traditional domestic responsibilities.

In the U.S. South, too, factors internal to the textile industry have influenced the labor force composition only in a larger regional context. Textiles continues to be a low-wage industry, so white males have been attracted to growing opportunities for better-paying manufacturing employment outside of textiles. Blacks, freed from agricultural labor by mechanization and freed to enter textiles by the civil rights movement, have filled the void in textiles. It is possible that lower wage rates for blacks have forced multiple family members into full-time employment, limiting black entry into service sector jobs, where about 68 percent of women worked part time or part of the year (U.S. Department of Commerce 1989b, table 653).

Juxtaposing these analyses of textile labor force composition trends in Great Britain and the United States has been hampered by differences in data sources and levels of analysis. Nonetheless, we have tried to match explanatory variables whenever possible. The resulting comparison, though hardly definitive, strongly suggests that studies of labor force composition should be framed by the intersection of labor process, industrial structure, and labor market.

9

Robotics, Electronics, and the American Textile Industry

Julia C. Bonham

For decades the American textile industry has been characterized by its product orientation, unskilled labor force, and low wages relative to other domestic industries. Recently, however, competition from inexpensive foreign imports has threatened its very survival and caused industry leaders to develop a new market orientation that emphasizes quality control and quick response to changing market conditions. Indeed, experts argue that American textile manufacturers must acknowledge that they have lost their competitive edge in the relatively stable, low-end, mass-produced product lines and must learn to cater to specialized, high-fashion markets featuring product diversity. For example, John N. Gregg, chief executive officer (CEO) of the Avtex Companies and chairman of the lobbying group Fiber, Fabric & Apparel Coalition for Trade (FFACT), noted in 1987 that the easy entry of developing nations into textile manufacturing will continue to put pressure on the American textile-apparel complex to do short-run, trendy, custom work: "My guess is that you will see the U.S. textile industry becoming more of a specialty supplier than a commodity business" ("John Gregg" 1987, p. 58).

The strategy of quick response or "just-in-time," which involves "compressing the pipeline from retailers all the way back to fiber producer" (Christiansen 1985, p. 15), emerged in 1985 in response to this growing perception. By "bridging the gap between fiber, fabric, apparel manufacturer and retailer" and ensuring "the right material at the right place at the right time" (Davidson 1987, p. 144), industry leaders argued that American textile manufacturers would be able to react quickly and effectively to the constantly changing demands of the top-end market. As L. A. Christiansen, the American Textile Manufacturing Institute's (ATMI) "New Generation" president, explained during a *Textile World* interview conducted in March 1988: "We were more manufacturing driven in the past. But we, as an industry, have begun to realize that it is time to be more market driven . . . developing our product line to fill areas where we perceive need but which are not as impacted by imports. As a result, we are changing the emphasis of the type of products we are running and the markets where we want to be involved" (Christiansen 1988a, p. 43). Robert M. Frazier of the industry advocacy firm Kurt Salmon suggested in 1985 that the payoff of the quick response strategy could be substantial: "Tightening the long information and product pipelines . . . could save $25 billion in the $100 billion consumer apparel system" (Christiansen 1985, p. 15).

This trend away from the traditional product orientation has led textile companies to seek out new technologies that are compatible with the goals of high quality control and quick response. According to Bob Swift, executive director of the Crafted with Pride in the U.S.A. Council, quick response reflects both a "technological and marketing response to the challenge of import competition . . . [that] doesn't count on negotiation, enforcement, or legislation for the survival of the U.S. textile/apparel industry" (Sheehy 1986, p. 47).

Even before industry leaders formally articulated the quick response strategy, American textile manufacturers had begun evaluating the role of the industrial robot in mill operations. In the early 1980s, they hoped that the new technology that had been so effectively applied in the U.S. automobile industry could become a quick fix for the domestic industry's dual problems of foreign competition and high labor costs relative to Asian competition. As one robotics expert expressed it in 1983, "Through the combined efforts of textile machinery manufacturers, robot manufacturers, and the textile industry in general, robotics can and will be a major force in keeping the U.S. textile industry strong and competitive" (Cahill 1987, p. 27).

Advocates gave two basic reasons for their positive outlook. First, the mechanical worker, unlike its human counterpart, could increase efficiency, cut costs, and improve product quality, while freeing management from the burden of dealing with costly labor issues (Buchanan 1986, p. 198). This argument featured the following points: the industrial robot does not take breaks or become distracted; it does not require expensive benefit packages; it has no family requiring health and life insurance; it does not become tired and can handle dangerous and boring jobs without fear or complaint; and it does not join unions or file grievances. Second, the industrial robot has a tremendous advantage over its hard-automation counterparts because it can be programmed to do a variety of tasks or to do the same task on materials of different size and composition (Buchanan 1986, pp. 197–98). In other words, it is flexible automation that does not need to be scrapped every time a manufacturer's product line changes. This latter characteristic, at least in theory, made the industrial robot the perfect technology for the quick response strategy.

By 1985, however, the American textile industry was no longer heralding the age of the industrial robot. Indeed, there has been little progress in the dissemination of this flexible automation since the industry's initial flirtation in 1983. By the late 1980s, experts seemed reluctant to estimate how long widespread adoption would take or even to state definitively that it would eventually happen (Cahill 1987, p. 27). Fortunately, during the mid-1980s, several successful electronics applications, first in the area of controls and later in the area of computer-aided manufacturing and design, revealed that technologies compatible with the industry's goals of high quality control and quick response and consistent with its new market orientation were nevertheless available. Although the keen interest in electronics applications centered on their relationship to quick response, the labor-saving feature of the new technology was never overlooked. As late as 1987, a *Textile World* editorial suggested that American textile manufacturers still associated automation with "how much labor 'we're going to cut' " (Christiansen 1987b, p. 15).

This chapter provides an overview of the questions and issues raised by the technological change under way in the American textile industry during the 1980s. It explains what an industrial robot is and why it is not suitable for most mill work. Then, it describes the electronics revolution in the American textile industry and assesses its impact on the competitive status of the U.S. industry. Finally, it identifies two labor-related problems that are likely to interfere with the swift changeover from the product to the market orientation—the incompatibility of the existing, poorly educated, and unskilled labor force with the new high technology, and the negative effect of the industry's reputation for low wages on its chance to compete with other industries as well as other sectors of the economy for the well-educated, sophisticated workers required by the new technology.

Theoretical Framework

During the late 1960s and early 1970s, historians of technology began to view technological change in its broadest context. They paid attention not only to how an invention was conceived and brought to commercial viability but also to how the new technology made its way into the economy and society. Their emphasis shifted from the exclusive study of the invention and development stages to the study of the pace and pattern of widespread dissemination. For example, Nathan Rosenberg, an economic historian by training, developed the concept of technological interdependence to explain how new technologies affect long-term economic growth. He argued that certain independently developing technologies are often "complementary" and consequently under the "right" conditions their industries of origin interact in a mutually beneficial way. He suggested that this phenomenon accounts for the emergence of capital goods industries and allows mature industries to take advantage of technological innovations that they could not develop on their own (either because of capital or knowledge constraints).

During the 1980s, textile manufacturers were able to introduce robots and electronics into their mills without spending precious capital on research and development because they adopted and adapted the technologies of robotics and, more significantly, of the electronics industry by way of the textile machinery industry. Rosenberg argued that technological interdependence, as manifested especially in the twentieth-century evolution of mutually beneficial interindustry relationships, accounts for much of the innovation under way (1972, pp. 3–33). This theory of technological change considers the political scene, economic conditions, prior practices, traditions, and the social environment as important in affecting when and to what degree interindustry activity takes place.

A decade later, historians of technology began developing models of technological change. Writing about the electrical power industry, Thomas P. Hughes, for example, argued that technological change can best be described using a systems approach. The process occurs in four stages: invention and development of the system, technological transfer from one locale to another, growth resulting from finding solutions to the critical technical problems, and technological momentum (1983, pp. 1–17). Some technologies, of course, lend themselves to systems analysis better than others. In the case of robotics and electronics applications in the American textile industry during the 1980s, the new technologies were systems oriented and yet they were introduced and continue to be introduced on a piece-meal basis.

Another model of technological change with relevance here comes from Edward W. Constant's study of the turbojet. He argued that there are basically two kinds of technological change: the improvement of the accepted tradition under new or more stringent conditions, and the innovation that occurs when the existing technology fails when subjected to new or more stringent conditions. Constant concluded that problems were solved either by intensive development of the existing technological system or by a random, ad hoc search for a radically new solution (1980). During the 1980s, changes in the old technology, which relied on high speeds and dedicated automation, did not solve the American textile industry's problems caused by unprecedented import competition and changing market conditions. Whether random or not, the search was on for a radically new technological solution.

The Industrial Robot in the Textile Industry

DESCRIPTION

In its current commercial form, an industrial robot can best be described as a reprogrammable, multijointed arm or manipulator equipped with a gripper or tool holder (Synder 1986, pp. 2–22). Indeed, in some respects the industrial robot takes the place of the human arm and to a much lesser extent the hand in the production process—moving material, parts, and tools through a series of predetermined motions to accomplish specific tasks. Because the industrial robot can be reprogrammed to adapt to new conditions and goals, experts call it flexible or advanced automation and contrast it with traditional applications, which are variously described as hard, fixed, or dedicated automation. Automatic doffers, piecers, and cleaners for open-end spinning and automatic doffers, splicers, and knotters used in winding are examples of hard automation. They are unifunctional and typically form an integral part of the production machine. In other words, when the production machine is scrapped, so are the automatic devices integrated into it.

Robots have three degrees of freedom that allow the arm to reach any point within the "work envelope" or operating range, which is the volume of space defined by the maximum extension of the arm in all directions. The revolute robot, for example, is a sophisticated anthropomorphic machine tool whose base, shoulder, elbow, and in some cases wrist rotate. It is superior to simpler robots in that it offers a comparatively large working volume with minimal space intrusion. It can also be programmed to avoid obstacles along its designated path: that is, it can reach over objects. This feature makes the revolute robot particularly desirable for textile applications because the work space in textile mills is often crowded and the machinery is frequently tiered.

All robots rely on a computer programmed with specialized instructions to tell them what to do. Some robots move an object to prespecified points in a predetermined order in what is called point-to-point control. Others move an object along a continuous path, transmitting precisely defined energy flows (forces and torques) to preassigned destinations. The robot "interacts continuously with its environment" (Synder 1986, p. 18) and thus can perform its task while interacting with a moving object such as a conveyor. Since many of the textile applications of the industrial robot require linkage to a conveyor system, continuous path control is desirable.

Regardless of the type of programming employed, the computer must receive information regarding present location and so forth in order to signal directions to the robot's arm. To this end, every robot joint (base, shoulder, elbow, wrist, and so on) is equipped with sensors that collect data about a joint's present situation so that the computer can generate control commands for the joint actuator, which drives the movement of the joint. Both hydraulic cylinders and electric motors are used as actuators.

The most distinguishing features of the industrial robot of the 1980s are its ability to be reprogrammed to suit different jobs and materials and to operate without human assistance. Despite these advantages, well suited to a rapidly changing market and labor cost problems, the industrial robot has not turned out to be readily adaptable to textile and apparel manufacturing.

DETERRENTS TO WIDESPREAD DISSEMINATION OF INDUSTRIAL ROBOTS

Immediately after the initial outpouring of interest in industrial robots in 1983, it became clear that they would not be the solution to the industry's problems. Robot manufacturers had shown little interest in the textile industry until 1983 (Krenek 1983, p. 57), and American textile manufacturers were completely ignorant of the new technology when it was presented to them at conferences and exhibitions. Automated Manufacturing '84, for example, was planned "to bring the latest technology from around the country to the Southeast, where much of the manufacturing expertise is still behind that of other industrial centers" ("AM '84" 1984, p. 19). This exhibition featured displays by prominent robot manufacturers, textile machinery builders, and computer companies. In 1984, *America's Textiles* described the response of southern textile manufacturers to the automated technologies: "The big questions were: How can I use this? Would it be worth the tremendous investment? . . . 'If the import situation is not resolved in the next few years, there won't be any apparel manufacturers to sell cloth to,' one textile manufacturer told *America's Textiles*. 'Then what am I going to do with a high-technology gadget like a robot?' " ("AM '84" 1984, pp. 19, 22).

In the early 1980s, robotics manufacturers and international textile machinery builders finally focused their attention on two elements of textile manufacturing—doffing and materials handling—that were still largely accomplished by human workers and could be performed by industrial robots. Although they developed industrial robots capable of doffing textile machines, this advance had little impact in the United States because American textile manufacturers preferred to adopt open-end spinning, which eliminated both the roving and winding processes required in ring spinning. In contrast, European and Japanese textile manufacturers favored ring spinning or the newer technologies of air-jet, rotor, and friction spinning to open-end spinning. Thus they found themselves having to doff roving, spinning, and winding machines. Savings in intermediate yarn storage, reduction in the number of bobbin boxes, and lower labor costs meant that the incentive to automate doffing using robots took on greater importance overseas ("Japanese Textile Machinery Makers Continue Assault" 1986, pp. 38–40).

American textile manufacturers were keenly interested in materials-handling applications, however. As the speeds and efficiencies of production machinery improved year by year, bottlenecks resulting from reliance on human workers to move materials at key junctures slowed down the process. In the early 1980s, case packing, palletizing yarn packages, loading and unloading operations, and creeling and sliver-can movement were among the potential applications under scrutiny. At a Clemson University conference on robotics held in the fall of 1983, E. M. Krenek of Platt Saco Lowell Robotics described how the industrial robot could be employed to palletize yarn packages: it "can grasp yarn packages in varying configurations, place them on a pallet in varying patterns, place a separator between pallet layers, repeat the process until the desired number of layers are in place, signal the conveyor to move the loaded pallet, and then place an empty pallet on the conveyor to start the process again" (Krenek 1983, p. 57). Although the textile industry found the application of robots to materials-handling jobs appealing, the robots' maximum load capacity of just six hundred pounds presented a formidable obstacle to widespread dissemination (O'Neil 1983, p. 61).

In addition to the interindustry problems, potential textile customers overestimated the ability or performance level of the mechanical worker relative to its human counterpart. Corporate executives held "a blue-sky image" that robots could solve all their manufacturing problems by eliminating most of the human labor force. The industrial robot could do neither. In most cases, it offers a simple one-to-one exchange—one robot for one human. Furthermore, the industrial robot certainly could not perform complicated actions. It could at best be thought of as "a functional idiot . . . deaf, dumb and blind: it has one arm and no hand, and its legs are tied to the floor" (Isaacs 1983, p. 37). This meant that they could not card, spin, or weave. They did not offer an alternative to the basic production machinery of textile manufacturing. Nor did they have the visual and tactile sensing capabilities necessary to perform many inspection chores required in textile processing.

A third deterrent to the swift and widespread dissemination of the new technology in textiles concerns the industrial robot's requirement of considerable support technology, including supply and take-away systems (rails, conveyor belts, indexers, and so on) as well as specialized end-of-arm tooling design. "Some believe, for example, that they can install a robot in a non-automated open-end spinning department and have it perform the tasks available with (fixed) automated systems—piecing, cleaning and doffing. The important thing to remember . . . is that a robot is only part of the system— 30% in some cases" (Isaacs 1983, p. 23).

In automobile plants, the problem of support technology was minimized by the presence of the assembly line, but in the textile industry the procurement of compatible support technology—a prerequisite for systems integration—represented a significant hidden investment in time and money. In the early years, manufacturers expecting to pay between $25,000 and $100,000 for an industrial robot were shocked to discover that they had to part with another $80,000 to $300,000 before the mechanical worker was operational (Isaacs 1983, p. 37). The explanation is simple. Textile machinery and plant layouts—aisle widths, ceiling heights, and the like—typically were designed and arranged with a human labor force in mind and thus required substantial physical alterations to take full advantage of the larger, heavier mechanized workers. As David Shardelow of the robot firm Cincinnati Milacron expressed the problem, "The use of robotics in the textile industry has been limited . . . primarily because the machinery now in place reflects manufacturing processes that have not changed in decades" (O'Neil 1983, p. 60).

A fourth reason robotics applications in textiles have been slow concerns the proprietary nature of the process as often practiced in the early 1980s. Individual textile manufacturing companies tended to join forces with machinery firms on specific projects or even to develop their own software and thus sustain substantial research costs, and they have not been eager to share the results of their labors (Isaacs 1983, p. 45).

The last deterrent to the broad-based adoption of industrial robots by textile manufacturers involves the new technology's compatibility with the quick response strategy. At first glance, American textile manufacturers seeking to minimize capital expenditures and provide quick turnaround were impressed by the flexibility of the mechanical worker. But because the robot had to be "taught" to do each job, a production run or batch had to be "large enough to repay for the teaching." And although theoretically the robot could learn its task from a computer program that established the movement of the arm through a set of coordinates, frequently it turned out to be preferable to provide manual instruction, relying on "a person guiding the robotic arm through the task the first time" (O'Neil 1983, p. 60). Going through this time-consuming and costly teaching process every time the product changed, especially in an industry betting its future on its ability to deliver goods "just in time," made the new technology inappropriate. Thus robots, with their high first cost (including support equipment), high operating costs, and long payback periods of five to fifteen years, did not offer a cost-effective alternative to traditional automation for short or small-volume runs (O'Neil 1983, p. 61).

Confronted with the very real limitations of the industrial robot of the 1980s, textile manufacturers shied away from widespread adoption. They were not, however, predisposed to limit their search for a technological solution to the import problem to robotics. Indeed, they exhibited a keen interest in a wide range of electronics applications, including electronic controls and computer-aided manufacturing and design. By 1985, the electronics revolution in the American textile industry was well under way.

The Electronics Revolution

Electronics had been well represented in textile mills since the mid-1970s, when computer monitoring of the production processes came of age. Actually, computer monitoring, which entailed equipping the production machinery with performance monitors capable of reading the status of the machine or the material in process, first entered mills on a very limited scale in the 1960s. It was then applied to machinery that had not changed much in fifty years and had been designed to be observed, serviced, and attended by human workers. In this early application, computer monitoring was only minimally effective. If computer technology was ahead of textile technology in the 1960s, by 1975 textile machinery had developed both in speed and sophistication to the point that the limits of the "manual observation team" were fast approaching. The potential of high-speed carding, automatic bale feeding, shuttleless weaving, and open-end spinning—all commercially viable technologies by 1975—could be met only with improved, more efficient monitoring and control systems. Computer monitoring provided the solution to the technological bottleneck facing the industry. As one observer expressed it, "Electronic monitoring provides the avenue through which machinery productivity, efficiency and quality data feed into a computer for use by plant management and operating personnel" (Cahill 1987, p. 26).

By 1983, textile manufacturers began expanding the use of computers at the monitoring stage to include the diagnostic function. Successful efforts by textile machinery builders during the 1970s and early 1980s to shorten the process chain (i.e., eliminate whole processes) and unprecedented increases in individual machine speeds created a new quality-control problem. High production rates made possible by the shortened process chain and dependence on fewer machines increased the potential to produce large volumes of defective goods (Tewkesbury 1984, pp. 66–67). But computers in combination with manual declaration boxes identified the causes of malfunctions. Human operators used the electronically generated data to correct problems (Cahill 1987, p. 27).

Beginning in 1985, the idea of computer networking at the monitoring stage gained favor. Indeed, the issue of computer networking had become so pronounced by the fall of 1987 that *Textile World* called upon North Carolina State University or the Textile Institute to host a forum on "factory computer standards for communicating between microprocessors on machines and monitoring, process control and host computer systems." The trade journal indicated that the American textile industry seemed to be placing more emphasis on machine-to-machine communication, known as computer-integrated manufacturing (CIM), than their counterparts in other parts of the world (Christiansen 1987c, p. 15).

Once computers operating at different levels were in use, a communication protocol, "a combination of hardware, software and rules which define the transmission of data between computers," became necessary. According to Richard C. Corson, group manager of the Institute of Textile Technology's manufacturing control systems, the protocols that had been accepted as standards in the late 1980s were not effective or relevant for all levels of communication between computers. Thus every manufacturer had to find a protocol that suited his particular need. The problem came when there were differences in protocols among computer systems used on process machinery. Corson called for the "standardization of communications to and from the machine level, so that users need not design or buy custom linkages and interfaces for use with multiple machines" (1987, p. 93). During the late 1980s, Burlington Industries produced a set of specifications, called MAP, to address the need for standardization in the communications technology of the industry ("MAP Provides the Computer Connection" 1987).

Concurrent with the move toward electronic networking at the monitoring stage came the push to relinquish to computers at least some of the responsibility for decision making at the process level. In the mid-1980s, textile manufacturers could choose from two types of computer-aided manufacturing (CAM). In the area of automated decision making, "intelligent" microprocessors, mounted directly on the machine, made "programmable decisions." They were capable of choosing without human aid an appropriate action from a set of routine responses by evaluating data relating to a given situation. According to one estimate, 80 percent or more of the day-to-day decisions made in textile manufacturing were of this nature. Before CAM enabled machines to make decisions regarding setting off alarms, adjusting machine settings, and other tasks, these decisions were made exclusively by human workers. The second application of CAM involved the creation of computer programs called expert systems, whose purpose was to capture some of the experience and knowledge of the most skilled human production specialists. During the late 1980s, the Institute of Textile Technology was

hard at work creating its first expert system, entitled Knowledge Diagnostic System (KDS), which was intended to act in an advisory capacity when confronted with processing problems (Cahill 1987, p. 27).

It is not an accident that the American textile industry's interest
in CAM coincided with the push by industry leaders to popularize
the quick response (QR) strategy. The incentive for introducing
CAM on a large scale came mainly from progressive textile manufacturers who believed in the philosophy of QR. By the late 1980s,
the entire industrial complex seemed to have embraced both QR
and CAM. Computer-aided design (CAD), which emerged in the
mid- to late 1980s, substantially shortened the design-to-production
time for those textile industries engaged in the creation of color designs, such as rug makers, printers, and converters. Without CAD, it
was not uncommon for eighteen months to lapse between the creation of a new design and its entry into the marketplace. With CAD,
the interval could be cut to weeks. Fieldcrest Mills, Inc., had pioneered the use of a new color CAD system for its Karastan rug business in 1982. The company found that CAD, which involved in this
case a digital imaging camera and an innovative color-description
technology, increased both contract and collection sales by allowing
the firm to respond swiftly to changing market demands and by improving operating efficiency. Larry Owens, president of Karastan
Rug Mills, explained the value of CAD:

> Dealers are always looking for exclusive patterns in their own
> markets. . . . Moreover, our options for taking advantage of those
> marketing opportunities were limited when it typically took us 18
> months to develop and bring a new design to the marketplace.
> One-of-a-kind samples of new designs were previously made by
> hand to show potential dealers. That was a comparatively slow
> and costly process. Now a high-speed color ink-jet plotter (a CAD
> system component) reproduces hard-copy samples in minutes at
> only a fraction of the old cost. ("Electronics Slashes Fieldcrest De-
> sign Times" 1986, pp. 59–60)

According to a company official, the camera scanned soft goods
such as one-of-a-kind, handmade Oriental rugs and translated their
color patterns into digital data that could be called up and displayed
at CAD work stations. *Textile World* summarized the advantages of
this approach: "Artists can manipulate these designs to create new
interpretations for reproduction. They also can choose to mix and
match elements from several designs to create interesting composite
patterns. The versatility and speed with which custom designs can

be created pay big dividends" ("Electronics Slashes Fieldcrest Design Times" 1986, p. 59).

The American dyeing, printing, and finishing industry had practiced the quick response approach for years. By early 1988, electronic devices were available for measuring and controlling speeds, temperature, tensions, and widths and for quick shutdowns. Also, a computerized formulation system that speeded up the color matching response time and gave precise recipe information for its automatic dye and chemical dispensing units was on the market. The system, which consisted of an optical sensor connected to a computer console and high-speed printer ("ITMA Dyeing and Finishing" 1988), helped ensure quick turnarounds and high quality control. These technological advances in the area of electronic processing control, when taken together, meant that plants were no longer "forced to rely on techniques garnered over 30–40 years of experience and slyly concealed in little black books" ("Process Control" 1987, p. 126). In other words, electronic controls had usurped the place of the experienced, skilled machine operator.

For the QR strategy to work, electronics applications in the American textile/apparel complex had to extend far beyond the manufacturing stage, for this approach required a high level of responsiveness at every point along the pipeline. According to Roger Milliken, chairman of Milliken & Company and of the Crafted with Pride in U.S.A. Council in 1987, the successful implementation of QR required the textile, apparel, and retail companies to put aside their long-standing adversarial relationships and work together in behalf of the entire industry ("Milliken" 1987). During the mid- to late 1980s, American textile leaders looked to advances in electronic communications technologies to bridge the gap between the fiber, textile, and apparel manufacturers and the retailers. For the textile manufacturer, QR meant expanding goals beyond cutting labor costs and increasing machinery speeds; it meant admitting that the competitiveness of the entire complex was the key to the salvation of the parts. In other words, the focus of the entire complex became saving the customer time and money.

According to Burlington chairman and CEO William A. Klopman, the best way to accomplish this goal was to "use computer linkage to help take up the slack in . . . [the chain that runs from fiber producer, through the textile manufacturer and apparel manufacturer, to the retailer and the consumer], and to provide customers quicker and better service through a combination of electronic communication, high technology and traditional human commitments to quality and customer relations." Speaking before several trade associations in November 1985, Klopman claimed that Burlington's computer linkage service allowed customers "to tap Burlington's computers (IBM) to obtain data such as cloth roll shading (using delta values for lightness, hue and chroma), width, roll length and shipping and billing information." This information provided the customer with "a look at the fabric even before it arrives, so cutting operations can be set up and scheduled in advance" (Byrd 1986, p. 61).

Proponents of QR hoped that the creation of computer data linkages between suppliers and customers might cut the total amount of time the product was in the pipeline from over sixty hours to thirty hours. But they acknowledged that this could occur only if computer linkage took place all along the pipeline ("EDI" 1986). To cut out paperwork and data entry errors, companies could adopt Electronic Data Interchange (EDI), which allows direct computer-to-computer exchange of standard business forms. "This means if you prepare business forms—orders, invoices, remittance advices, etc.—in a computer, and your trading partners copy the information into their computers," you can avoid the time and money involved in the transmission of forms through the mail as well as the data entry errors on the customer end ("EDI" 1986, p. 50). According to Robert Crosby, marketing systems project leader for American Hoechst, "at least 70% of one computer's input was another computer's output. And 25% of a transaction's cost is data entry and reentry" ("EDI" 1986, p. 50). In addition to the indirect benefits of reduced inventory investment, improved customer service, increased sales productivity, and streamlined manufacturing processes, EDI's direct benefits "include clerical processing reduction, telephone communications, transcribing, data entry, document matching, reduced clerical errors and reduced order cycle time" ("EDI" 1986, p. 56).

If EDI handled the proliferation of paperwork that came with a decision to ship to major customers on a weekly rather than monthly basis or to adopt an as-needed-based inventory system, then bar coding was the means for QR. In the shipping and receiving departments, bar-coded incoming supplies, raw materials, and finished goods coupled with bar-coded warehouse locations provided instantly accurate inventory records. For those companies processing gray goods or finished goods by lot, bar coding provided a fast, continuous method of tracking them on their trip through the factory. In addition, bar coding facilitated fixed-asset accounting. But the most significant advantage came in the area of customer service by increasing the speed and accuracy with which products could be traced, located, and controlled ("Bar-coding" 1985).

In 1988, the Charlotte-based textile consulting firm Ernst & Whinney conducted a survey of textile and apparel executives on the benefits of quick response ("Are You Doing Enough?" 1988). More than 60 percent of the respondents expected QR to provide significant benefits to retailers and apparel manufacturers, while 50 percent and 30 percent expected significant gains for textile manufacturers and fiber producers, respectively. The survey also asked participants to identify impediments to the successful implementation of QR. One-fourth to one-half of the respondents considered problems involving trust and commitment among participating firms as well as basic information deficiencies to be major deterrents.

If this survey is representative, then it is clear that the American textile/apparel industry had not yet reached consensus on the value of QR in 1988. And yet QR had clearly captured the interest of industry leaders by 1985. In the trade literature, there was a clear sense that the idea acquired momentum because it offered a systematic approach to solving the labor and marketing problems that had emerged during this period of steep foreign competition.

Technology and Industrial Choices

During the 1980s, technological change became a major ingredient in the American textile industry's recipe for increased competitiveness. American textile manufacturers acknowledged the need for technological innovation and exhibited a willingness to mobilize the capital required to introduce technological innovations when they felt such an investment was worthwhile.

There are five points that make this observation particularly noteworthy. The first three have to do with technological change, while the last two concern labor. First, since the 1920s, the rate of technological innovation has been relatively low in the American textile industry. Observers point to low profit margins and the availability of cheap labor to explain this historical trend (Hughes 1976). Thus the keen interest in technological innovation represented an important break with the past. Second, textile manufacturers were selective in their decisions regarding technological change; they studied and dismissed the industrial robot because it did not address the problems facing the industry in the 1980s. Third, there was an unspoken danger associated with the industry's commitment to rely on new technologies to implement QR. By the late 1980s, the American textile machinery industry no longer competed with its foreign counterparts in the sophisticated, high-tech sector of their industry (Office of Technology Assessment 1987, p. 74). Consequently,

American textile manufacturers found themselves increasingly dependent on foreign machinery makers for their survival.

Fourth, during the 1980s, profit margins were still low and United States manufacturers were forced by competition to cut their already low prices ("U.S. Textiles Will Throw Counterpunch" 1986). The traditional labor force, poorly educated and unskilled, was still available. The labor force shrank between 1980 and 1985 (Office of Technology Assessment 1987, p. 7) but not because the workers found better opportunities in other industries or sectors of the economy. Plant closings and mergers, a result of foreign competition as well as technological change, accounted for the depopulation of the American textile industry in the last decade ("1980s" 1987). Fifth, and finally, textile workers were introduced to a new technological threat to their livelihoods in the 1980s. According to industry leaders, dramatically reduced demand for American products in the stable, low-end markets and high labor costs relative to the competition in Asia fueled the keen interest among manufacturers in a technological fix that would reduce their labor needs.

Potential technological solutions could involve improvements to the existing machinery, such as additional hard automation applications, or they could involve trying radical new technologies, such as robotics and electronics applications. Initially, the focus was on labor-saving technology, whether conventional or radical. The swift takeover of the traditional low-end markets by foreign competitors tipped the scale in favor of the new flexible technologies as manufacturers realized that their marketing options had been severely curtailed. The new technologies, which originated outside the industry, were more capital intensive than traditional technologies and harder to understand. And yet pressing economic considerations made their unique characteristic of flexibility a high priority for new technologies.

The Impact of Automation on Workers

According to industry experts, the fully automated factory, variously referred to as flexible manufacturing and "lights out" manufacturing, represents the last phase of the electronics revolution (Christiansen 1987b). As the industry moves into the decade of the 1990s, this goal has not yet been realized. But important steps in this direction were taken during the 1980s.

During the 1980s, American textile manufacturers were uninterested in the relationship between the new electronic technologies and their workers. When they believed that large numbers of industrial robots would be used in American mills, they forged a consensus opinion regarding the impact of the new technology on the work force. They acknowledged that the new automation would destroy some production jobs but argued that a healthy domestic textile industry would create many new jobs in the service sector (Bonham 1986). Although industry leaders understand that the electronics revolution means that fewer workers will assume more responsibility, they have made no definitive statement regarding the impact of CAD-CAM and electronic controls on labor.

One reason for the silence may be that the labor situation in the case of the electronics revolution is far more complex than in the case of the industrial robot. It is not simply a question of finding a way to rationalize the dismissal of many production workers. The widespread use of electronic controls and CAD-CAM will put white-collar and blue-collar workers alike out of work, especially if the new electronic technologies are applied all along the pipeline. Moreover, the electronics revolution in the American textile industry will force manufacturers to choose between hiring a new breed of worker, one who is well enough educated to be able to interact with computers effectively and to adapt easily to constantly changing conditions in the workplace, and retraining the existing, largely unskilled, and often illiterate labor force. According to one industry leader, the success of one company over the competition in the future will depend in part on management's ability to "substantially develop both its operating and technical personnel" (Christiansen 1988b, p. 15). On this point, Sir Clive Jeanes, director general of Milliken Industrials Europe, commented in spring 1988: "The old model believes in specialization of labor; you train people to do just one or a very few of the elements, in a search for production efficiency. The new model believes this sort of compartmentalization is not efficient, and that people should have multiple skills and be cross-trained to do more than one job." Jeanes concludes that the new labor model will require textile manufacturers to see their labor force as "a valuable resource of knowledge and experience to be tapped" (Christiansen 1988b, p. 15).

It is clear that whenever possible many American textile manufacturers will apply the new model to a new work force. Comments from industry leaders indicate that they believe that few from the existing pool of textile workers can be expected to make the transition to the high-technology factory. In an interview for *Textile World*, Daniel K. Frierson, CEO of Dixie Yarns and president of ATMI, provided insight into the reasoning process:

I don't think there is any question about it: The textile machinery
we're buying today is much more sophisticated than we have traditionally bought. For example, in the dyehouse across the street
we have computerized and automated our dyeing process. A fellow over there who has operated those machines another way for
40 years had a hard time converting to the new machinery—they
all did. But now that everyone sees how it works, they're excited
about the new technology and are glad to be a part of it.

   However, as we bring up new people and other people in (from
the outside), we need people who are more sophisticated in computerization and technology. (Christiansen 1988a)

Having made the choice to employ new workers in the high-
technology mills, textile manufacturers should be hard at work trying to locate and attract well-educated people to an industry with a
long-standing reputation for paying low wages. If the new work
force is not forthcoming, electronic controls and CAD-CAM cannot
be introduced on a large scale. But there has been little commentary
on this point in the trade literature, perhaps because the idea of
paying these new workers who will operate modern, high-tech machines a wage that reflects their skill is not appetizing.

Textile World editor L. A. Christiansen did pen a succinct yet
thoughtful comment on the next step toward producing and sustaining a labor force capable of meeting the unique demands of the
new technology of the electronics revolution: "The implications are
clear for today's management, educational infrastructure and machinery suppliers: Work together to deliver more training, more education, more teamwork, more involvement, more respect, more
incentives—a new philosophy" (Christiansen 1988b, p. 15).

The chance for the displaced textile workers of the next decade to
enjoy a bright future or at least a decent one depends on state and
federally funded educational and retraining programs (Office of
Technology Assessment 1987, p. 105). But because these workers are
so poorly educated in the basics and tend to be located in rural regions throughout the South, the effectiveness of such programs is
questionable. There may be one ironic twist to the story, however. If
the American textile manufacturers' reputation for paying low
wages prevents them from attracting the workers of their choice,
they may be forced to try to bring the existing labor force along into
the era of advanced automation.

10

The Deindustrialization of the Textile South: A Case Study

John Gaventa and Barbara Ellen Smith

The textile industry, once embraced as the salvation of rural areas wracked by war and a breakdown of the agricultural economy, now condemns many southern mill towns to decline. Throughout the 1980s, plant closings in the rural South wiped out the economic base of one mill town after another. In the more modern plants of the larger companies, automation further reduced the size of the work force. Between 1970 and 1985, 155,000 jobs were eliminated in the textile industry, a decline of 25 percent (Avery and Sullivan 1985, p. 36). These trends are symptomatic of larger forces at work: the development of truly international production arenas, communication, and markets, which together have spurred a competitive scramble for the lowest possible production costs in the labor-intensive textile industry.

One hundred years ago, the rural South promised rock-bottom production costs to local investors hoping to edge out their northern competitors. Waterways in the rolling hills of the piedmont in central

The case study reported here is based on Gaventa 1988. Part of the chapter is adapted from "From the Mountains to the *Maquiladoras*: A Case Study of Capital Flight and Its Impact on Workers" by John Gaventa in *Communities in Economic Crisis: Appalachia and the South*, edited by John Gaventa, Barbara Ellen Smith, and Alex Willingham, © 1990 by Temple University. Reprinted by permission of Temple University Press.

North Carolina, northern South Carolina, and north Georgia were the favored location for the new factories. The impoverished farm population provided the cheap labor that gave southern textile manufacturers the competitive advantage they required. Race discrimination barred blacks from all but a few menial jobs in the new mills and reinforced their indebted status as sharecroppers and tenant farmers. Over half and in some mills as many as 80 percent of the workers were white women and their children. Their labor fueled the industrial revolution that transformed the region—at least ideologically—into the New South (Smith 1986).

Textile manufacturers in the Northeast, the original hub of the industry in the United States, soon began to desert the mill towns of Massachusetts and other northeastern states and move south. The mathematics were irresistible: wages were nearly one-third lower than in the North. By 1927, North Carolina exceeded Massachusetts in the number of textile workers and the value of their products (Mitchell and Mitchell 1930). The first major migration of capital for the U.S.-based textile industry had occurred, but it would not be the last.

Immediately following World War II, a second wave of southward migration began. Between 1950 and 1970, nearly 300,000 jobs were lost in the textile mills of the Northeast, while employment continued to grow in the South (Avery and Sullivan 1985, p. 35). At the same time, the apparel industry began an extensive move south. By 1970, 40 percent of all apparel workers were in the South, up from 17 percent in 1950 (North American Congress on Latin America 1977, p. 1). North Carolina consolidated its position as the premier textile-producing state in the country; by 1970, over 280,000 workers, nearly one-third of the industry total, were employed in the textile mills of North Carolina (Avery and Sullivan 1985, p. 35).

The economic boom enjoyed by many industries in this period eventually produced a labor shortage in the relatively low-wage textile mills. Prompted by the civil rights movement, during the 1960s textile manufacturers increasingly turned to the black workers they had historically spurned. In a decade when many other manufacturing industries dramatically increased their labor productivity through technological innovation, productivity in textiles rose only slightly. Persistent reliance on low-wage labor and the associated failure to update the production process partly explain textile and apparel manufacturers' present vulnerability to international competition.

By the 1970s, the handwriting was on the wall: the U.S. textile industry had to "modernize or die," said Ellison S. McKissick, Jr., president of the American Textile Manufacturing Institute (Office of Technology Assessment 1987, p. 18). Textile and apparel production in the newly industrializing countries of the Third World has been rising rapidly and is encroaching on markets once claimed by U.S. producers. Investors from all over the world, including the United States, are attracted to textile production in Hong Kong, Korea, and other locations for many of the same reasons that entrepreneurs were lured to the South in the late nineteenth century: the availability of cheap—especially female—labor, the low skill requirements, the relatively small capital outlays required to begin production, and the expanding markets. Governments in developing countries typically view their domestic textile and apparel industries as a cornerstone of the industrialization process and aggressively protect them through tariffs, quotas, and in some cases outright bans on the importation of certain products. As a result of these dynamics, imports into the U.S. textile market doubled between 1973 and 1985 and now account for one-third of U.S. consumption. In the apparel industry, an even higher proportion of the domestic market, 48 percent, is claimed by imports (Office of Technology Assessment 1987, p. 4).

These trends have triggered a massive shakeout in the U.S. textile industry. The American Textile Manufacturers Institute estimates that in just four years, 1981–84, 231 plants closed nationwide (Office of Technology Assessment 1987, pp. 3, 19). Some companies, notably medium-sized firms without the capital to modernize and without a specialized market niche, have gone out of business. Others have followed the time-honored strategy of moving their capital to a cheaper production site—out of the country. Capital is far more mobile in the apparel sector than in textiles proper, but mobility is a resurgent trend in both. In 1983, Dan River and West Point Pepperell were among the first major textile manufacturers to initiate foreign production, and others have followed their lead (Standard and Poor's 1984).

International competition has also spurred a somewhat belated campaign to automate the textile production process. Although labor productivity is still only one-half the overall average in manufacturing, productivity growth in textiles exceeds that in all other manufacturing industries. Today, the U.S. textile industry is one of the most productive in the world (Office of Technology Assessment 1987).

Despite investments of $1.5 billion per year in new plants and equipment, the outlook for a U.S.-based textile industry is grim. As the U.S. Office of Technology Assessment warned in 1987: "Unless policy action is taken in the next few years, there is reason to be concerned about the very existence of many parts of the industry" (p. 3). Technology available in the United States can also be used in countries where other costs of production, especially wages, are far lower. (Indeed, much of the equipment that is transforming the textile production process is produced overseas.) The perception that a highly automated production process requires relatively skilled technicians to operate—implying an advantage for production in the United States rather than the Third World—may be largely a myth. Some evidence suggests that Third World producers (including, of course, many U.S.-based multinationals) are investing in automated equipment not only to ensure consistent product quality but also to deskill the production process. One U.S. producer of high-tech machinery used in apparel production commented that he sold "the first two belt-loop machines that we built to Singapore. It's pitiful. We couldn't even sell them here. . . . They can go from zero to our quality without training—by buying equipment. That's the key. They can hire a girl off the street and she'll do as well at a tenth the cost as someone who's been doing it for 20 years" (McGrayne 1984).

For southern textile workers and their communities, these developments threaten to end a way of life. Rural mill towns, especially those distant from metropolitan centers, are turning into ghost towns. Women, most notably rural blacks, are especially hard hit by the job loss. Although textile mills are low wage by manufacturing standards, they pay better than the unskilled jobs in the lower rungs of the service sector to which many laid-off women workers must turn. A reduced standard of living, forced migration, and the breakdown of rural communities are now the legacy of a capitalist industrialization process that once promised to create a New South.

Deindustrialization in the Global Context

The problems posed by the global movement of the textile industry are examples of the broader issues associated with capital mobility, which have been debated in an outpouring of literature by sociologists, political economists, and others in recent years. In the United States, the debate has been particularly vigorous in two streams of literature: those dealing with the intranational movement of industry, especially as seen in the Sunbelt-Snowbelt controversies that emerged in the 1960–70s; and those dealing with the international movement of industry from the industrialized core countries to the developing countries, which yields a "new" or "changing" division of labor.

Traditional economic theory holds that capital mobility takes place as firms seek locations with favorable comparative advantages. Capital movement is seen as a means for spurring economic growth, through which inequalities are leveled among differing regions (Summers 1984). The neo-Marxist approach "links the geographic restructuring of industry to the broader political economic forces of capital accumulation and economic crisis." "Thus, capital mobility is the process by which capital shifts its stock and investment from a less favorable to a more favorable social structure of accumulation. Since the social structure of accumulation varies spatially, and industry has become increasingly mobile, geographic location is a leading means to reestablish conditions of profitability" (Jaffee 1986, pp. 298, 300).

Both of these perspectives regarding the spatial location of manufacturing investment were evident in the debate during the late 1960s and early 1970s about the decline of the Snowbelt and the rise of the Sunbelt (Estall 1980; Sawers and Tabb 1984; Till 1973). As plant closings and industrial decline hit the manufacturing belt of the Northeast (termed the Frostbelt or the Snowbelt) and Midwest (Rustbelt), manufacturing jobs grew in the South. Between 1970 and 1977, the North lost almost 1 million jobs, while more than two hundred thousand new jobs in manufacturing were created in the South. "By 1977 the share of the old core area in total U.S. manufacturing employment had been reduced to about 50 percent compared with 66 percent in 1950. The southern share, meanwhile, had grown from approximately 20 percent to 30 percent" (Estall 1980, p. 372).

As we have seen, the shift in manufacturing from the North to the South is exemplified by the textile and apparel industries, which are among the largest and most mobile of manufacturing industries. In 1950, almost two-thirds of all apparel workers in the United States were employed in the Northeast. By 1974, this number had dropped to slightly over one-third (35.7 percent). The South meanwhile gained apparel jobs, raising its share of apparel employment from 16.7 percent in 1950 to 44.2 percent in 1974. In the North, New York City alone lost sixty-eight thousand jobs in the apparel sector between 1958 and 1970—a decline of 28 percent (North American Congress on Latin America 1977, pp. 10–11).

By the 1970s and 1980s, however, the debates over the movement of capital to the South were being overtaken by the rapid movement of industry out of the country altogether. Drawing upon the world systems perspective developed by Immanuel Wallerstein and others, the concept of the "new" or "changing" division of labor emerged to explain the movement of manufacturing from the First World, or industrialized core countries, to the Third World. Examining the movement of textiles from Germany to the Third World, Folker Fröbel, Jürgen Heinrichs, and Otto Kreye (1980), whose book first coined the concept of the new international division of labor, wrote:

> Perhaps the clearest expression of structural changes in the world economy which can be observed in the mid-1970s is the relocation of production. . . . The development of the world economy has increasingly created the conditions (forcing the development of the new international division of labor) in which the survival of more and more companies can only be assured through the relocation of production to new industrial sites, where labor power is cheap to buy, abundant and well disciplined; in short through the transnational reorganization of production. (1980, pp. 9, 15)

This situation has emerged because of the coming together of three preconditions: a huge reservoir of disposable labor in the developing world; the development of production processes based on fragmentation and routinization of production (Fordism and Taylorism); and the development of techniques of communication and transportation so that production processes can be coordinated on a global scale. Fröbel and associates argue that "the coincidence of these three preconditions (which are supplemented by other, less important ones), has brought into existence a world market for labor and a real world industrial reserve army of workers, together with a world market for production sites" (1980, p. 13).

The shifts in production have also been encouraged by shifts in state policy from import substitution as a way to overcome dependency on core countries to the development of goods for export. In certain developing countries, especially Mexico, Taiwan, Singapore, Hong Kong, and the Philippines, export processing zones were created which offered tax, labor, and environmental concessions for the assembly of products by multinationals with cheap Third World labor. Initially, industries that relied mainly on low-skill assembly line labor, such as garments and electronics, flocked to the newly industrializing countries (NICs). In more recent years, other industries, such as manufacturers of auto parts, radios, televisions, and watches, have joined the ranks of these "footloose" or runaway industries (Grunwald and Flamm 1985; Harrison and Bluestone 1988; Nash and Fernandez-Kelly 1983).

Arguments concerning the new or changing division of labor have been further developed by those who suggest that it is also characterized by a feminization of the production process. In addition to state incentives, the multinational corporations have taken advantage of the vast reserve army of Third World women workers (created in part by declining rural economies), who have provided cheap labor and are perceived by the corporations to be more "docile" and "nimble-fingered" than their First World counterparts. Employment of women has been especially pronounced in the electronics and textile and garment sectors (Nash and Fernandez-Kelly 1983; Porpora, Lim, and Prommas, 1989; Robert 1983). As June Nash and Maria Fernandez-Kelly summarize, "The vanguard of industrial investment in the world capitalist system is in the lowest paid segment of those countries paying the lowest wages. Young women in developing countries are the labor force on this frontier just as women and children were in the industrialization of England and Europe in the nineteenth century" (1983, p. x).

In the past, analysts of development and underdevelopment have tended to view the global production process as vertically integrated, such that workers within the Third World extracted the raw materials necessary for production of manufacturing goods in the First World. Within this vertical hierarchy, workers in the core benefited from the exploitation of workers in the periphery. The internationalization of the production process, however, breaks down the vertical hierarchy of labor between First World and Third World workers, challenging the privileged position of First World workers. As Fröbel, Heinrichs, and Kreye point out: "Workers in the already industrialized countries are now placed on a world-wide labor market and forced to compete for their jobs with their fellow workers in the developing countries. Today with the development of a worldwide market in production sites, the traditional industrialized and the developing countries have to compete against one another to attract industry to their sites" (1980, p. 13).

In the United States, increased foreign production has had a major impact on the labor market and, as a consequence, on the bargaining position of U.S. workers. Bennett Harrison and Barry Bluestone point out how rapid this expansion has been in recent years: "In 1965, total direct U.S. investment abroad—investment in factories, office buildings, machine tools, and office equipment— was less than $50 billion. It took only ten years to reach $124 billion. And in just the next five, it surpassed $213 billion. The profits that came back to U.S. corporations from their subsidiaries grew even faster, from $5.2 billion in 1965 to more than $424 billion in 1980" (1988, pp. 26–27, referring to Berberoglu 1987).

These trends in turn have prompted warnings of the "hollowing" and the "deindustrialization" of America. These arguments contend that the internationalization of production has contributed to the restructuring of the economies of First World countries, weakening the bargaining position of both workers and localities vis-à-vis corporations (Harrison and Bluestone 1988; Nash and Fernandez-Kelly 1983; Perucci et al. 1988). Robert Ross and Kent Trachte argue that "the shift of productive facilities to low-wage sites in the periphery or semi-periphery . . . has had a sharp impact on the employment and security of formerly more or less secure, core, monopoly workers. . . . Workers in some of the core countries find themselves in competition for access to capital and to buyers of their labor power across the world span. This competition provides a new tool for capital in its relation to labor, the threat to move" (1983, p. 402).

These trends may be seen in the following case study of a seat belt sewing and manufacturing operation, which moved from Michigan, to Tennessee, to Alabama, and then to Mexico, each time in search of cheaper labor and a more favorable business climate.

A Case in Point

The Allied Signal Seat Belt Company, originally the Jim Robbins Company of Royal Oak, Michigan, came to Knoxville, Tennessee, in 1965, attracted by "a progressive attitude and desire to work" on the part of local laborers. The "cooperative spirit" displayed by the city (Barrett 1967), which helped the company acquire land and a building as well as cut through red tape for utilities, was also a factor. Perhaps most important, however, was the wage differential between the two locations. In 1972, according to the Census of Manufacturers, the average wage for production workers in the industry in Knoxville was $2.58 an hour, almost half the $5.04 an hour that comparable workers received in the Detroit area.

During the 1960s and 1970s, Allied Signal's Knoxville operations flourished, with employment in various plants rising from one hundred in 1965 to close to three thousand in 1979. By 1980, the company ranked with two other apparel firms, Levi-Strauss and Standard Knitting Mills, as the city's largest industrial employers. Local papers heralded Knoxville as the Seat Belt Capital of the World.

The atmosphere of industrial growth began to change very quickly in the 1980s. Between late 1979 and 1981, the company laid off over two thousand workers. More layoffs followed from 1983 to

1985, bringing employment down to two to three hundred workers. In 1981, company officials publicly attributed the layoffs to the deepening effects of the recession on the automotive industry. By 1983, as the country climbed out of the recession, the company blamed the slump of new U.S. car sales and increased imports. According to a 1983 Allied Corporation press release, moves had to be made to "maintain the firm's competitive position as one of the leading independent suppliers of seat belts to the North American automotive industry." "Costs of upgrading the local operations [were] prohibitive," a company representative said.

Though spokespeople publicly stated that the company could not afford to reinvest in Knoxville, it was investing handsomely in a new facility in Greenville, Alabama, a rural, nonunion area eager to acquire new industry. Between 1980 and 1985, Allied carried out three expansions there and increased its Alabama work force three-fold—from 300 in 1980 to 960 in 1985. The company was attracted by a "large and motivated workforce." The strong work ethic of the local labor force was complemented by the "upbeat, co-operative ready-to-serve attitude of local officials and business leaders" ("Planning for Expansion" 1985), who provided revenue bond financing for a new building and initial recruitment and training of local workers. As in the move to Tennessee, differences in wages were also a factor. Butler County, where Greenville is located, is more rural than Knoxville and has fewer unions, a larger percentage of minorities, and fewer other industrial competitors. In 1982, wages for manufacturing workers in Butler County were approximately 60 percent of those for comparable workers in Knoxville.

ECONOMIC BLACKMAIL

Rather than reinvest in equipment and retraining in Knoxville, the company moved to a new area that offered nonunion, lower-wage labor and favorable state subsidies. Moreover, as the company increased its facilities in Alabama, it used the threat of further layoffs and movement of capital to extract concessions from the Knoxville work force.

Workers at Allied Signal's Knoxville plant had successfully unionized in 1967, shortly after the company located in the area. During the subsequent period of growth, labor-management relations were relatively stable. By the 1980s, "the company increasingly used job blackmail against us, playing the Knoxville workers off against the Alabama employees," said one local union official. Workers in

Knoxville were told that if they took a reduction in wages and benefits and accepted "flexible job language" in their contract, some of
the jobs would be reinstated. At first, workers rejected the demands
for concessions, but by 1983, desperate for jobs, they accepted.
Some workers were rehired, but at a wage of about $5.30 per hour,
less than when they had been laid off three years before. "We're
hoping it will be a start of a major turnaround," said one union
official. "It's definitely a trend going in the right direction" (Nauman 1983). The optimism did not last long. Soon after a few jobs
returned from Alabama, they were transferred again—this time to a
new plant in the *maquiladora* zone along the Mexican-U.S. border.

In Mexico, the *maquiladoras* or border zones have emerged as the
result of a development policy that is by now familiar: the effort to
recruit industry from the North.[1] The word *maquilar* means to assemble. The *maquiladoras* are companies located along the Mexican
border which assemble products with Mexican labor for reexport
back to the United States or other countries.

Originally, the *maquiladora* zones were established to combat unemployment along the border. Through a strategy somewhat similar
to that employed by state and local governments in the southern
United States, the Mexican Border Industrialization Program was
established in 1965. Industrial parks were built and offered as sites
to plants. Advertisements about low-cost labor promoted the favorable business climate to companies in the North. In December 1965
there were 12 *maquiladora* enterprises along the border with 3,087
workers. By 1974 the number of plants had grown to 209 with
29,000 workers (Bustamente 1983). By the 1980s, the border program began to take on new significance both as a strategy for industrialization and as a source of foreign exchange desperately needed
to repay foreign debts. Devaluation of the peso made labor costs
even more attractive. From 1982 to 1986, the border zones experienced phenomenal growth. By 1986, there were almost one thousand companies in the area, employing 300,000 workers; predictions
are that employment will triple again by the mid-1990s, to some 1
million workers.

The seat belt company, by now part of the large international
Bendix conglomerate, chose the town of Aqua Prieta, one of the
smaller and newer of the *maquiladora* towns located directly across

---

1. Some of the information about the *maquiladoras* is based on papers presented at
a conference sponsored by El Colegio de la Frontera Norte entitled "The *Maquiladora*
Industry: Structural Change and Regional Development," Tijuana, Mexico, Sept. 21–
23, 1987.

the border from Douglas, Arizona, for its new facility.[2] In recent years, more than twenty manufacturing plants have located in the town, almost all sewing, electronics, automotive parts, or other labor-intensive operations from the United States.

The Allied Bendix plant opened on January 1, 1986. According to sources in the plant, the company employs about five hundred people and is growing. In addition to the work that had been carried out in Knoxville, by 1987 new production lines were being brought in from Alabama, and employment was expected to rise to six or seven hundred workers. Like other *maquiladora* plants, this one is dedicated to sewing and assembly and is deeply interlocked in production with the Knoxville and Greenville plants. The webbing is sewn in Knoxville and shipped to Greenville, where the other parts and components are added and shipped to Aqua Prieta. There, in repetitive, noisy assembly line work, the workers cut the webbing and assemble the seat belts for shipment back to Greenville for U.S. distribution.

The wages are minuscule compared to those in the United States. Workers in this plant, as in others along the Mexican border, work nine-and-a-half-hour days for a total of about $3.50 a day, or 37 cents an hour, one-sixteenth of the wages workers received for comparable work in Knoxville. Because of U.S. tariff laws, import duty is charged only on the value added to the product in Mexico, a minor amount given the wage rates. Because the component parts are made in the United States, they are not taxed upon reentry.

Although the wages appear low to the U.S. visitor, the jobs are welcomed by the local workers and the community. Bumper stickers on the cars by the plant read in Spanish "I love Bendix." Local merchants are glad for the revenues. Even the local union, which is tied into the official national union, scarcely questions the arrangement. In short, the business climate is extremely favorable. As one U.S. resident along the border remarked, "If you think economic boosterism is big in your part of the world, you haven't seen anything until you come here."

THE IMPACT ON WORKERS

While the new Mexican venture was growing, workers laid off from the Knoxville seat belt plant faced severe economic difficulties. In 1986, 170 of these laid-off hourly workers were surveyed when they

2. Observations about Aqua Prieta are based on a personal visit and interviews, Sept. 24–26, 1987.

applied for Trade Readjustment Act benefits, following the move of
the company to Mexico in 1985. The sample of displaced workers is
90 percent female, as are most apparel workers in the South. Their
racial characteristics reflect that of Knox County: only 14 percent are
black. They are older workers, with an average age of forty-six years.
About two-thirds live in the urban area of Knoxville, and the rest are
evenly divided between surrounding small towns and rural areas.
For about half, their job at Allied was the primary source of income
for their household, and a little fewer than half had dependents.

These workers did not fare well following the plant closing, despite their position in a Sunbelt state. Some fifteen months after
being laid off, 44 percent remained unemployed, although 92 percent reported attempting to find jobs elsewhere.

Of those workers who found new jobs, reemployment meant
downward mobility. Fewer than half were able to get full-time work;
53 percent were working at part-time jobs. Average wages dropped
from $5.76 an hour in the seat belt company to $3.70 an hour, a loss
of $2.06 an hour. When they worked at Allied, none of the workers
earned less than $5.00 an hour. For those who have obtained new
jobs, 91 percent are earning less than $5.00 an hour. The union jobs
they lost provided health care benefits. For 91 percent there is no
union at their new jobs, and only 48 percent are covered under a
health insurance plan.

Of the workers who have obtained new jobs, 28 percent found
work in other textile or garment plants. Most are doing sewing or
assembly work as they had at the seat belt company—but for
smaller firms, which pay less, are generally nonunion, and are located in rural areas. Another 34 percent obtained low-paying and
low-skill service jobs, mainly as cleaners, guards, or custodians, food
service workers, or child care or health care workers in workplaces
or people's homes. Some obtained jobs in other manufacturing industries or as sales clerks and cashiers in retail trade.

The impact of the layoffs has been especially severe on older
workers, women, and families with only one primary earner in the
household. To counter the hardships of displacement, workers have
turned to the informal economy and to traditional forms of survival,
made possible in part by the somewhat rural culture of the area.
After their unemployment benefits ran out, remarkably few of the
workers, only 18 percent of the total, drew food stamps. For many,
family and kin were a key to survival; spouses as well as extended
family members found extra jobs, sent money, or offered housing.
Within the region, workers, especially rural workers, historically

have turned to the land to raise food to supplement low wages and to survive hard times. Twenty-two percent of the workers interviewed reported that they gardened or farmed, often freezing or canning their produce. Many of these workers also turned to the informal economy to make a few extra dollars through odd jobs— making quilts, selling belongings at local flea markets, painting houses, or hawking magazine subscriptions.

But for many workers, this informal system has not provided protection against severe hardship. For instance, almost one-quarter of the workers faced large medical expenses while laid off. One woman, aged thirty-seven, had three teenaged children, all of whom had medical emergencies: one son broke his arm, and the other two were involved in car and motorcycle accidents. Facing a debt of $18,000, she had to declare bankruptcy.

Loss of income has also had an impact on housing. More than one-third of the workers interviewed had a mortgage on their homes, and almost one-quarter had monthly rent payments. No cases of foreclosure were reported, but some had to sell their homes and rent apartments or move in with relatives.

And they are not alone. Many workers with large medical bills or housing costs have gone into debt, used up their savings, worked extra jobs, or depended on relatives' help to meet their expenses. Many cut back on basic needs for themselves and their children— clothing, food, transportation, and electricity. Others have dipped into savings that were intended to provide for their security in the future. The uncertainties of unemployment or of working at minimum wage jobs take their toll in less tangible ways as well. Almost half (48 percent) of the workers reported psychological problems such as stress and depression.

Toward New Strategies

The case of the Allied workers is not unique. Displaced apparel and textile workers throughout the South face similar circumstances, as do hundreds of thousands of other manufacturing workers throughout the country who have fallen through the cracks of economic restructuring. Plant closings and layoffs have prompted warnings of "the deindustrialization of America" and have caused major disruptions in workers' lives and communities, ranging from long- and short-term unemployment and underemployment to foreclosures on homes and associated family and mental stress (Bluestone and Harrison 1982).

Until recently, however, the situation of displaced textile workers—relatively more of whom are female, black, and rural than their
counterparts in the steel or auto industries—had gone relatively un-
noticed in the national debate on plant closings. Their invisibility
resulted in part from the dominant image of the Sunbelt that
emerged in the 1970s as a bright spot on the national landscape,
where an economic boom offset the declining Frostbelt or Rustbelt
of the industrialized North.

In the late 1980s, however, a series of reports warned that plant
closings had become a significant economic problem for the South.
In "Shadows in the Sunbelt," MDC, a research firm in North Carolina, warned that "after two decades of reasonably solid growth,
many rural communities are now finding themselves in serious trouble" (1986, p. 4). Moreover, the traditional economic development
policy of luring industries such as textile plants from the North no
longer works. "The situation is analogous to the great buffalo hunts
of the last century. The stampede of plants to the South is definitely
over—especially for the rural areas that lack a skilled workforce,
transportation and cultural amenities. Yet the hunters continue in
their pursuit, hoping to bag one of the remaining hides" (MDC
1986, p. 10).

The end of the great stampede of textiles and other industries to
the South has created a problem for the economic development
strategies of the region. Labor-intensive industries that once might
have come to the South are now moving elsewhere, and many of the
region's traditional employers, such as textiles, are also fleeing.
Southern economic historian James Cobb has noted that "there is
grim irony in the fact that the South, having worked so diligently to
create a business climate attractive to footloose industries, should
now find its economic future threatened by an increase in industrial
mobility" (1986, p. 98).

If the deindustrialization of the textile South poses threats to the
traditional industrial recruitment strategy of economic development,
it also poses new challenges for southern textile workers. In a climate of plant closings, job blackmail becomes a potent force against
union organization and workers' demands. Labor must not only
fight defensive battles to save at-risk manufacturing jobs and hold
the line against wage and benefit concessions, it must simultaneously
organize new service sector and part-time jobs to obtain improved
wages and benefits.

Nationally, such organizations as the Tri-State Conference on
Steel, the Federation for Industrial Renewal, plant closing organiza-

tions, and others have met these challenges by joining with community groups and local policy makers in unified campaigns to press for passage of legislation that requires early warning of plant closings; to take over ailing plants and run them as worker- or community-owned enterprises; to get more involved in the economic development process by participating in local industrial boards, state economic development agencies, and economic development initiatives; and to establish coalitions with workers and communities in other parts of the country and in other countries to counter economic blackmail.

In Tennessee, the Amalgamated Clothing and Textile Workers Union (ACTWU) has begun to play such a role. In 1988, in response to the closings at Allied and other mills across the state, ACTWU's Georgia-Tennessee-Alabama Joint Board joined with the Commission on Religion in Appalachia and the Highlander Research and Education Center to form the Tennessee Industrial Renewal Network (TIRN). In June 1989, this labor, church, and community coalition held a conference in Chattanooga in the wake of several textile plant closings there. More than one hundred workers, policy makers, and church and community leaders attended, helping to launch TIRN as a statewide worker-community coalition to help address the issues of plant closings and economic development policy in the state. To date, TIRN and ACTWU have worked to teach workers how to spot the early warning signs of a plant closing and how to use the limited rights under the newly passed Worker Adjustment and Retraining Notification Act and the Economic Dislocation and Worker Adjustment Assistance Act. Following closings of the Thatcher plant in Chattanooga and the Furtex plant in Jacksboro, they explored avenues for saving plants through worker or other buyouts. Following the loss of hundreds of jobs with the closing of the Standard Knitting Mill, once Knoxville's largest employer, they demanded better job-training opportunities and organized to force the city government to intervene.

At the national level, ACTWU and other unions have helped lead the fight for plant closing laws and fairer and more coherent industrial policies. Slowly, too, ACTWU has moved beyond a stance of attempting to protect jobs through limiting imports to recognizing the need to press for international labor standards that reduce wage competition worldwide. At the Chattanooga conference, ACTWU's Vice-President John Hudson described the challenge:

How do we build the strength to make some of these changes? This is ultimately a question of how we as workers, communities

and victims get some political power, isn't it? First, we have to
agree that we can't do that unless we do it in coalition. None of us
is strong enough to do it alone; I think labor has begun to learn
that lesson after being bludgeoned for the last twenty years. We
have to identify those forces that should be able to coalesce, forge
a basis of unity among us, and in the case of plant closings, overcome the passivity and isolation that occurs when people lose
their jobs. . . .

There is a generation of workers now coming into their own
who want the union to be more than shopfloor nannies. They
want unions to stand for something, to put forward a vision of
what this country should be like. These workers want us to join
forces with others who share the same values both in this country
and around the world—community groups, religious organizations, civil rights groups. (Tennessee Industrial Renewal Network
1989, pp. 15–16)

Such initiatives represent a marked shift in the traditional role of
textile unions in the South. Changing economic and social conditions have thrust textile workers beyond traditional fights for a fair
share of the economic pie and for job protection on the shop floor
into new coalitions and new demands for a role in the economic
development process, at the local level and globally. From the closings of textile mills and the decline of communities in the South
may spring new seeds of economic democracy—seeds that must find
a way to grow in the rocky legacy of textile industry domination and
paternalism.

PART V

Conclusion

11

Facing Extinction?

Rhonda Zingraff

This industry has been dying for the last 40 years. It's like a dinosaur. First, the tail goes, then, the head. ("Takeover Fever" 1988, p. 2D)

R eaders of recent reports on the southern textile industry may be understandably skeptical or confused about the industry's future. Is it dying, or is it developing into a more modern and competitive industry? One headline says, "Factory's Shutdown Tears Fabric of Small Company Town" (Pyatt 1985). Another announces, "Takeover Fever Hits Reeling U.S. Textile Industry" (1988). But in the midst of such bleak reports, we also notice "Textile Industry Enjoying Revival" (Wayne 1988). These headlines hint at the rapid and far-reaching changes that have engulfed southern textiles, but they do not begin to convey the complexity of the situation. For a comprehensive picture, it is necessary to examine the relationships between mill workers and mill owners, between the mills and the towns, between the towns and the regional markets, and between the markets and the global economy.

These relationships are scrutinized by both historians and sociologists. We share a professional skepticism about analyses found in the mass media. We wonder what has been overlooked or what else should be investigated. A report that is short on description may mislead, regardless of intent. A description that lacks analysis may confuse, regardless of its accuracy.

An informed interpretation of the changing textile industry must join knowledge of its historical development with appraisals of its contemporary performance. The careful skeptic must follow the trail of class and community relationships to the beginning of cotton cultivation in the U.S. South. In particular, we must understand how the rural, agricultural context of the Old South, the organization of the early mill village, the gender-based labor distinctions, and the castelike racial division in the region reflected social forces of domination and subordination. In addition, we must analyze how these forces combined to nurture the industry's growth and its current problems.

The preceding chapters in this volume offer historical and sociological assessments of these complex and unfolding relations. From the initial concern with textile industrialization and labor recruitment, through the appraisal of paternalism and worker mobilization, to the final examination of contemporary problems, they recognize that forces for change and for social control are at work simultaneously. This chapter concentrates on current developments in southern textiles but first highlights the most salient background themes.

Development of the Southern Textile Industry

The history of textile manufacturing in the South as an adjunct to the production of cotton predates the Civil War (Mitchell 1921). The availability first of slave labor and later of wage labor made cheap by the vacillating markets for raw cotton attracted investment to cotton mills. When cotton prices fell, southern planters recognized that textile production could be a means of diversification as well as a strategy to counter New England's grip on the manufacture of goods. Likewise, when cotton prices were low, white labor was driven from the farm to the mill as a strategy to survive. Hoping for better market prices, farm families continued cultivation, while women and children worked in the mill. Because these families relied on both agricultural and industrial sources of income, mill owners could set wages for textile work below labor's minimal reproduction costs. As documented by Gullickson and Wood in this volume, this low-wage formula became the cornerstone of textile industrialization in the piedmont.

Mills operated on a small scale until the resurgence of the industry in the years following the Civil War. As early as 1846, however, William Gregg adopted an English practice by establishing the first mill village in Graniteville, South Carolina (Simpson 1948). This significant development constituted a physical and social symbiosis of mill and town. Adjacent to the mill would be housing for workers' families, stores for buying provisions, schools for basic education, and churches for worship. Mill villages remained oddities until post-war Reconstruction, but then, as Simon details in his chapter, they expanded rapidly until the 1920s.

During the post–Civil War period, mill villages were bolstered in their development by both financial and cultural forces in the war-torn South. The South was financially crippled, but recovery through indebtedness to the North was a loathsome prospect to those in the defeated Confederacy. For the South to "rise again," the use of local capital was much preferred. Thus local investments in mills and mill villages were viewed as a "civic virtue" (Wood 1986). Local chambers of commerce and newspapers encouraged community investment in cotton mills as dutiful and admirable. Small business proprietors and professionals responded by placing their savings in the service of their communities.

As mills came to dominate the southern economy, southerners became accustomed to linking the mills' prosperity with their own. The negative connotations of paternalism were dismissed by insisting that mills make better citizens and that better citizens make better families, schools, churches, and communities (Andrews 1987). Similarly, as Freeze explains earlier in this volume, paternalistic management has been viewed as a benevolent accommodation to the needs of a largely female labor force.

In addition to providing financial support to southern communities, the mills benefited from the socioeconomic distinctions characteristic of southern race relations. Mill villages attracted poor whites. Black labor was used in the mills only if there was a shortage of white labor, and black families were not allowed to live in mill villages. Thus the villages became close-knit white communities. Mill villages offered social and economic security to people unable to survive by farming and preserved a climate of racial stratification during the Jim Crow years for southern yeomen who held no other competitive advantage over blacks.

Class Domination in the Mill Villages

Mill villages secured post–Civil War patterns of racial subordination, but they also reflected the emerging structure of class domination. The struggles surrounding the accumulation of capital and the control of labor are partially unveiled by the contrasting accounts of mill village life and partially by the record of union activities.

Facing allegations that mill owners had exploited and abused mill worker families, the American Cotton Manufacturers Association supported a retrospective study in the 1940s of mill villages in an attempt to defend their value to the region (Simpson 1948). The mill village family, including children, worked at the mill. In the absence of child labor laws before the Great Depression, this arrangement was described by the mill owners as mutually beneficial, inasmuch as the entire family enjoyed the amenities and securities of the village community. The owners tried to develop "good" moral character by requiring workers to avoid alcohol, attend church, complete their basic schooling, and learn responsibility from intelligent men: "The cotton mill operative, not unlike thousands of others in this country, is negligent in planning his financial life and budgeting. Too many live on a day-to-day basis and, of course, often find themselves in embarassing (sic) financial conditions, with few places from which to secure the needed assistance" (Simpson 1948, p. 113).

The manufacturers association study explained that the mill villages, far from being exploitative, were actually a financial liability for the owners. Owners could have sold the houses to the workers to cut their own costs. They expected to provide the workers with improved citizenship and community ties via home ownership. "Sometimes this has been distasteful to the cottonmill operative, however, who as a renter enjoys mobility, and who prefers something of the life of a nomad" (Simpson 1948, p. 126).

What owners saw as negligent planning and nomadic tendencies others describe as functional autonomy. Oral histories indicate that the combination or alternation of farm and factory labor sustained a family's independence, which, by limiting worker subordination, frustrated the owners (Hall et al. 1986). Workers who used mill jobs to supplement farm income were inclined to leave the mill when they had earned enough to manage or had become sufficiently irritated by factory conditions. At times in the early stages of southern textile development, mills had to send agents out to recruit laborers. The recruiters carried promises of a cash payroll to the rural poor and unemployed, who were viewed as "sensitive, proud and stubborn people" (Andrews 1987, p. 15).

Workers who did not farm and who relied heavily on their mill wages sometimes evidenced a different sort of autonomy: they were prone to absenteeism or low productivity if their wages were sufficient to satisfy simple needs. Thus the welfare programs established in the mill villages were designed to heighten materialistic consumer interests and thereby increase the mill families' dependence on the wages only regular and consistent work would bring. Despite such efforts, worker autonomy continued to complicate labor control strategies. What finally provided textile manufacturers with abundant and reliably productive labor was the effect of the agricultural depression of the 1920s. Desperate for work, farming families flocked to textiles (Byerly 1986; Hall et al. 1986).

Between 1880 and 1929, profits in the mills were high, ranging from 30 to 75 percent, and the growth of capital in southern textiles enabled firms to compete successfully in national and international markets. The industry relocated from New England to the Southeast because of the regional differences in rates of surplus value. Northern firms were drawn to the labor benefits of the southern states, where no laws limited the labor of women and children and where unions were widely discredited as obstacles to economic growth. In the mill village, if a worker acted contrary to the employer's desires, everyone in the family could lose his or her job and be evicted from the mill village house. The reputation of mill workers as a "docile labor force" traces to the control landlord-bosses could exercise. This alleged docility, especially in light of unionization efforts, merits review as another feature of class domination.

Labor Unrest and Union Organizing Efforts

The Knights of Labor attempted to organize textile workers during the 1880s, and an American Federation of Labor (AFL) affiliate, the National Union of Textile Workers, tried to organize strikes around the turn of the century. These efforts were failures, owing to a combination of flawed leadership, desperate but not united workers, meager resources, and the absence of legal supports (Hodges 1986). Collective bargaining was not legally protected until the New Deal.

The National Recovery Act was intended to keep the lid on class antagonisms, but the industry responded to the Depression by finding ingenious ways to reduce labor costs. Putting mill hands on the stretch-out forced fewer individuals to operate more looms. Workers lost control over the pace of their work and with it the latitude for social relations in the mill. Franklin Roosevelt received letters from workers who described conditions in the mills in terms that resemble an exposé of white slavery (Hall et al. 1986). Meanwhile, the depression in southern agriculture intensified, blocking the earlier cohort's escape route to the farm. In this situation, the general strike by workers in the summer of 1934 stands as a staggering statement not of docility but of determination.

The strike was organized by the United Textile Workers, which had been formed by the AFL following the collapse in 1900 of the

NUTW. Within a few weeks, approximately four hundred thousand workers left the mills. The "docile labor force" virtually closed down the industry. Workers who remained on the job were described by one woman as more desperate, hardly content or docile: "It is true that every textile worker in the south would walk out of the mill today if they were not afraid of starvation. I don't *believe* that God intended people to suffer as we have suffered . . . the life of the average textile worker is a tragic thing" (Hall et al. 1986, pp. 281–82).

Mill executives and townspeople were panicked by the strike, and governors responded by imposing military control. The fourteen thousand troops dispatched in the Carolinas made clear with machine guns and bayonets which side state authority favored. The strike was over after twenty-two days, the activists were purged from the textile labor force, the unions lost credibility, the workers who remained on the payroll were demoralized, and the mill owners were provoked to rationalize further their strategies for production and labor control (Hall et al. 1986; Hodges 1986; Wood 1986). According to the president of the UTW, workers got "a raw deal instead of a New Deal" (Hodges 1986, p. 133).

Up until World War II, industry further strengthened itself by divestiture of the mill villages. New Deal legislation, such as the Fair Labor Standards Act, significantly reduced the regional wage differential in America, effectively increasing the costs of maintaining mill villages in the South. Workers were offered the "choice" of either purchasing their houses or leaving the mills. Home ownership in this context was established through wage withholding arrangements, which reduced industrial costs for both labor and capital. The breakup of mill communities undermined the social basis of worker unity and thus curtailed the likelihood of further challenges. Industrial expansion favored decentralized, rural locations, where underemployment and surplus agricultural labor offered enduring advantages for the accumulation of capital (Wood 1986).

Unionization was not entirely derailed by the catastrophe of 1934. With support from the Congress of Industrial Organizations (CIO), the Textile Workers Organizing Committee (TWOC) pressed on with an agenda for collective bargaining. The agenda was not well received, however. One organizer expressed his distress in especially vivid language: "The South, geographically and physically speaking, is a part of the United States of America. Socially speaking, it is separated considerably from the rest of the country by mountains of pride and rivers of prejudice and valleys of ignorance and swamps of reactionary stupidity and every now and then washed out with floods of lawlessness" (Hodges 1986, p. 38).

Trying always to gain a stronger foothold, the TWOC became an affiliate of the CIO in 1939 and was known thereafter as the Textile Workers Union of America. It was the TWUA that organized the 1958 Harriet-Henderson strike described by Frankel in this volume. The union emerged from the Henderson disaster deeply defeated but not quite dead. Sixteen years later, J. P. Stevens workers voted for TWUA representation in Roanoke Rapids, North Carolina. Merging with the Amalgamated Clothing Workers of America (ACWU), the TWUA became the Amalgamated Clothing and Textile Workers of America (ACTWU) in 1976 (Rowan and Barr 1987).

The textile industry was restructured as well, beginning with consolidations during the Depression. Firms enjoyed guaranteed profits during World War II via cost-plus government contracts. In the postwar decade, they emerged as major corporations, having accomplished wide-scale vertical integration of production with distribution and sales and horizontal integration through the acquisition of numerous small firms, especially in the South. The success of unionization drives in the North provided a reason for capital to flee, and southern leaders, eager to recruit industry, kept their promises of an inexpensive and unorganized labor supply (Johnson and Scurlock 1986b; Wood 1986). Southern state policies equated good government with the maintenance of right-to-work laws and the avoidance of capital-intensive, high-wage industry relocations to the region. By designing pro-industry tax incentive schemes, state governments revealed their active interdependence with the region's textile interests (Truchil 1988). By the end of the 1970s, the four largest corporations in North Carolina were Burlington Industries, Cannon Mills, J. P. Stevens, and Cone Mills, all low-wage, labor-intensive textile giants. The South had outgrown King Cotton, but its heirs had come of age and were about to grow unwieldy.

Transformation of the Southern Textile Industry

The textile industry grew to maturity by benefiting from the hardships of a predominantly rural, agricultural, racially divided population (Byerly 1986). Even as the paternalistic mill villages declined and the small, locally owned firms gave way to large, bureaucratic corporations, local communities remained dependent on the textile industry. This dependence brought benefits and costs. Farming families got needed jobs, although clearly they did not need brown lung

disease and exploitative working conditions. As the chapter by Judkins and Dredge explains, the threats to workers' health have been
serious, and compensation was not easily secured. Likewise, community developments, such as streets, housing, schools, hospitals, and
shopping centers, materialized out of the economic potential mills
created, but there is no doubt that single-industry towns are inher-
ently weak. Such communities are always at risk of being the industry's economic hostage. From a distance, the employment rates and
indicators of community growth suggest a relationship of reciprocal
advantage between the textile industry and the South, but the recent case of Ware Shoals, South Carolina, shows that workers have
clear cause to challenge the reciprocity thesis.

Ware Shoals was one of hundreds of small towns across the Carolinas whose destiny was entirely dependent on the company, in this
case the Riegel Textile Corporation. In 1982, eight hundred workers were laid off; in 1984, another nine hundred were laid off; by
the end of 1985, after eighty years of operation, the firm shut
down. For the citizens of this community, there followed not only
severe unemployment but also mortgage foreclosures, empty stores,
an eroding tax base, and outmigration of the residents who would
have otherwise provided a vital small town population. Older members of the community, those over age fifty, found themselves in especially hopeless circumstances. Using a pickup truck to operate a
vegetable stand at a local service station, one couple explained how
inadequate weekly unemployment compensation was to finance job
hunting elsewhere. The collapse of this local economy left hundreds
of families in a local trap (Pyatt 1985).

Details from a single community, however, cannot convey the scope
of the changes during the 1980s. A *New York Times* article in 1987
reported that, in the preceding decade, eight hundred textile plants
had disappeared (Barmash 1987). Government records documented
the loss of 700,000 jobs nationally in textiles between 1972 and 1984.
In the first half of the 1980s alone, 242,000 jobs were lost, 38,200 of
them in North Carolina and 6,200 in Virginia (Mayfield 1985). Industry experts disagreed on where to place the blame, but all expected
continued job losses (Office of Technology Assessment 1987).

In Ware Shoals, the Riegel Textile Corporation blamed imports.
The AFL-CIO has a rule of thumb, not accepted by the Labor Department, that every $1 billion gap in imports over exports means a
loss of twenty-five thousand jobs in this country (Johnston 1985).
Testimony from numerous sources suggests that this formula is accurate and especially applicable to textiles. Why? Because "virtually

every nation in the world has at least a rudimentary textile industry—in order to serve its domestic market, provide jobs, and earn
foreign exchange" (Office of Technology Assessment 1987, p. 81).

Increasingly, the fates of textiles and apparels are intertwined.
Domestic textile production suffers a direct blow to demand as the
supply of imported apparel reduces the market for domestic apparel. Likewise, domestic apparel workers may retain some jobs by
way of the containment of materials costs made possible with imported textiles. Interestingly, in some areas of the South, workers
laid off from textiles have sought employment in local apparel
firms. Reports of developments in the apparel industry thus become
more and more germane to the analysis of southern textiles.

In China, for example, textile exports have become the most important source of hard currency, and China's national goals for
modernization of textiles include matching Western levels of production in the next few years ("China Pushes Textile Automation"
1988). The effect of escalating international production is further
compounded by the differential in labor costs: "At $6.71 per hour
in 1985, a full-time U.S. textile mill products worker earned just under $14,000 per year; in contrast, his/her average hourly earnings
were more than 33 times higher than a comparable Chinese worker
earning 20 cents per hour. At $5.73 per hour in 1985, a full-time
U.S. apparel worker earned just under $12,000 per year, but that
was approximately 28 times more than the comparable Chinese
worker earning 20 cents per hour" (Office of Technology Assessment 1987, p. 87).

Comparisons such as these led the Office of Technology Assessment of the U.S. Congress (1987) to report that for every billion
yards of fabric and apparel imported, one hundred thousand American job opportunities are lost. The *Economist* published a graph in
1986 showing the import-export deficits for the industry. It was entitled "In Tatters: America's Textiles and Clothing." With a yearly
increase in imports of 17 percent since 1980 and a yearly domestic
market growth of only 2 percent, the reason for such pessimism is
obvious ("America's Textile Industry" 1986, p. 80).

The threat from imports is not new. At a 1901 dinner meeting
of the Southern Manufacturers Club in Charlotte, North Carolina,
the speaker's topic was "The Oriental Question." The concern at the
time was raw cotton from China (Walker 1985). Decades later, in
1935, textile industrialists persuaded President Roosevelt to establish an agreement with Japan for a voluntary limit on Japanese exports. The need for such an agreement evaporated during and

immediately after World War II, when the United States had the
only major intact textile industry in the world. By the mid-1950s, a
resurgence of production in Japan led the United States to seek another export quota agreement. Japan cooperated, but others eager
for international trade advantages did not agree to limits (Brandis
1979). Hong Kong, in particular, became a source of imports of
such volume that today it heads the list, followed by China, Taiwan,
Korea, and Japan (Johnston 1985). For women's and children's apparel, Sri Lanka must be included as well (Reid 1986).

Comparative figures over time indicate the degree of import penetration. In the mid-1950s, 5 percent of women's and children's apparel sold in the U.S. market were imported; by the mid-1980s, the
figure had risen to 52 percent. The International Ladies' Garment
Workers' Union (ILGWU) has lost fully half its membership in the
last two decades (Reid 1986). During that same time, textile product
imports increased 428 percent (Rowan and Barr 1987, p. 20). The
Amalgamated Clothing and Textile Workers Union insists that international trade developments have had a greater effect on textile
workers than on any other group (Walker 1985). Expressing essen-
tial agreement with the union on this point, Ellison S. McKissick, Jr.,
president of the American Textile Manufacturers Institute, wrote to
the *Wall Street Journal* in 1985 that three hundred thousand jobs had
been lost since 1980 in fibers, textiles, and apparel because of one-
way trading. The American Dream, argued McKissick, cannot be
fulfilled in the Far East (1985, p. 25E).

Efforts to control the flow of imports have continued, but they
have been insufficient to offset a steady loss of strength in the domestic industry. President John F. Kennedy called for an agreement
in 1961; President Lyndon Johnson followed suit in 1967; and the
Multifiber Act (MFA), passed in 1974 under President Gerald Ford,
is still in force, although it is widely violated. In 1986, President
Ronald Reagan vetoed legislation designed specifically to protect
the textile industry from import imbalances, to the jeers of textile
industry interests but to the cheers of free trade advocates (Krueger
1987; Toner 1986), who argue that quotas and tariffs raise prices for
U.S. consumers. For every job protected in this country by import
controls, the American public is said to pay $86,000 in excess con-
sumer costs. By this logic, protectionist laws are outrageous and the
jobs they are designed to save, with wages below $7.00 per hour, are
hardly worth the cost. Workers should not have difficulty finding
other work at a similarly low wage ("The Great Textile Robbery"
1987). It would be interesting to introduce advocates of this view-

point to the South Carolina couple selling vegetables from the back of their pickup truck.

An analysis published by the Southern Regional Council in Atlanta in 1986 explained that "the climate for workers in the sunny south is rather chilly" (Marshall 1986, p. 2). Growing numbers of people are working full time, year-round and are earning below poverty wages. States in the Southeast offer the least protection for workers and have the greatest percentage of poor households of any region in the country (Johnson and Scurlock 1986b). North Carolina was one of six states recognized in a 1988 Senate Budget Committee report for undergoing "downward wage polarization" because of the growth in jobs paying below poverty-level wages ("Low-Paying Jobs on the Rise" 1988). Consequently, the prospects for thousands of workers laid off by the textile industry, albeit from low-wage jobs, must be recognized as grim. In particular, production workers, approximately 68 percent of the textile labor force, are extremely vulnerable to losses of both income and dignity. Because of their low levels of training and skill, their best prospects are probably absorption into the less desirable positions in the service sector (Brannon et al. 1986). Their worst prospects, of course, are chronic unemployment and personal impoverishment. The case study by Gaventa and Smith and the analysis of displaced workers by Penn and Leiter in this volume reveal precisely how costly plant closings can be for workers.

The debates about imports, labor costs, job losses, and plant shutdowns are matched by angry charges and countercharges about mill management, modernization, and mergers (Office of Technology Assessment 1987). In language strikingly similar to descriptions of decline in the domestic steel and auto industries, analysts claim that textile problems have been "self-inflicted" ("America's Textile Industry" 1986, p. 79). Flawed choices about investments and production, they say, have seriously weakened the domestic industry during a time when it was faced with increasing competition from abroad. While Asian exporters were moving toward more capital-intensive production because they recognized that even cheaper labor costs elsewhere were undercutting their advantage in world markets, the American textile industry was averse to reinvesting its profits in research and development or in plant modernization. Of all the jobs lost by American workers, estimates are that only one-third of them were attributable to imports; the other two-thirds were allegedly the result of technological backwardness (Ezell 1987). Additionally, production for maximum quantity instead of maximum flexibility has backfired. Few buyers are interested in fabric rolls of thirty-five hundred yards; many buyers, especially for the fashion market, seek hundred-yard rolls. Thus, though industry leaders complain about predatory pricing and dumping, blaming the government for failure to protect them, their own laggard practices may explain their decline ("America's Textile Industry" 1986).

By the mid-1980s there were obvious signs that the industry was struggling to close the technological gap. Bonham's contribution to this volume explains the managerial choices involved in belatedly matching textile technology to market requirements. Through the adoption of shuttleless or air-jet looms and automated guided vehicles, some plants began a drive to modernize as their path to salvation. Computerization enables producers to adopt a "quick response" system, wherein enhanced communication between textile and apparel manufacturers and retail outlets facilitates rapid adjustments to changing needs and tastes in the market. Furthermore, producers may keep a low inventory to avoid risks of overstocking, while cutting the time from order to delivery by two-thirds (Friedman 1987). Modernization, however, requires billions of dollars industrywide and is an option only financially strong companies can consider. While "marginal" companies perish, larger, more diversified corporations restructure (Rowan and Barr 1987; Office of Technology Assessment 1987; Wayne 1988). While workers were pleading for consumers to "buy American," the industry, ironically, was buying machinery made in Japan, Germany, Belgium, Switzerland, and Italy to reduce labor requirements. A motto for the leadership in the textile industry might be "buy foreign and fire American" (Clendinen 1985, p. 8L).

Apparel production is not as amenable to automation as textiles, but new technologies can help "reduce the labor time per garment and cut down on the operator/equipment ratio in the production process" (U.S. Department of Commerce 1986, pp. 43–44). Consequently, while the "Crafted with Pride in America" slogan was appearing on the airwaves of the United States to promote consumer awareness and the Textile Fiber Products Identification Act was amended to ensure that advertisements and catalogs would identify product origins, the industry was seeking to escape from American labor costs by automation and increased reliance on overseas assembly of fabric cut in the United States. Indeed, the future of the apparel industry, according to experts, must be high-technology, capital-intensive, twenty-four-hours-a-day, seven-days-a-week production, and in this scenario a large work force is viewed as a signal of company weakness (Walker 1985).

Without losing sight of displaced workers, it is also important to consider the plight of currently employed workers. Placing workers on short-time and stretch-out simultaneously reduces their earnings while increasing their productivity. Government figures confirm that labor productivity in the industry has been increasing though wages have fallen. When Hanes raised the production rate for employees in Sparta, North Carolina, for example, productivity improved, but 40 percent of the workers took home less money. Many of these same workers also went home with tendinitis and carpal tunnel syndrome (Schoonmaker 1985). The earnings potential for workers who retain their jobs is complicated by changes in the regional economy. Some projections were for personnel improvements and income gains based on the growth of more capital-intensive and better-paying industries in the Sunbelt (Rowan and Barr 1987). Yet the clearer pattern in the South is the growth of low-paying, low-quality jobs. The terms of this labor market appear to favor the buyer far more than the seller.

Unionization is one response that might be expected of beleaguered workers. Union drives in southern textiles, however, have yielded few successes and many painfully divisive defeats. The six-year battle waged by J. P. Stevens after workers in Roanoke Rapids, North Carolina, had voted for ACTWU as their representative illustrates the industry's intransigence regarding unionization. Even as the company was being cited by the National Labor Relations Board as the worst violator of labor laws in the nation's history, it was spending millions of dollars to avoid signing a contract with ACTWU. Unlike previous union struggles in the South, no one died because of the hostilities, but the sense of sacrifice was high and the gains were meager (Serrin 1985). Nonetheless, during the dark days of the mid-1980s, faced with the stretch-out and reduced buying power, Cannon workers mobilized for an election. The company's new owner, David Murdock, a financier from California, threatened the workers that the cost of a union contract to the corporation would force him to sell. Murdock assured employees at the time that with perseverance, together, without a union, Cannon would remain profitable and their jobs would be secure (figure 11.1 contains Murdock's letter to employees). Clearly afraid that Murdock would sell, workers vetoed the union. A few weeks later, Murdock sold nearly all of Cannon to Fieldcrest.

FIGURE 11.1.   Text of Letter to Cannon Mills Employees

August 8, 1985

DEAR CANNON EMPLOYEES:

I am pleased that one of the problems you and I have had to endure since last July will soon come to an end. As we have encouraged them to do repeatedly, ACTWU has finally filed their petition for a union election at Cannon. At long last, you will have the opportunity to say, "NO, now go away and leave us alone!" I repeat my statement made to you in my July 23, 1984 letter when ACTWU distributed their first propaganda: "The company's position is clear—*we are absolutely opposed to unionization* as Cannon Mills believes the best way to provide maximum employment opportunity and security to Cannon employees is for management and employees to communicate and work together to give customers the best possible service and highest quality products." My position will never change.

You know without my telling you, that Cannon, in particular, and the textile industry, in general, is in serious trouble. Our market base has been invaded by imports. And, our international business has fallen from $55 million four years ago to less than $24 million in 1984 because of the strength of the U.S. dollar abroad. There was only a certain amount of business to be had by all American textile manufacturers; now there is even less because imports from low-wage countries continue to pour in. In spite of all of our efforts, our government has done nothing to stem the tide of imports, and, despite their claims, ACTWU has not been very successful or effective in fighting them. In order to try to save their companies, other manufacturers who formerly marketed apparel, decorative fabrics, industrial fabrics, etc., are invading Cannon's markets in towels, sheets, bedspreads and the other products we make. So, we now have more domestic competition for our markets in addition to that from imports.

Cannon, as well as other domestic textile manufacturers, has attempted to reverse the impact of imports by intensive capital investments for overall improvements, reorganizing and downsizing, and working closely with employees to reduce costs and improve efficiencies. There have even been some mergers of textile companies, and will undoubtedly be more, as well as major restructuring of others, all designed to form stronger and more competitive companies. I have followed this trend with interest and have, in fact, had discussions with several major textile companies concerning the advantages of combining financial resources of our respective businesses with the goal of forming a stronger, more competitive company able to compete with foreign and domestic companies and provide the retention of a maximum number of textile jobs for our employees. The union says a sale of Cannon is taking place and a new owner will soon take over. *This is*

absolutely not true. As stated, I have discussed merger with several textile companies, but none of these talks has resulted in a possible combination which, in my opinion, would benefit all of us, and such talks
have ended. For our mutual benefit and protection, I have no choice
except to continue to explore all opportunities for Cannon to emerge
as a stronger company with a business we can all rely upon to provide
stability and future job security.

One of my goals since coming to Cannon has been to improve the
quality of life for employees and persons in the plant communities. I
believe, as the saying goes, "actions speak louder than words," and I
have put my words into action at Cannon. I have actively supported
the new Senior Citizens Center—area parks—the new library now
under construction—Cannon Memorial YMCA and Community Center for which ground was broken on July 19. I have also spent millions
of dollars to revitalize Kannapolis into Cannon Village and bring
more business into the area for everyone. In addition, in 1984 Cannon contributed more than $380,000 to United Ways, not including
amounts already committed to the building programs previously mentioned, and continues its support this year. Has ACTWU demonstrated its interest in you or your quality of life in such a manner? I
think not.

Cannon Mills Company is not operating profitably at the present
time. In fact, I have put an additional $12 million of my own funds
into the company during 1985. I have directed the financial people to
pull exact figures together and we will be giving you detailed information about our operating profits.

I ask that you seriously consider this important decision and not
allow ACTWU to divide us at a time when, more than ever, we need
to work together and have confidence in each other. Mutual trust and
respect is the only way a team can be successful. Working together we
have made a lot of progress.

I am strongly and totally opposed to this union coming in because
they have nothing worthwhile to offer you. I have no intention of see-
ing this union come in here and tear down what you and I are trying
to build. I hope you feel the same way.

David H. Murdock

ac

Mergers and speculative investments in the industry have been al-
tering the labor market across the Southeast. The costs associated
with modernization and the losses from imports have resulted in
heavy debts even for the major firms. These debts were managed,
in some cases, through mergers and selective plant closings or sales.
In 1983, there were fifteen major publicly held textile enterprises in

the United States; five years later there were three: West Point Pepperell in Georgia, Fieldcrest Cannon in North Carolina, and Springs
Industries in South Carolina.

Burlington Industries, which had been the nation's largest textile
firm, negotiated a leveraged buyout in September 1987. The sale to
management, backed by Morgan Stanley, had several important consequences. It further reduced the number of publicly held companies in the domestic textile industry, a trend that has been viewed
with alarm because the shift of decision making away from public
shareholders typically shifts the concern from productivity to speculative financing and debt management (Bruck 1989). Not only does
this reduce public accountability, it also results in widespread sales of
productive assets and job losses. In Burlington's case, the buyer expected to raise $900 million from the sale of Burlington businesses
and assets ("Morgan Stanley-Led Group Buys Burlington" 1987).
Even before the completion of the buyout, in July 1987, 525 jobs
were eliminated, involving all departments in the Greensboro,
North Carolina, headquarters, and the entire research and development center in Jamestown, North Carolina, was closed ("Burlington
to Cut 525 Jobs" 1987).

J. P. Stevens, another of the long-standing giants, was also purchased, by West Point Pepperell, and then sold off in pieces to satisfy corporate debts ("Takeover Fever" 1988). West Point Pepperell
has since been bought for $1.56 billion by William Farley, who al-
ready held controlling stock in Fruit of the Loom and whose plans
for West Point Pepperell are to divest $1.3 billion in assets in less
than two years. He needs the money to cover interest payments on
debts from his other companies ("Farley Plans Major Sales" 1989).
Only time will tell if a similar fate awaits the remaining "dinosaurs."
According to a report issued by the Office of Technology Assessment, "An industry of many small firms is giving way to oligopolistic
markets, or at least to monopolistic competition. A large number of
firms engaging in price competition with similar if not identical
markets is a fading economic possibility for the U.S.-based industry"
(1987, p. 33). One analyst argued that the government should alter
its antitrust laws and let firms "cooperate" rather than compete.
They could then establish productive networks, reduce unemployment, raise wages, and strengthen exports, just as firms in Europe
have done (Eldersheim 1989).

The mastermind of the J. P. Stevens buyout was a thirty-six-year-
old financial wizard who had never been in the plants or met any of
the people whose lives were embedded in the mills and the towns.

The youthful Thomas C. Foley negotiated solely with Whitney Stevens, the great-great-grandson of the founder of the company, whose final annual salary was $754,000. As a result of their deal, Stevens received severance benefits worth $2.0 million and sold his stock for $12.2 million. "Foley acknowledges he knows little about piloting a textile company, in part because he has spent most of his career buying and selling companies rather than running them" (Kenneson 1988, p. 5I).

Men like Foley, Farley, and Murdock may embody something fearsome or something magnificent about the spirit of American enterprise, depending on one's point of view. Such men may also represent a sharp edge in the political economy of the late twentieth century. This could be a competitive edge internationally, but as a structural edge domestically, it has increased fortunes and undercut lives. It may yet sever the remaining threads by which the textile industry dangles.

Is textile production in the United States facing extinction? Has the tail gone to be followed by the head? Analysts in the nation's capital now describe textiles as a "sunset industry" (Reid 1986). With the international trade in consumer goods, societies need not plan for domestic production of all their supplies. Perhaps the textile industry is losing its niche in the modern American landscape, just as the dinosaurs lost theirs in prehistoric times.

Executives of the industry insist that they do have a future in the United States. Evolution into a capital-intensive oligopoly may save this dinosaur (Walker 1985). Recent data support this view. In 1985, industrial production was 31.2 percent higher than in 1967, even with sizable employment losses (Rowan and Barr 1987, p. 9). Similarly, 1986 and 1987 were the two best years ever for profits and volume (Wayne 1988). The modernization that may be credited for this performance, however, has cost communities and workers dearly and has encumbered firms with debts that may not be manageable without a continued frenzy of corporate, and often foreign, buyouts. Indeed, the reactive, ad hoc conduct of the U.S. government in these affairs leaves the fate of textiles and apparel in America deeply dependent on decisions made by other governments (Office of Technology Assessment 1987). Could extortion rather than extinction be the fear of the future?

Sometimes the disruption of families, communities, and markets seems so threatening that fears cannot be clearly focused. An atmosphere of crisis develops, and the outcome remains uncertain to the actors on the stage. Each time society undergoes major shifts in production, "there are cries of despair from those who prefer the status quo, and cries of hope from the left. Each sees the old primary industries in trouble, and so foresees the end of capitalism and of the world order which it has built. And each time, there are losers, but also winners. . . . Not only workers, but the owners and managers of the old, established industries complain most loudly, and the regions in which they are located suffer most" (Chirot 1986, p. 223).

From this broad perspective, the hardships faced by the textile communities of the South are the inevitable growing pains of an increasingly dynamic and sophisticated global economy. Alternatively, the hardships of textile and apparel workers around the globe call the whole calculus of change into question: which people in which regions are actually suffering the most; are the fates of southern U.S. textile workers tied to the fates of their employers or to the fates of other, far distant workers in the global community? Commenting on our "postindustrial" social order in *The Great U-Turn*, Harrison and Bluestone observe that our enterprises have been "merged and acquired, downsized, deindustrialized, multinationalized, automated, streamlined, and restructured" and that the blunt results are that "the rich have gotten richer, the poor poorer, and life for the middle class more and more precarious" (1988, p. 22). This trend is apparent domestically and internationally. A good deal more than the southern textile industry could be hanging by a thread.

References

Abrams, Philip. 1982. *Historical Sociology*. Ithaca: Cornell University Press.

Acheson, T. W. 1985. "The National Policy and the Industrialization of the Maritimes, 1880–1910." In *Atlantic Canada after Confederation*, edited by P. A. Buckner and David Frank, pp. 176–201. Fredericton, N.B.: Acadiensis Press.

Adams, Edith. Interview by Linda Frankel. Southern Oral History Project, Southern Historical Collection, University of North Carolina, Chapel Hill.

"AM '84: Bringing Automation to Textiles." 1984. *America's Textiles* (May): 19, 22.

"America's Textile Industry: Holding Its Salvation in Its Own Hands." 1986. *Economist*, April 5–11, pp. 79–82.

Andrews, Mildred Gwin. 1987. *The Men and the Mills: A History of the Southern Textile Industry*. Macon, Ga.: Mercer University Press.

Applewhite, Marjorie M. 1954. "Sharecropper and Tenant in the Courts of North Carolina." *North Carolina Historical Review* 31: 134–49.

Archives Départementales de la Seine Maritime (ADSM)

    6MP5110: Description of the Department, *an* IX

    6MP5122: Cotton Industry, *an* X (1801–2), 1809

    6MP5154: Departmental Reports on Manufacturing, 1855; Parish and Civil Registers, 1751–1850

    L367: Enumerated Census, Canton of Auffay, *an* IV (1796)

    6M23: Enumerated Census, Canton of Totes, 1841

    6M64: Enumerated Census, Canton of Totes, 1846

    6M83: Enumerated Census, Canton of Totes, 1851

    6M1100: Industrial Census, Seine-Infèrieure, 1847

    Civil Registers, Auffay, 1801–50

    Municipal Council Records, Auffay, 1832–50

Archives Nationales (AN)

    F12 560: M. Latapie, "Réflexions préliminaires sur un mémoire intitulé Voyage de Rouen ou observations sur l'état actuel des arts et manufactures de Rouen, Elbeuf, Louviers, Evreux et Andely faites dans le mois de mai, juin et juillet 1773"

F12 650: M. Goy, Inspecteur des Manufactures à Rouen, Rapport, 1782

F12 4705: Child Labor Reports, Rouen, 1837

F12 4713: Factory Inspectors Reports, Rouen, 1843

F12 4755, 4722, 4719: Responses to proposed revisions in the 1841 child labor law, Rouen, 1867

F12 4476C: Industrial Census, Seine-Infèrieure, 1847

"Are You Doing Enough on Quick Response?" 1988. *Textile World* (May): 49–50, 52, 56, 59.

Arnett, Ethel Stephens. 1955. *Greensboro, North Carolina: The County Seat of Guilford*. Chapel Hill: University of North Carolina Press.

Atkinson, J., and N. Meager. 1986. *Changing Working Patterns*. London: National Economic Development Office.

Avery, David, and Gene D. Sullivan. 1985. "Changing Patterns: Reshaping the Southeastern Textile-Apparel Complex." *Economic Review of the Federal Reserve Board of Atlanta* 70: 34–38.

Baldwin, J. A. 1899. "Mills and Morals." *Southern and Western Textile Excelsior* 6 (Dec. 17).

Balliett, Carl J. 1925. *World Leadership in Denims: Through Thirty Years of Progress*. Baltimore: Proximity Manufacturing Co.

"Bar-coding—Textiles Takes a Closer Look." 1985. *Textile World* (Nov.): 40–41.

Barmash, Isadore. 1987. "Merger Talk in Textiles." *New York Times*, Aug. 21 (late ed.), p. D4.

Barrett, Bob. 1967. "Robbins Plans New Unit in Knoxville." *Knoxville News Sentinal*, Oct. 30, p. A1.

Beatty, Bess. 1984. "Textile Labor in the North Carolina Piedmont: Mill Owner Images and Mill Worker Response, 1830–1900." *Labor History* 25: 485–503.

——. 1986. "The Edwin Holt Family: Nineteenth Century Capitalists in North Carolina." *North Carolina Historical Review* 63: 511–35.

Beaulieu, Lionel J. 1988. *The Rural South in Crisis: Challenges for the Future*. Boulder, Colo.: Westview Press.

Bell, Daniel. 1974. *The Coming of Post-Industrial Society*. London: Heinemann.

Bendix, Reinhard. 1974. *Work and Authority in Industry: Ideologies of Management in the Course of Industrialization*. Berkeley: University of California Press.

Benson, Susan Porter. 1988. *Counter Cultures: Saleswomen, Managers, and Customers in American Department Stores, 1890–1940*. Urbana: University of Illinois Press.

Berberoglu, Berch. 1987. *The Internationalization of Capital*. New York: Praeger.

Berkstresser, Gordon A., III. 1987. Personal communication. Raleigh: School of Textiles, North Carolina State University.

Berman, Dan. 1978. *Death on the Job*. New York: Monthly Review Press.

Bernstein, Irving. 1960. *The Lean Years: A History of the American Worker, 1920–1933*. Boston: Houghton Mifflin.

Billings, Dwight B., Jr. 1979. *Planters and the Making of a "New South": Class, Politics, and Development in North Carolina, 1865–1900.* Chapel Hill: University of North Carolina Press.
Billings, Dwight B., Jr., and Kathleen M. Blee. 1986. "Bringing History Back In: The Historicity of Social Relations." In *Current Perspectives in Social Theory*, vol. 7, edited by John Wilson and Scott G. McNall, pp. 51–68. Greenwich, Conn.: JAI Press.
Blauner, Robert. 1964. *Alienation and Freedom: The Factory Worker and His Industry.* Chicago: University of Chicago Press.
Bluestone, Barry, and Bennett Harrison. 1982. *The Deindustrialization of America: Plant Closings, Community Abandonment, and the Dismantling of Basic Industry.* New York: Basic Books.
Bode, Frederick A., and Donald E. Ginter. 1986. *Farm Tenancy and the Census in Antebellum Georgia.* Athens: University of Georgia Press.
Bonham, Julia C. 1986. "American Society in the Age of Advanced Automation: Trends and Prospects." In *Automation and Robotics in the Textile and Apparel Industries*, edited by Gordon A. Berkstresser, III, and David Buchanan, pp. 275–328. Park Ridge, N.J.: Noyes Publications.
Bookman, Ann, and Sandra Morgen, eds. 1988. *Women and the Politics of Empowerment.* Philadelphia: Temple University Press.
Bouloiseau, M. M. 1956. "Aspects socieaux de la crise cotonnière dans les campagnes rouennaises en 1788–1789." *Actes de 81ᵉ Congrès National des Sociétés Savantes, Rouen-Caen, 1956.* Paris: Presses Universitaires de France.
Boyte, Harry. 1972. "The Textile Industry: Keel of Southern Industrialization." *Radical America* 6 (2): 4–49.
Brandis, R. Buford. 1979. "Textile Import Quotas: A Short History." American Textile Manufacturing Institute, International Trade Division Report. May.
Brannon, Yevonne, Rick Shields, John Hice, Arthur Fahrner, Robert Fearn, and Jack Wilson. 1986. "Employment and Training Needs of N.C. Textile Workers." Raleigh: Center for Urban Affairs and Community Services, North Carolina State University.
Braudel, Fernand. 1980. "History and Sociology." In *On History*, edited by Fernand Braudel, pp. 64–82. Chicago: University of Chicago Press.
Braverman, Harry. 1974. *Labor and Monopoly Capital: The Degradation of Work in the Twentieth Century.* New York: Monthly Review Press.
Brenner, Robert. 1977. "The Origins of Capitalist Development: A Critique of Neo-Smithian Marxism." *New Left Review* 104: 25–92.
Briggs, Martha Tune. 1975. "Mill Owners and Mill Hands in an Antebellum North Carolina County." M.A. thesis, University of North Carolina, Chapel Hill.
Brody, Charlotte. 1981. Interview by Bennett Judkins, March 8, Raleigh, North Carolina.
Bruck, Connie. 1989. "The World of Business: The Old Boy and the New Boys." *New Yorker*, May 8, pp. 81–96.

Buchanan, David. 1986. "Directions of Technological Change in the Fiber,
    Textile and Apparel Industry." In *Automation and Robotics in the Textile and
    Apparel Industries*, edited by Gordon A. Berkstresser, III, and David
    Buchanan, pp. 189–222. Park Ridge, N.J.: Noyes Publications.
Burawoy, Michael. 1979. *Manufacturing Consent: Changes in the Labor Process
    under Monopoly Capitalism*. Chicago: University of Chicago Press.
"Burlington to Cut 525 Jobs at Two Sites." 1987. *New York Times*, July 7 (late
    ed.), p. D4.
Bustamente, Jorge A. 1983. "Maquiladoras: A New Face of International
    Capitalism on Mexico's Northern Border." In *Women, Men, and the New
    International Division of Labor*, edited by June Nash and Maria Patricia
    Fernandez-Kelly, pp. 224–56. Albany: State University of New York
    Press.
Byerly, Victoria. 1986. *Hard Times Cotton Mill Girls: Personal Histories of Wom-
    anhood and Poverty in the South*. Ithaca: ILR Press.
Byrd, Richard H. 1986. "OTTO +2 = QR at BI." *Textile World* (Feb.): 61,
    63, 64.
Cabarrus County. 1843. Records of the Pleas and Quarter Sessions of the
    County Court, Concord. North Carolina State Archives, Raleigh.
Cahill, Cornelius. 1987. "The Textile Automation Puzzle: Fitting the Pieces
    Together." *America's Textiles International* 16 (April): 26–27.
Calavita, Kitty. 1983. "The Demise of the Occupational Safety and Health
    Administration: A Case of Symbolic Action." *Social Problems* 30: 437–48.
Calhoon, Robert M. 1979. "A Troubled Culture: North Carolina in the New
    Nation." In *Writing North Carolina History*, edited by J. J. Crow and Larry
    E. Tise, pp. 76–110. Chapel Hill: University of North Carolina Press.
Canada. 1885. "Reports Relative to Manufacturing Industries in Existence
    in Canada." House of Commons *Sessional Papers*, 37, 37a.
———. 1912. *Census of Canada 1911*. Vol. 4. Ottawa: Office of the Census.
———. 1938. Royal Commission on the Textile Industry, *Report*. Ottawa:
    King's Printer.
Carlton, David L. 1982. *Mill and Town in South Carolina, 1880–1920*. Baton
    Rouge: Louisiana State University Press.
Carnoy, Martin, and Derek Shearer. 1980. *Economic Democracy*. White Plains,
    N.Y.: M. E. Sharpe.
Carrigan, John Warren. 1843–62. Family Papers, Manuscripts Department,
    Perkins Library, Duke University, Durham, N.C.
Cash, Wilbur J. 1941. *The Mind of the South*. New York: Knopf.
Cauchois, André. 1929. *Démographie de la Seine-Inférieure*. Rouen: Laine.
Cecil-Fronsman, Bill. 1983. "The Common Whites: Class and Culture in
    Antebellum North Carolina." Ph.D. dissertation, University of North
    Carolina, Chapel Hill.
Census of the United States. 1860. Population Schedule Manuscripts, North
    Carolina State Archives, Raleigh.
Chafe, William H. 1980. *Civilities and Civil Rights*. New York: Oxford Uni-
    versity Press.

Chandler, Alfred D., Jr. 1977. *The Visible Hand: The Managerial Revolution in American Business.* Cambridge: Belknap Press of Harvard University Press.

"China Pushes Textile Automation." 1988. *Raleigh News and Observer*, May 1, p. 5I.

Chirot, Daniel. 1977. *Social Change in the Twentieth Century.* New York: Harcourt Brace Jovanovich.

————. 1986. *Social Change in the Modern Era.* San Diego: Harcourt Brace Jovanovich.

Christiansen, L. A. 1985. "QR—PDQ!" *Textile World* (Nov.): 15.

————. 1986. "Business as Usual?" *Textile World* (April): 15.

————. 1987a. "ITMA: Lights-Out Manufacturing?" *Textile World* (May): 15.

————. 1987b. "Automation: The Hidden Plusses." *Textile World* (Aug.): 15.

————. 1987c. "Needed: A Forum on How Machines Communicate." *Textile World* (Oct.): 15.

————. 1988a. "ATMI 'New Generation' President Takes Charge." *Textile World* (March): 43–44, 47–48.

————. 1988b. "Technology Bottleneck: People?" *Textile World* (May): 15.

Clark, Daniel James. 1989. "The TWUA in a Sourthern Mill Town: What Unionization Meant in Henderson, North Carolina." Ph.D. dissertation, Duke University.

Clark, Gregory. 1987. "Why Isn't the Whole World Developed? Lessons from the Cotton Mills." *Journal of Economic History* 47: 141–73.

Clark, Peter B., and James Q. Wilson. 1961. "Incentive Systems: A Theory of Organizations." *Administrative Science Quarterly* 6: 129–66.

Clawson, Dan. 1980. *Bureaucracy and the Labor Process: The Transformation of U.S. Industry, 1860–1920.* New York: Monthly Review Press.

Clendinen, Dudley. 1985. "Textile Mills Squeezed in Modernization." *New York Times*, Oct. 26, p. 8.

Cobb, James C. 1984. *Industrialization and Southern Society, 1877–1984.* Lexington: University Press of Kentucky.

————. 1986. "The Southern Business Climate: A Historical Perspective." *Forum for Applied Research and Public Policy* 1 (Summer): 94–101.

Concord Manufacturing Company. 1839–60. "Board of Directors Minute Book." Southern Historical Collection, University of North Carolina, Chapel Hill.

Cone, Bernard M. 1912. "Some Phases of Welfare Work." *Textile Bulletin*, July 4, p. 4.

Cone, Ceasar, II. 1983. Interview conducted by Harry Watson, January 7. Southern Oral History Project, Southern Historical Collection, University of North Carolina, Chapel Hill.

Cone, Ceasar, II, and Benjamin Cone. 1981. Interview conducted by E. P. Douglas, July 23. Southern Oral History Project, Southern Historical Collection, University of North Carolina, Chapel Hill.

"Cone Group of Mills Carry Out Large Rehabilitation Program and Increase Capacity." 1928. *Textile World* (Feb.): 397, 400, 401.

Conn, Robert, and Howard Covington. 1980. "Brown Lung: A Case of Deadly Neglect." *Charlotte Observer*, Feb. 3–10.

Constant, Edward W. 1980. *The Origins of the Turbojet Revolution*. Baltimore: Johns Hopkins University Press.

Conway, Mimi. 1979. *Rise Gonna Rise: A Portrait of Southern Textile Workers*. Garden City, N.Y.: Anchor Press/Doubleday.

Cook, John Harrison. 1925. *A Study of the Mill Schools of North Carolina*. New York: Teachers College, Columbia University.

Cordier, M. Alphonse. 1864. *La crise cotonnière dans la Seine-Inferièure: Ses causes et ses effets*. Rouen: Lapierre.

Corson, Richard C. 1987. "Requirements for Factory Computer Network Communications." *Textile World* (Oct.): 93, 107.

"Cotton Manufactures." 1892. *Monetary Times* 26 (Sept. 9): 278–79.

Cowles, Calvin. 1856. Business and Personal Papers, Southern Historical Collection, University of North Carolina, Chapel Hill.

Cramer, M. Richard. 1978. "Race and Southern White Workers Support for Unions." *Phylon* 39: 311–21.

Crosby, Faye J. 1982. *Relative Deprivation and Working Women*. New York: Oxford University Press.

Danhof, Clarence. 1964. "Four Decades of Thought on the South's Economic Problems." In *Essays in Southern Economic Development*, edited by Melvin L. Greenhut and F. Tate Whitman, pp. 7–68. Chapel Hill: University of North Carolina Press.

Dardel, Pierre. 1939. *Histoire de Bolbec des origines à Bolbec des origines à la Révolution: Le commerce et l'industrie à Bolbec avant 1789*. Rouen: Lestringant.

Davidson, W. A. B. 1987. "Robotics for All at 1987 Bobbin Show." *America's Textiles International* (Sept.): 144–45.

Davies, J. C. 1962. "Toward a Theory of Revolution." *American Sociological Review* 27: 5–14.

"The Deep River Factories." 1848. *Greensboro Patriot*, Aug. 18.

DeHart-Mathews, Jane. 1984. "The Status of Women in North Carolina." In *The North Carolina Experience: An Interpretive and Documentary History*, edited by Lindley S. Butler and Alan D. Watson, pp. 427–51. Chapel Hill: University of North Carolina Press.

DeLottinville, Peter. 1979. "The St. Croix Cotton Manufacturing Company and Its Influence on the St. Croix Community, 1880–1892." M.A. thesis, Dalhousie University.

Denman, William N. 1974. "The Black Lung Movement: A Study in Contemporary Agitation." Ph.D. dissertation, Ohio University.

DePauw, Jacques. 1976. "Illicit Sexual Activity and Society in Eighteenth-Century Nantes." Translated by Elborg Forster and Patricia M. Ranum. In *Family and Society*, edited by Robert Forster and Orest Ranum, pp. 145–91. Baltimore: Johns Hopkins University Press.

Dominion Annual Register and Review. 1883. Toronto: Hunter and Rose.

Dublin, Thomas. 1979. *Women at Work*. New York: Columbia University Press.

Durham, Eula, and Vernon Durham. 1978. Interview by James Leloudis, November 29. Southern Historical Collection, University of North Carolina, Chapel Hill.

Dworkin, Gerald. 1972. Paternalism. *Monist* 56: 65–84.

Earle, Conville, and Ronald Hoffman. 1980. "Foundations of the Modern Economy: Agriculture and the Costs of Labor in the United States and England, 1800–1860." *American Historical Review* 85: 1055–84.

"EDI: Let Computers Do Your Talking." 1986. *Textile World* (Dec.): 50, 56.

Edwards, Richard C. 1979. *Contested Terrain: The Transformation of the Workplace in the Twentieth Century.* New York: Basic Books.

Eisinger, Peter K. 1973. "The Conditions of Protest Behavior in American Cities." *American Political Science Review* 67: 11–28.

Eldersheim, Elizabeth H. 1989. "A Strategy for American Industry." *New York Times*, March 26, p. 3F.

"Electronics Slashes Fieldcrest Design Times." 1986. *Textile World* (Dec.): 59–60.

Elias, P. 1989. *A Study of Trends in Part-Time Employment, 1971–1986.* London: Department of Employment.

Ellis, Marion A. 1985. "Unions Have Found Few Footholds in N.C. Industry." *Charlotte Observer*, Sept. 29.

———. 1986. "Losing 'The Big One' at Cannon Mills a Sign of Rough Year for the Unions." *Charlotte Observer*, Jan. 20.

Ellis, Marion A., and David Olmos. 1985. "Cannon Union Vote Likely to Echo throughout Textiles." *Charlotte Observer*, Sept. 29.

Engels, Friedrich. 1962 [1845]. *The Condition of the Working Class in England in 1844.* Moscow: Foreign Languages Publishing House.

Equal Employment Opportunity Commission. 1966–81. *Job Patterns For Minorities and Women in Private Industry.* Washington, D.C.: U.S. Government Printing Office.

———. 1985–88. "EEO-1 Employment Analysis Report Program" (EARP). Unpublished statistics.

Escott, Paul D. 1985. *Many Excellent People: Power and Privilege in North Carolina.* Chapel Hill: University of North Carolina Press.

Estall, Robert. 1980. "The Changing Balance of the Northern and Southern Regions of the United States." *American Studies* 14: 365–86.

Evrard, Fernand. 1947. "Les ouvriers du textile dans la région rouennaise (1789–1802)." *Annales historiques de la Révolution française* 108: 349–50.

Ezell, Walter K. 1987. "A Concerted Campaign Helps U.S. Textile Industry Comeback." *Christian Science Monitor*, July 16, p. 21.

"Farley Plans Major Sales after Acquiring Pepperell." 1989. *Wall Street Journal*, April 6, p. 10A.

Feree, Myra Marx, and Frederick D. Miller. 1985. "Mobilization and Meaning: Toward an Integration of Social Psychological Perspectives on Social Movements." *Sociological Inquiry* 55: 38–61.

Feuer, L. S. 1969. *The Conflict of Generations.* New York: Basic Books.

Fiorito, Jack, and C. R. Greer. 1982. "Determinants of U.S. Unionism: Past Research and Future Needs." *Industrial Relations* 21: 1–32.

Fite, Gilbert, and Jim Reese. 1965. *An Economic History of the United States*. 2d ed. Boston: Houghton Mifflin.

Fohlen, Claude. 1956. *L'industrie textile au temps du Second Empire*. Paris: Plon.

Foner, Phillip S. 1979. *Women and the American Labor Movement*. New York: Free Press.

Forbes, Ernest R. 1977. "Misguided Symmetry: The Destruction of Regional Transportation Policy for the Maritimes." In *Canada and the Burden of Unity*, edited by D. J. Bercuson, pp. 60–86. Toronto: Macmillan.

Fotian, N. 1979. "Paternalism." *Ethics* 89: 191–98.

Frankel, Linda J. 1984. "Southern Textile Women: Generations of Survival and Struggle." In *My Troubles Are Going to Have Trouble with Me: Everyday Trials and Triumphs of Women Workers*, edited by Karen Brodkin Sacks and Dorothy Remy, pp. 39–60. New Brunswick: Rutgers University Press.

———. 1986. "Women, Paternalism and Protest in a Southern Textile Community: Henderson, North Carolina, 1900–1950." Ph.D. dissertation, Harvard University.

Frederickson, Mary. 1982. "Four Decades of Change: Black Workers in Southern Textiles, 1941–1981." *Radical America* 16 (Nov.–Dec.): 27–44.

Freeman, Jo. 1979. "Resource Mobilization and Strategy." In *The Dynamics of Social Movements*, edited by Mayer N. Zald and John D. McCarthy, pp. 167–89. Cambridge, Mass.: Winthrop.

Freeze, Gary R. 1988. "Model Mill Men of the New South: Paternalism and Methodism in the Odell Cotton Mills of North Carolina, 1877–1908." Ph.D. dissertation, University of North Carolina, Chapel Hill.

Friedman, Amy. 1987. "Textiles." *Financial World*, Jan. 6, p. 55.

Fröbel, Folker, Jürgen Heinrichs, and Otto Kreye. 1980. *The New International Division of Labour: Structural Unemployment in Industrialized Countries and Industrialization in Developing Countries*. New York: Cambridge University Press.

Frost, James D. 1982. "The 'Nationalization' of the Bank of Nova Scotia, 1880–1910." *Acadiensis* 12: 3–38.

Fuchs, Rachel. 1984. *Abandoned Children*. Albany: State University of New York Press.

Gamson, William A. 1968. *Power and Discontent*. Homewood, Ill.: Dorsey.

———. 1975. *The Strategy of Social Protest*. Homewood, Ill.: Dorsey.

Gaventa, John. 1988. *From the Mountains to the Maquiladoras: A Case Study of Capital Flight and Its Impact on Workers*. New Market, Tenn.: Highlander Center.

Gaventa, John, Barbara Ellen Smith, and Alex Willingham, eds. 1990. *Communities in Economic Crisis: Appalachia and the South*. Philadelphia: Temple University Press.

Genovese, Eugene D. 1976. *Roll Jordan, Roll: The World the Slaves Made*. New York: Vintage Books.

Gerringer, Carrie. 1979. Interview by Douglas DeNatale, August 11. Southern Historical Collection, University of North Carolina, Chapel Hill.

Gert, Bernard. 1979. "The Justification for Paternalism." *Ethics* 89: 199–210.

Gert, Bernard, and Charles M. Culver. 1976. "Paternalistic Behavior." *Philosophy and Public Affairs* 6: 45–57.

Giddens, Anthony. 1979. *Central Problems in Social Theory*. London. Macmillan.

Gilman, Glen. 1952. *Human Relations in the Industrial Southeast*. Chapel Hill: University of North Carolina Press.

Goldsmith, Frank, and Lorin E. Kerr. 1982. *Occupational Safety and Health*. New York: Human Sciences Press.

Goodloe, Robert L. 1881. Family Papers. Southern Historical Collection, University of North Carolina, Chapel Hill.

"The Great Textile Robbery." 1987. *New York Times* (editorial), Oct. 26 (late ed.), p. A18.

Griffin, Richard W. 1954. "North Carolina: The Origin and Rise of the Cotton Textile Industry, 1830–1880." Ph.D. dissertation, Ohio State University.

———. 1960. "Poor White Laborers in Southern Cotton Factories, 1789–1865." *South Carolina Historical Magazine* 61: 15–35.

Grunwald, Joseph, and Kenneth Flamm. 1985. *The Global Factory: Foreign Assembly in International Trade*. Washington, D.C.: Brookings Institution.

Gullickson, Gay L. 1986. *The Spinners and Weavers of Auffay: Rural Industry and the Sexual Division of Labor in a French Village, 1750–1850*. New York: Cambridge University Press.

Gurney, Joan Neff, and Kathleen J. Tierney. 1982. "Relative Deprivation and Social Movements: A Critical Look at Twenty Years of Theory and Research." *Sociological Quarterly* 23: 33–47.

Gurr, Ted Robert. 1970. *Why Men Rebel*. Princeton: Princeton University Press.

Gusfield, Joseph R. 1970. *Protest, Reform and Revolt: A Reader in Social Movements*. New York: Wiley.

Gutman, Herbert. 1977. *Work, Culture, and Society in Industrializing America: Essays in American Working-Class and Social History*. New York: Vintage Books.

Hahn, Steven. 1982. "Common Right and Commonwealth: The Stock-Law Struggle and the Roots of Southern Populism." In *Region, Race and Reconstruction: Essays in Honor of C. Vann Woodward*, edited by J. Morgan Kousser and James M. McPherson, pp. 51–88. New York: Oxford University Press.

Hall, Bob. 1978. "The Brown Lung Controversy." *Columbia Journalism Review* 16 (6): 27–35.

Hall, Jacquelyn Dowd. 1986. "Disorderly Women: Gender and Labor Militancy in the Appalachian South." *Journal of American History* 73: 354–82.

Hall, Jacquelyn Dowd, Robert Korstad, and James Leloudis. 1986. "Cotton Mill People: Work, Community, and Protest in the Textile South, 1880–1940." *American Historical Review* 91: 245–86.

Hall, Jacquelyn Dowd, James Leloudis, Robert Korstad, Mary Murphy, Lu Ann Jones, and Christopher B. Daly. 1987. *Like a Family: The Making of a Southern Cotton Mill World*. Chapel Hill: University of North Carolina Press.

Hardin, Grover. 1980. Interview by Allen Tullos, July 19, Charlotte, N.C. Southern Historical Collection, University of North Carolina, Chapel Hill.

Hareven, Tamara K. 1982. *Family Time and Industrial Time: The Relationship between the Family and Work in a New England Industrial Community.* Cambridge: Cambridge University Press.

Hargett, Edna Y. 1979. Interview by James Leloudis, July 19, Charlotte, N.C. Southern Historical Collection, University of North Carolina, Chapel Hill.

Harris, Candee. 1985. "The Magnitude of Job Loss from Plant Closings and the Generation of Replacement Jobs: Some Recent Evidence." *Annals of the American Academy of Political and Social Science* 475 (Sept.): 15–27.

Harrison, Bennett, and Barry Bluestone. 1988. *The Great U-Turn: Corporate Restructuring and the Polarizing of America.* New York: Basic Books.

Hartmann, Heidi. 1976. "Capitalism, Patriarchy, and Job Segregation by Sex." *Signs* 1: 137–69.

Harvey, David. 1982. *The Limits to Capital.* Chicago: University of Chicago Press.

Harwood, Geoff. 1985. *A Survey of Textile and Related Education in Britain.* London: Association of Livery Companies.

Hearden, Patrick J. 1982. *Independence and Empire: The New South's Cotton Mill Campaign, 1865–1901.* DeKalb: Northern Illinois University Press.

Henderson [N.C.] City Directory. 1902. Interstate Directory Co.

Henderson Daily Dispatch (HDD). Henderson, North Carolina. Letters to the Editor:
Forsythe, Olive, June 9, 1959
Hale, Mildred, June 4, 1959
Jackson, Luther, and Charlie Raines, Nov. 8, 1958
Journigan, Annie, June 19, 1959
Langley, Mildred, March 19, 1959
Roberson, Esther, March 19, 1959
Roberson, Gibb, April 7, 1959
Turner, Annie, May 1, 1959
Wilder, Lois, Feb. 20, 1959

"The Henderson Story." 1960. *America's Textile Reporter*, Feb. 4 (special collection).

Herring, Harriet L. 1929. *Welfare Work in Mill Villages: The Story of Extra-Mill Activities in North Carolina.* Chapel Hill: University of North Carolina Press.

———. 1949. *The Passing of the Mill Village.* Chapel Hill: University of North Carolina Press.

Higgs, Robert. 1971. *The Transformation of the American Economy, 1865–1914.* New York: Wiley.

Hodges, James A. 1986. *New Deal Labor Policy and the Southern Cotton Textile Industry, 1933–1941.* Knoxville: University of Tennessee Press.

Hoffer, Eric. 1951. *The True Believer*. New York: Harper & Row.

Hoover, Calvin B., and B. U. Ratchford. 1951. *Economic Resources and Policies in the South*. New York: Macmillan.

Hopkins, George W. 1982. "Occupational Health and the Miners: The Black Lung Revolt." Paper presented at the Annual Meeting of the Organization of American Historians, Philadelphia, April 2.

Hufton, Olwen. 1975. "Women and the Family Economy in Eighteenth-Century France." *French Historical Studies* 9: 1–22.

Hughes, Chip. 1976. "A New Twist for Textiles." *Southern Exposure* 3: 73–79.

Hughes, Thomas P. 1983. *Networks of Power: Electrification in Western Society, 1880–1930*. Baltimore: Johns Hopkins University Press.

Isaacs, McAllister, III. 1983. "Are You Ready for Robots?" *Textile World* (April): 35, 37.

"ITMA Dyeing and Finishing: Sophistication, Automation." 1988. *Textile World* (Jan.): 45–46, 48–50.

Jackson, Luther. Interview by Linda Frankel. Southern Oral History Project, Southern Historical Collection, University of North Carolina, Chapel Hill.

Jaffee, David. 1986. "The Political Economy of Job Loss in the United States, 1970–1980." *Social Problems* 33: 297–315.

Janiewski, Dolores. 1985. *Sisterhood Denied: Race, Gender, and Class in a New South Community*. Philadelphia: Temple University Press.

"Japanese Textile Machinery Makers Continue Assault on Spinning and Weaving Technologies." 1986. *America's Textiles International* (June): 38–40.

Jenkins, J. Craig. 1983. "Resource Mobilization Theory and the Study of Social Movements." *Annual Review of Sociology* 9: 527–53.

Jenkins, J. Craig, and C. Perrow. 1977. "Insurgency of the Powerless." *American Sociological Review* 42: 249–68.

"John Gregg: TW's 1987 Textile Leader of the Year." 1987. *Textile World* (Oct.): 43, 46, 48–49, 52, 55, 58.

Johnson, Guion G. 1937. *Antebellum North Carolina: A Social History*. Chapel Hill: University of North Carolina Press.

Johnson, Kenneth, and Marilyn Scurlock. 1986a. "The Climate for Workers." *Southern Exposure* 14: 28–31.

———. 1986b. "The Climate for Workers: Where Does the South Stand?" *Southern Changes* 8 (4–5): 3–15.

Johnston, Oswald. 1985. "Link between Trade Deficit, Jobs Debated." *Los Angeles Times*, Nov. 15, sec. 4, pp. 1, 5.

Judkins, Bennett M. 1986. *We Offer Ourselves as Evidence: Toward Workers' Control of Occupational Health*. Westport, Conn.: Greenwood Press.

———. 1990. "Workplace Democracy and Occupational Health." *Humanity and Society* 14: 35–53.

Kealey, Gregory. 1973. *Canada Investigates Industrialism: The Royal Commission on the Relations of Labour and Capital in Canada, 1889*. Toronto: University of Toronto Press.

Kenneally, James J. 1981. *Women and American Trade Unions*. Montreal: Eden Press Women's Publications.

Kenneson, Kim. 1988. "Deal-Maker, 36, Key in Stevens' Undoing." *Raleigh News and Observer*, May 1, pp. 1I, 5I.

Kessler-Harris, Alice. 1982. *Out To Work: A History of Wage-Earning Women in the United States*. New York: Oxford University Press.

Key, V. O. 1949. *Southern Politics in State and Nation*. New York: Vintage Books.

King, J. Crawford, Jr. 1982. "The Closing of the Southern Range: An Exploratory Study." *Journal of Southern History* 48: 53–70.

Kirby, Jack T. 1987. *Rural Worlds Lost: The American South, 1920–1960*. Baton Rouge: Louisiana State University Press.

Klandermans, Bert. 1984. "Mobilization and Participation: Social-Psychological Expansions of Resource Mobilization Theory." *American Sociological Review* 49: 583–600.

Kleinig, John. 1983. *Paternalism*. Totowa, N.J.: Rowman & Allanheld.

Kornhauser, Ruth. 1961. "Social Determinants and Consequences of Union Membership." *Labor History* 2: 30–61.

Krenek, E. M. 1983. "Robotics in the Textile Industry." *America's Textiles* (Nov.): 57–60.

Krueger, Bill. 1987. "Textile Aid a Priority for Lawmakers." *Raleigh News and Observer*, March 1, p. 1D.

Kuznets, Simon. 1973. *Population, Capital, and Growth: Selected Essays*. New York: Norton.

Lahne, Herbert J. 1944. *The Cotton Mill Workers*. New York: Farrar and Rinehart.

Lamphere, Louise. 1987. *From Working Daughters to Working Mothers: Immigrant Women in a New England Industrial Community*. Ithaca: Cornell University Press.

Landes, David S. 1969. *The Unbound Prometheus: Technological Change and Industrial Development in Western Europe from 1750 to the Present*. London: Cambridge University Press.

Layton, Clara. N.d. Interview conducted by Ida Moore, Federal Writers Project of the Works Progress Administration. Southern Historical Collection, University of North Carolina, Chapel Hill.

Lears, T. J. Jackson. 1985. "The Concept of Cultural Hegemony: Problems and Possibilities." *American Historical Review* 90: 567–93.

Leary, Marty R. 1987. "The Power of Public Opinion: The Commerical Elite and the Textile Question in Greensboro, North Carolina, 1870–1934." Honors thesis, University of North Carolina, Chapel Hill.

Leiter, Jeffrey. 1982. "Continuity and Change in the Legitimation of Authority in Southern Mill Towns." *Social Problems* 29: 540–50.

———. 1986. "Reactions to Subordination: Attitudes of Southern Textile Workers." *Social Forces* 64: 948–74.

———. 1989. "The Wages of Aging: Time-Related Determinants of Earnings in the Southern Textile Context." Paper presented at the Meeting of the American Sociological Association, San Francisco, August 13.

Leloudis, James. 1986. "Oral History and Piedmont Mill Villages, 1880–1940. *International Journal of Oral History* 7 (3): 163–80.

Lemert, Ben F. 1933. *The Cotton Textile Industry of the Southern Appalachian Piedmont.* Chapel Hill: University of North Carolina Press.

Levainville, J. 1911. "Les ouvriers du coton dans la région de Rouen." *Annales de Géographie* 20: 52–64.

———. 1913. *Rouen: Etude d'une agglomeration urbaine.* Paris: Armand Colin.

Levenstein, Charles, Dianne Plantamura, and William Mass. 1987. "Labor and Byssinosis." In *Dying for Work: Workers' Safety and Health in Twentieth Century America,* edited by David Rosner and Gerald Markowitz, pp. 208–23. Bloomington: Indiana University Press.

Lloyd, Cynthia B., ed. 1975. *Sex, Discrimination, and the Division of Labor.* New York: Columbia University Press.

Lloyd, Peter E., and John Shutt. 1983. "Industrial Change in the Greater Manchester Textiles-Clothing Complex." North West Industry Research Unit, Department of Geography, Manchester University.

"Low-Paying Jobs on the Rise, Report Says." 1988. *Raleigh News and Observer,* Sept. 27, p. 1D.

Lublin, Joann S. 1982. "Union Organizer Faces Harder Job than Ever in Recession-Hit South." *Wall Street Journal,* Aug. 3, p. 1.

Maddox, James G., E. E. Liehafsky, Vivian W. Henderson, and Herbert M. Hamlin. 1967. *The Advancing South: Manpower Prospects and Problems.* New York: Twentieth Century Fund.

Mandle, Jay R. 1978. *The Roots of Black Poverty: The Southern Plantation Economy after the Civil War.* Durham, N.C.: Duke University Press.

Marglin, Stephen A. 1974. "What Do Bosses Do?" *Review of Radical Political Economics* 6 (2): 33–60.

Marley, Harold. 1930. "A Southern Textile Epoch." *Survey* 65: 17–20, 55, 58.

Mars, Isidore. 1857. *Auffay, ou le vieil Isnelville.* Rouen: Lecointe Frères.

———. 1876. *Derniers souvenirs du bon vieux temps d'Auffay depuis 1793 jusqu'à 1840 environ.* Dieppe: Paul Lepetre & Cie.

Marshall, F. Ray. 1967. *Labor in the South.* Cambridge: Harvard University Press.

———. 1986. "The Climate for Workers in the U.S.: Summary of a Study by the Southern Labor Institute and a Special Project of the Southern Regional Council." *Southern Changes* 8 (4–5): 1–2.

Martin, Frank. N.d. Interview conducted by Ida Moore, Federal Writers Project of the Works Progress Administration. Southern Historical Collection, University of North Carolina, Chapel Hill.

Marwell, Gerald, and Pamela Oliver. 1984. "Collective Action Theory and Social Movements Research." In *Research in Social Movements, Conflict and Change,* vol. 7, edited by Louis Kriesberg, pp. 1–27. Greenwich, Conn.: JAI Press.

Martin, Arieta. Interview by Linda Frankel. Oral History Project, Southern
  Historical Collection, University of North Carolina, Chapel Hill.
Marx, Karl. 1976. *Capital*. Vol. I. Harmondsworth, Eng.: Penguin Books.
———. 1977. *Capital*. Vol. 3. Moscow: Progress Books.
———. 1978. *Capital*. Vol. 2. Harmondsworth, Eng.: Penguin Books.
Mathias, Peter. 1969. *The First Industrial Nation: An Economic History of Britain, 1700–1914*. New York: Scribner.
Mayfield, Dave. 1985. "Textile Makers Confront Troubles." *Virginian Pilot* (Norfolk), Dec. 29, p. 1E.
McCann, L. D. 1981. "The Mercantile-Industrial Transition in the Metal Towns of Pictou County, 1857–1931." *Acadiensis* 10: 29–64.
McCarthy, John D., and Mayer N. Zald. 1973. *The Trend of Social Movements in America: Professionalization and Resource Mobilization*. Morristown, N.J.: General Learning Press.
———. 1977. "Resource Mobilization and Social Movements: A Partial Theory." *American Journal of Sociology* 82: 1212–41.
McDonald, Joseph A., and Donald A. Clelland. 1984. "Textile Workers and Union Sentiment." *Social Forces* 63: 502–21.
McGrayne, Sharon. 1984. "Hanging on by a Thread." *Knoxville News Sentinal*, Oct. 7, Business section, p. 1.
McHugh, Cathy L. 1988. *Mill Family: The Labor System in the Southern Cotton Textile Industry, 1880–1915*. New York: Oxford University Press.
McIntosh, Jay. 1985. "Cannon-Textile Union Fight Said 'Far from Gentlemanly.' " *Charlotte Observer*, Aug. 12.
McKissick, Ellison S., Jr. 1985. Letter. *Wall Street Journal*, Sept. 4, p. 25E.
McLaurin, Melton A. 1971. *Paternalism and Protest: Southern Mill Workers and Organized Labor, 1875–1905*. Westport, Conn.: Greenwood Press.
"MAP Provides the Computer Connection." 1987. *Textile World* (May): 45, 47.
MDC, Inc. 1986. *Shadows in the Sunbelt: Developing the Rural South in an Era of Economic Change*. Chapel Hill: MDC, Inc.
Mendels, Franklin. 1972. "Proto-industrialization: The First Phase of the Industrialization Process." *Journal of Economic History* 32: 241–61.
Michelet, Jules. 1860. *La femme*. Paris: Hachette.
Mill, John Stuart. 1925. *A System of Logic*. London: Longmans.
"Milliken: Retailers Are Getting Behind QR." 1987. *Textile World* (Oct.): 32.
Mitchell, Broadus. 1921. *The Rise of the Cotton Mills in the South*. Baltimore: Johns Hopkins University Press.
Mitchell, Broadus, and George Sinclair Mitchell. 1930. *The Industrial Revolution in the South*. Baltimore: Johns Hopkins University Press.
Mitchell, Dorothy. 1913. "Annual Outing of the Cone Mills Is a Wonderful Success This Year." *Charlotte Evening Chronicle*, July 12.
Mitchell, George Sinclair. 1931. *Textile Unionism and the South*. Chapel Hill: University of North Carolina.
Mollat, Michel, ed. 1979. *Histoire de Rouen*. Toulouse: Edouard Privat.
Montgomery, David. 1979. *Workers' Control in America*. New York: Cambridge University Press.

Moody, Kim. 1990. "The Bad Deal: Bargaining in the 1980's." *Labor Notes* (Jan) 7–10

"Morgan Stanley-Led Group Buys Burlington Industries." 1987. *Wall Street Journal*, Sept. 1, p. 19E.

Morland, Kenneth. 1958. *Millways of Kent*. New Haven, Conn.: College and University Press.

Musker, Semple Moore. 1979. Interview, May 17. Southern Oral History Project, Southern Historical Collection, University of North Carolina, Chapel Hill.

Nash, June, and Maria Patricia Fernandez-Kelly. 1983. *Women, Men, and the New International Division of Labor*. Albany: State University of New York Press.

Nauman, Matt. 1983. "Allied Revs for Revival." *Knoxville Journal*, Nov. 23.

Navarro, Vicente. 1983. "Work, Ideology and Science: The Case of Medicine." In *Health and Work under Capitalism*, edited by Vicente Navarro and Daniel M. Berman, pp. 1–35. Farmingdale, N.Y.: Baywood.

Naylor, Thomas, and James Clotfelter. 1974. *Strategies for Change in the South*. Chapel Hill: University of North Carolina Press.

Newby, Howard. 1975. "The Deferential Dialectic." *Comparative Studies in Society and History* 17: 139–64.

———. 1977. *The Deferential Worker*. London: Allen Lane.

Newman, Dale. 1978. "Work and Community Life in a Southern Textile Town." *Labor History* 19: 204–25.

———. 1980. "Textile Workers in a Tobacco County: A Comparison between Yarn and Weave Mill Villages." In *The Southern Common People: Studies in Nineteenth-Century Social History*, edited by Edward Magdol and Jon L. Wakelyn, pp. 345–68. Westport, Conn.: Greenwood Press.

———. 1981. "The Myth of the Contented Southern Mill Worker." In *Perspectives on the American South: Annual Review of Society, Politics, and Culture*, vol. 1, edited by Merle Black and John Shelton Reed, pp. 187–204. New York: Gordon and Breach Science Press.

Nicholls, William H. 1960. "Southern Tradition and Regional Economic Progress." *Southern Economic Journal* 26: 187–98.

Nicholson, Roy H. 1952. *Wesleyan Methodism in the South*. Syracuse, N.Y.: Wesleyan Publishing House.

"1980s: Consolidations, Bankruptcies, Mergers, Buyouts, Imports, Imports, and—(Surprize!) Rejuvenation." *America's Textiles International* 16 (June): 176–78, 180, 182, 186.

Noiret, Charles. 1836. *Mémoires d'un ouvrier rouennais*. Rouen: François.

Norris, G. M. 1978. "Industrial Paternalist Capitalism and Local Labour Markets." *Sociology* 12: 469–89.

North American Congress on Latin America. 1977. "Capital's Flight: The Apparel Industry Moves South." *NACLA Report on the Americas* 11 (March): 1–33.

North Carolina Bureau of Labor and Printing. 1900–7. *Annual Reports*. Raleigh.

North Carolina Department of Labor and Printing. 1910–26. *Annual Reports*. Raleigh.

North State Video. N.d. "Something That Brought Us Together: The Harriet-Henderson Strike of 1958." Video documentary. Durham, N.C.

"Nova Scotia Cotton Company." 1885. *Morning Herald* (Halifax, Nova Scotia), Aug. 6, p. 3.

Oberschall, Anthony. 1973. *Social Conflict and Social Movements.* Englewood Cliffs, N.J.: Prentice-Hall.

———. 1978. "Theories of Social Conflict." *Annual Review of Sociology* 4: 291–315.

Office of Population Censuses and Surveys. 1971. *Census of Employment.* London: Her Majesty's Stationery Office.

———. 1987. *Census of Employment.* London: Her Majesty's Stationery Office.

Office of Technology Assessment, U.S. Congress. 1987. *The U.S. Textile and Apparel Industry: A Revolution in Progress-Special Report.* Washington, D.C.: U.S. Government Printing Office.

Olphe-Galliard, G. 1913. "Les industries rurales à domicile dans la Normandie Orientale." *La Science Sociale* (Dec.): 1–75.

Olson, Mancur. 1965. *The Logic of Collective Action: Public Goods and the Theory of Groups.* Cambridge: Harvard University Press.

O'Neil, Peggy. 1983. "Robotics in Textiles: Feasible Now?" *America's Textiles* (Nov.): 60–62.

Oppenheimer, Valerie Kincade. 1970. *The Female Labor Force in the United States.* Berkeley: Institute of International Studies, University of California.

"OTA Report Is Critical of Workplace Protection." 1985. *Nation's Health* (May-June): 73.

Page, Myra. 1929. *Southern Cotton Mills and Labor.* New York: Workers Library Publishers.

Parsons, Talcott. 1961. *Theories of Society,* vol. 1. Glencoe, Ill.: Free Press.

Penn, Roger D. 1985. *Skilled Workers in the Class Structure.* New York: Cambridge University Press.

———. 1990. *Class, Power and Technology: Skilled Workers in Britain and America.* Oxford: Polity Press.

———. 1991. "Technical Change and Gender Relations in Contemporary Rochdale." In *Gender and Employment in Modern Britain,* edited by A. Scott. Oxford: Oxford University Press.

Penn, Roger, and Hilda Scattergood. 1985. "Deskilling or Enskilling?: An Empirical Investigation of Recent Theories of the Labour Process." *British Journal of Sociology* 36: 611–30.

———. 1987. "Corporate Strategy and Textile Employment: A Comparison of Two British Multinationals." Paper presented to the Annual Meeting of the Southern Sociological Society, Atlanta, April 11. Available as Lancaster University Social Change and Economic Life Research, Working Paper No. 12.

Pepper, Lil. Interview for the Federal Writers Project of the Works Progress Administration. Southern Historical Collection, University of North Carolina, Chapel Hill.

Perrow, Charles. 1979. "The Sixties Observed." In *The Dynamics of Social Movements*, edited by John D. McCarthy and Mayer N. Zald, pp. 192–211. Cambridge, Mass.: Winthrop.

Perrucci, Carolyn C., Robert Perrucci, Dena B. Targ, and Harry B. Targ. 1988. *Plant Closings: International Context and Social Costs*. New York: Aldine de Gruyter.

Perry, Joseph B., and Meredith David Pugh. 1978. *Collective Behavior*. St. Paul: West Publishing.

Phillips, Anne, and Barbara Taylor. 1980. "Sex and Skill: Notes towards a Feminist Economics." *Feminist Review* 6: 79–88.

Pinchbeck, Ivy. 1969 [1930]. *Women Workers and the Industrial Revolution, 1750–1850*. New York: Augustus Kelly.

Pinkney, David. 1958. *Napoleon III and the Rebuilding of Paris*. Princeton: Princeton University Press.

Planning a Clinic: Planning, Preparation and Follow Up: Building the Organization through Screening Clinics. N.d. Pamphlet provided to staff of the Brown Lung Association.

"Planning for Expansion." 1985. *Nation's Business* (May): 40J–40K.

Pope, Liston. 1942. *Millhands and Preachers: A Study of Gastonia*. New Haven: Yale University Press.

Porpora, Douglas V., Mah Hui Lim, and Usanee Prommas. 1989. "The Role of Women in the International Division of Labour: The Case of Thailand." *Development and Change* 20: 269–94.

Potter, David M. 1947. "The Historical Development of Eastern-Southern Freight Rate Relationships." *Law and Contemporary Problems* 12: 416–48.

Potwin, Marjorie A. 1927. *Cotton Mill People of the Piedmont: A Study in Social Change*. New York: Columbia University Press.

"Process Control Will Govern Finishing Exhibits." 1987. *Textile World* (Sept.): 126, 142, 147.

Pyatt, Rudolph A., Jr. 1985. "Factory's Shutdown Tears Fabric of Small Company Town." *Washington Post*, Oct. 14, p. WB1.

Pyke, Frank. 1987. "Labour Organization and the Use of Time." Mimeo. Department of Sociology, Manchester University.

Ragan, Robert A. 1969. *The Pioneer Cotton Mills of Gaston County, N.C., 1848–1904*. Gastonia, N.C.: Privately published.

Raynor, Bruce. 1977. "Unionism in the Southern Textile Industry: An Overview." In *Essays in Southern Labor History*, edited by Gary M. Fink and Merl E. Reed, pp. 80–99. Westport, Conn.: Greenwood Press.

Reddy, William M. 1984. *The Rise of Market Culture*. New York: Cambridge University Press.

Reich, Michael. 1981. *Racial Inequality*. Princeton: Princeton University Press.

Reid, Alexander. 1986. "In Hard Times, Garment Union Places Hopes on New Leadership." *New York Times*, June 3 (late ed.), pp. B1, B4.

Reid, Donald. 1985. "Industrial Paternalism: Discourse and Practice in the Nineteenth Century." *Comparative Studies in Society and History* 3: 579–607.

Reif, Linda, Michael D. Schulman, and Michael J. Belyea. 1988. "The Social Bases of Union Support: An Analysis of Southern Textile Workers." *Journal of Political and Military Sociology* 16: 57–75.

Reybaud, Louis. 1862. *Rapport sur la condition morale, intellectuelle et materielle des ouvriers qui vivent de l'industrie du coton.* Paris: Institut Imperial de France.

Rhyne, Jenning J. 1930. *Some Southern Cotton Mill Workers and Their Villages.* Chapel Hill: University of North Carolina Press.

Robert, Annette. 1983. "The Effects of the Changing International Division of Labour on Female Workers in the Textile and Clothing Industries." *Development and Change* 14: 19–37.

Rogers, Ethel. Interview by Linda Frankel. Southern Oral History Project, Southern Historical Collection, University of North Carolina, Chapel Hill.

Rosenberg, Nathan. 1972. "Factors Affecting the Diffusion of Technology." *Explorations in Economic History* 10: 3–33.

Ross, Robert, and Kent Trachte. 1983. "Global Cities and Global Classes: The Peripheralization of Labor in New York City." *Review: A Journal of the Fernand Braudel Center for the Study of Economies, Historical Systems, and Civilizations* 6: 393–431.

Rowan, Richard L. 1970. *The Negro in the Textile Industry.* Philadelphia: Industrial Research Unit, Wharton School, University of Pennsylvania.

Rowan, Richard L., and Robert E. Barr. 1987. *Employee Relations: Trends and Practices in the Textile Industry.* Philadelphia: Industrial Research Unit, Wharton School, University of Pennsylvania.

Roy, Donald F. 1965. "Change and Resistance to Change in the Southern Labor Movement." In *The South in Continuity and Change,* edited by John C. McKinney and Edgar T. Thompson, pp. 225–47. Durham, N.C.: Duke University Press.

Rush, Gary B., and R. Serge Denisoff. 1971. *Social and Political Movements.* New York: Appleton-Century-Crofts.

Sacks, Karen Brodkin. 1988. *Caring by the Hour: Women, Work and Organizing at Duke Medical Center.* Urbana: University of Illinois Press.

Sawers, Larry, and William K. Tabb. 1984. *Sunbelt-Snowbelt: Urban Development and Regional Restructuring.* New York: Oxford University Press.

Schoonmaker, Mary Ellen. 1985. "Wearing down the Workers." *In These Times,* July 10–23, p. 10.

Schulman, Michael D. 1983. "Systems of Control over Labor in Rural Textile Communities: The Case of the American South." *Rural Sociologist* 2: 295–301.

Schulman, Michael D., Rhonda Zingraff, and Linda Reif. 1985. "Race, Gender, Class Consciousness and Union Support: An Analysis of Southern Textile Workers." *Sociological Quarterly* 26: 187–204.

Scott, James C. 1985. *Weapons of the Weak: Everyday Forms of Peasant Resistance.* New Haven: Yale Universtiy Press.

Scott, Joan Wallach. 1988. " 'L'ouvrière! Mot impie, sordide . . .': Women Workers in the Discourse of French Political Economy, 1840–1860." In *Gender and the Politics of History*, pp. 139–63. New York: Columbia University Press.

Serrin, William. 1985. "Union at Stevens, Yes; Upheaval, No." *New York Times*, Dec. 5, p. A18.

Sheehy, Jan. 1986. "Crafted with Pride Dazzles America." *Textile World* (May): 38–39, 42, 44, 47.

Simon, Bryant. 1989. " 'I Believed in the Strongest Kind of Religion': James Evans and Collective Action at the Cone Mills of Greensboro, 1900–1930." Paper presented at the University of North Carolina at Charlotte History Forum, April 1.

Simon, Jules. 1861. *L'ouvrière*. Paris: Hachette.

Simpson, Richard L. 1981. "Labor Force Integration and Southern U.S. Textile Unionism." In *Research in the Sociology of Work*, vol. 1, edited by Richard L. Simpson and Ida H. Simpson, pp. 383–403. Greenwich, Conn.: JAI Press.

Simpson, William Hays. 1948. *Southern Textile Communities*. Charlotte, N.C.: Dowd Press.

Sion, Jules. 1909. *Les paysans de la Normandie Orientale: Pays de Caux, Bray, Vexin Normand, Vallée de la Seine. Etude géographique*. Paris: Armand Colin.

Skocpol, Theda. 1984. "Sociology's Historical Imagination." In *Vision and Method in Historical Sociology*, edited by Theda Skocpol, pp. 1–21. New York: Cambridge University Press.

Sloan, Cliff, and Bob Hall. 1980. "It's Good to Be Home in Greenville." In *Working Lives: The Southern Exposure History of Labor in the South*, edited by Marc S. Miller, pp. 229–43. New York: Pantheon.

Smelser, Neil J. 1959. *Social Change in the Industrial Revolution: An Application of Theory to the British Cotton Industry*. Chicago: University of Chicago Press.

———. 1962. *Theory of Collective Behavior*. New York: Free Press.

Smith, Adam. 1976 [1776]. *An Inquiry into the Nature and Causes of the Wealth of Nations*. Chicago: University of Chicago Press.

Smith, Barbara Ellen. 1983. "Black Lung: The Social Production of Disease." In *Health and Work under Capitalism*, edited by Vicente Navarro and Daniel M. Berman, pp. 39–54. Farmingdale, N.Y.: Baywood.

———. 1986. *Women of the Rural South: Economic Status and Prospects*. Lexington, Ky.: Southeast Women's Employment Coalition.

———. 1987. *Digging Our Own Graves: Coal Miners and the Struggle over Black Lung Disease*. Philadelphia: Temple University Press.

Smith, Robert S. 1960. *Mill on the Dan: A History of Dan River Mills, 1882–1950*. Durham, N.C.: Duke University Press.

Snyder, Wesley E. 1986. "Overview of Robotics." In *Automation and Robotics in the Textile and Apparel Industries*, edited by Gordon A. Berkstresser, III, and David Buchanan, pp. 2–22. Park Ridge, N.J.: Noyes Publications.

Standard and Poor's. 1984. *Industry Surveys*. Vol. 2. July.

Stelzer, Irwin M. 1961. "The Cotton Textile Industry." In *The Structure of American Industry: Some Case Studies*, 3d ed., edited by Walter Adams, pp. 42–73. New York: Macmillan.

Stinchcombe, Arthur L. 1978. *Theoretical Methods in Social History*. New York: Academic Press.

Summers, Gene F. 1984. "Deindustrialization: Restructuring of the Economy: Preface." *Annals of the American Academy of Political and Social Science* 475 (Sept.): 9–14.

"Takeover Fever Hits Reeling U.S. Textile Industry." 1988. *Raleigh News and Observer*, May 31, p. 2D.

Tarrow, Sidney. 1981. "Struggling to Reform: Social Movements and Policy Change during Cycles of Protest." Occasional Paper 15. Center for International Studies, Cornell University, Ithaca, N.Y.

Tennessee Industrial Renewal Network. 1989. "Responding to Plant Closings in Tennessee." Conference Report. Knoxville.

Terrill, Tom E., and Jerrold Hirsch. 1978. *Such as Us: Southern Voices of the Thirties*. Chapel Hill: University of North Carolina Press.

Tewkesbury, Charles G. 1984. "Managing Technological Change in Our Industry." *America's Textiles* (May): 66–67.

Textile Workers Union of America (TWUA) holdings. Harriet-Henderson Files, Wisconsin State Historical Society, Madison.

Thompson, E. P. 1963. *The Making of the English Working Class*. New York: Vintage Books.

———. 1967. "Time, Work-Discipline, and Industrial Capitalism." *Past and Present* 38: 56–97.

Thompson, Holland M. 1900. "Life in a Southern Mill Town." *Political Science Quarterly* 15: 1–11.

———. 1906. *From the Cotton Field to the Cotton Mill: A Study of the Industrial Transition in North Carolina*. New York: Macmillan.

———. 1920. *The New South: A Chronicle of Social and Industrial Evolution*. New Haven: Yale University Press.

Thornton, Patricia. 1986. "The Problem of Out-Migration from Atlantic Canada, 1871–1921: A New Look." *Acadiensis* 15: 3–33.

Thurow, Lester G. 1975. *Generating Inequality: Mechanisms of Distribution in the U.S. Economy*. New York: Basic Books.

Till, Thomas. 1973. "The Extent of Industrialization in Southern Nonmetro Labor Markets in the 1960s." *Journal of Regional Science* 13(3): 453–61.

Tilly, Charles. 1978. *From Mobilization to Revolution*. Reading, Mass.: Addison-Wesley.

———. 1981. *As Sociology Meets History*. New York: Academic Press.

Tilly, Louise A., and Joan W. Scott. 1978. *Women, Work and Family*. New York: Holt, Rinehart and Winston.

Tilly, Louise A., Joan W. Scott, and Miriam Cohen. 1976. "Women's Work and European Fertility Patterns." *Journal of Interdisciplinary History* 6: 447–76.

Tindall, George B. 1967. *The Emergence of the New South, 1913–1945*. Baton Rouge: Louisiana State University Press.

Tippett, Thomas. 1931. *When Southern Labor Stirs*. New York: J. Cape and H. Smith.

Toner, Robin. 1986. "Campaign in Textile Belt Focusing on Trade." *New York Times*, Sept. 25 (late ed.), p. D24.

"A Town in America Named 'Revolution.' " 1929. Translation. *Jewish Daily Forward*, Sept. 14, 3 ff.

Le travail et l'enfant au XIXe siècle. 1978. Val de Marne.

Truchil, Barry E. 1988. *Capital-Labor Relations in the U.S. Textile Industry*. New York: Praeger.

Turner, Herbert A. 1962. *Trade Union Growth, Structure and Policy*. London: George Allen & Unwin.

"Union Membership Declines by 62,000 Workers in U.S." 1988. *Charlotte Observer*, Jan. 23, p. 5A.

"Unions Report Fewest Strikes in 39 Years." 1986. *Charlotte Observer*, March 2.

U.S. Department of Commerce. 1982. *Census of Manufactures*. Industry Series. Washington, D.C.: U.S. Government Printing Office.

———. 1986. *1986 U.S. Industrial Outlook*. Washington, D.C.: U.S. Government Printing Office.

———. 1989a. *Census of Manufactures*. Preliminary Report. Industry Series 1987 (MC87–1–22b[P]). Washington, D.C.: U.S. Government Printing Office.

———. 1989b. *Statistical Abstract of the United States, 1989*. 109th ed. Washington, D.C.: U.S. Government Printing Office.

U.S. Department of Labor, Bureau of Labor Statistics. 1974. *Technological Change and Manpower Trends in Six Industries*. Bulletin 1817. Washington, D.C.: U.S. Government Printing Office.

———. 1985. *Employment, Hours, and Earnings, 1909–84*. Washington, D.C.: U.S. Government Printing Office.

———. 1988. *Employment, Hours, and Earnings: Supplement*. Washington, D.C.: U.S. Government Printing Office.

"U.S. Textiles Will Throw a Counterpunch in 1986." 1986. *Textile World* (Jan.): 38–40, 43–45.

Vance, Truman. 1910. "How a Man Went to Meet His Labor Problems." *Independent*, March 17. Harriet Laura Herring Papers, Box 5, Folder 378, Southern Historical Collection, University of North Carolina, Chapel Hill.

Vatter, Harold G. 1975. *The Drive to Industrial Maturity: The U.S. Economy, 1860–1914*. Westport, Conn.: Greenwood Press.

Villermé, Louis-René. 1840. *Tableau de l'état physique et moral des ouvriers employés dans les manufactures de coton, de laine, et de soie*. Paris: Jules Renouard.

Vinson, John. N.d. Interview by Ida Moore for the Federal Writers Project of the Works Progress Administration. Southern Historical Collection, University of North Carolina, Chapel Hill.

Walker, Ruth. 1985. "U.S. Textile Firms Insist They Have a Future." *Christian Science Monitor*, Aug. 26, p. 17.

238 REFERENCES

6
Wallerstein, Immanuel. 1980. *The Modern World-System II: Mercantilism and the Consolidation of the European World-Economy, 1600–1750.* New York: Academic Press.

Ware, Norman. 1964 [1924]. *The Industrial Worker, 1840–1860: The Reaction of American Industrial Society to the Advance of the Industrial Revolution.* Chicago: Quadrangle.

Wayne, Leslie. 1988. "Textile Industry Enjoying Revival." *Raleigh News and Observer,* Feb. 16, p. 1D.

Webb, James. 1851. Business and Personal Papers. Southern Historical Collection, University of North Carolina, Chapel Hill.

"The Welfare Work at Proximity Mills, Greensboro, NC." 1906. *Mill News.* Harriet Laura Herring Papers, Box 5, Folder 376, Southern Historical Collection, University of North Carolina, Chapel Hill.

Westbrook Family. N.d. Interview by Ida Moore for the Federal Writers Project of the Works Progress Administration. Southern Historical Collection, University of North Carolina, Chapel Hill.

Wiener, Jonathan M. 1978. *Social Origins of the New South: Alabama, 1860–1885.* Baton Rouge: Louisiana State University Press.

Wilder, Lois. Interview by Linda Frankel. Southern Oral History Project, Southern Historical Collection, University of North Carolina, Chapel Hill.

Wilder, Lucille. Interview by Linda Frankel. Southern Oral History Project, Southern Historical Collection, University of North Carolina, Chapel Hill.

Williamson, Jeffrey G. 1965. "Regional Inequality and the Process of National Development: A Description of the Patterns." *Economic Development and Cultural Change* 13 (2): 3–84.

———. 1974. *Late Nineteenth-Century American Development.* London: Cambridge University Press.

Williamson, Joel. 1984. *The Crucible of Race: Black-White Relations in the American South Since Emancipation.* New York: Oxford University Press.

Wood, Phillip J. 1986. *Southern Capitalism: The Political Economy of North Carolina, 1880–1980.* Durham, N.C.: Duke University Press.

———. 1989a. "Barriers to Capitalist Development in Maritime Canada, 1870–1930: A Comparative Perspective." In *Canadian Papers in Business History,* edited by Peter Baskerville, pp. 33–57. Victoria: Public History Group.

———. 1989b. "Marxism and the Maritimes: On the Determinants of Regional Capitalist Development." *Studies in Political Economy* 29: 123–53.

———. 1989c. "The Paradoxical Maritimes: On the Neo-Classical Competitive Model of Capitalist Development in Maritime Canada." Paper presented to the Atlantic Provinces Political Studies Association, University of Prince Edward Island, Oct. 13–15, 1989.

Woodman, Harold D. 1977. "Sequel to Slavery: The New History Views the Postbellum South." *Journal of Southern History* 43: 523–54.

———. 1979. "Post-Civil War Southern Agriculture and the Law." *Agricultural History* 53: 319–37.

Woodward, C. Vann. 1971 [1951]. *Origins of the New South, 1877–1913.* Baton Rouge: University of Louisiana Press.

Wright, Gavin. 1986. *Old South, New South: Revolutions in the Southern Economy since the Civil War.* New York. Basic Books.

Wright, Lacy. 1975. Interview by Bill Finger and Chip Hughes, March 10. Southern Oral History Project, Southern Historical Collection, University of North Carolina, Chapel Hill.

Wright, Scott, and Martha Clark. 1979. "The South Moves South." *Southern Exposure* 7 (1): 101–6.

Zahavi, Gerald. 1983. "Negotiated Loyalty: Welfare Capitalism and the Shoeworkers of Endicott Johnson, 1920–1940." *Journal of American History* 71: 602–20.

——. 1988. *Workers, Managers, and Welfare Capitalism: The Shoeworkers and Tanners of Endicott Johnson, 1890–1959.* Urbana: University of Illinois Press.

Zald, Mayer N., and Roberta Ash. 1966. "Social Movement Organizations: Growth, Decay and Change." *Social Forces* 44: 327–41.

Zald, Mayer N., and Michael A. Berger. 1978. "Resource Mobilization in Organizations: Coup d'Etat, Insurgency, and Mass Movements." *American Journal of Sociology* 83: 823–61.

Zald, Mayer N., and David Jacobs. 1978. "Compliance/Incentive Classifications of Organizations: Underlying Dimensions." *Administration and Society* 9: 403–24.

Zald, Mayer N., and John D. McCarthy, eds. 1987. *Social Movements in an Organizational Society.* New Brunswick: Transaction Books.

Contributors

JULIA C. BONHAM holds a Ph.D. in American civilization from Brown University. She is an adjunct member of the History and Multidisciplinary Studies faculties at North Carolina State University. She is the author, with Gary Kulik, of *Rhode Island: Inventory of Historical Engineering and Industrial Sites*, published by the Historic American Engineering Record in 1978.

BART DREDGE is a doctoral candidate in sociology at the University of North Carolina at Chapel Hill. A member of the faculty of Furman University, he is working on an organizational study of the Brown Lung Association.

LINDA FRANKEL received her Ph.D. in sociology from Harvard University. She is the author of *Broken Threads: Women's Work and Protest in a Southern Textile Community*, forthcoming from the University of Illinois Press.

GARY R. FREEZE received his Ph.D. in American history from the University of North Carolina at Chapel Hill. He is an assistant professor of history and government at Erskine College. His publications include "God, Cotton Mills, and the New South Myths: A New Perspective on the Community Crusade in Salisbury, N.C., 1887–1888," forthcoming in *Continuity and Change in the New South: Essays in Honor of George Brown Tindall*.

JOHN GAVENTA holds a Ph.D. in political sociology from Oxford University. He is an assistant professor of sociology at the University of Tennessee and director of the Highlander Research and Education Center. He is the author of *Power and Powerlessness: Quiescence and Rebellion in an Appalachian Valley*, published by the University of Illinois Press in 1980.

GAY L. GULLICKSON received her Ph.D. in modern European history from the University of North Carolina at Chapel Hill. She is an associate professor of history at the University of Maryland and the author of *The Spinners and Weavers of Auffay: Rural Industry and the Sexual Division of Labor in a French Village, 1750–1850*, published in 1986 by Cambridge University Press.

BENNETT M. JUDKINS earned his Ph.D. in sociology at the University of Tennessee. He is a professor of sociology at Meredith College and the author of *We Offer Ourselves as Evidence: Toward Workers' Control of Occupational Health*, published by Greenwood Press in 1986.

JEFFREY LEITER holds a Ph.D. in sociology from the University of Michigan. He is an associate professor of sociology at North Carolina State University. His publications include "Reactions to Subordination: Attitudes of Southern Textile Workers," published in *Social Forces* in 1986.

ROGER PENN received his Ph.D. in sociology from Cambridge University. He is a senior lecturer in sociology at Lancaster University and the author of *Class, Power and Technology: Skilled Workers in Britain and America*, published by St. Martin's Press in 1990.

MICHAEL D. SCHULMAN holds a Ph.D. in sociology from the University of Wisconsin. He is a professor of sociology at North Carolina State University. His publications include "Race, Gender, Class Consciousness and Union Support: An Analysis of Southern Textile Workers," with Rhonda Zingraff and Linda Reif, published in 1985 in *Sociological Quarterly*.

BRYANT SIMON is a doctoral candidate in history at the University of North Carolina at Chapel Hill, where he is working on a dissertation on labor and politics in South Carolina during the New Deal era. He has published in *Labor Conflict in America: An Encyclopedia* and has an article forthcoming in *Labor's Heritage*.

BARBARA ELLEN SMITH earned her Ph.D. in sociology from Brandeis University. She is an assistant professor of sociology at Marshall University and the author of *Digging Our Own Graves: Coal Miners and the Struggle over Black Lung Disease*, published by Temple University Press in 1987.

PHILLIP J. WOOD holds a Ph.D. in political studies from Queen's University in Kingston, Ontario, where he is an associate professor. He is the author of *Southern Capitalism: The Political Economy of North Carolina, 1880–1980*, published by Duke University Press in 1986.

RHONDA ZINGRAFF received her Ph.D. in sociology from Bowling Green State University. She is an associate professor of sociology at Meredith College and the author, with Michael Schulman, of "Social Bases of Class Consciousness: A Study of Southern Textile Workers with a Comparison by Race," published in *Social Forces* in 1984.

Index